Additional praise for GU

"Sara Roahen's *Gumbo Tales* makes you want to spend a week—immediately—in New Orleans."

—Jeffrey A. Trachtenberg, *Wall Street Journal*

"Roahen has written a surprisingly informative, engaging, and amusing book about the cooking of New Orleans."

—Jonathan Yardley, *Washington Post Book World*

"[Roahen's] culinary tour succeeds repeatedly in defining the indefinable with grace, wit and passion—especially in regards to the city's alluring, complex flavors and aromas. . . . Those familiar with the city will smile and nod along; readers who've never had the pleasure may find themselves making travel arrangements long before the last page." —*Publishers Weekly*, starred review

"With humor and clarity, [Roahen] uses food as a vehicle through history, providing fascinating chapters on the contributions of Italian and Vietnamese populations to the cosmopolitan menu."

—Elliot Mandel, *Booklist*

"*Gumbo Tales* is an endearing collection from the seven years [Roahen] spent in the Crescent City, learning to embrace its unapologetically decadent cuisine. It is part culinary history, part memoir, and part homage to places that have since been erased."

—Sarah Hepola, *Salon*

"What makes *Gumbo Tales* more than just another food or restaurant guide is the personal passages, including stories about the author's Washington upbringing, her New Orleans friends and the city's many iconic personalities, and in the margins, the intimate and near-existential relationship she developed with New Orleans and its denizens." —Tim Whitaker, *Philadelphia Weekly*

"Sara Roahen in her brand-new *Gumbo Tales* takes the King Cake for pouring out her heart and soul for the Crescent City. . . . Roahen is funny, strange, and, like a new New Orleanian, gets right under your skin. I can't wait for what else she's got in that brain of hers."

—Kim O'Donnel, *Washington Post*

"Sara Roahen's empathetic tales of time at table in New Orleans will break your heart and rile your stomach. If you wish to understand why and how food matters in this papal city of American cookery, trust her palate, trust her pen."

—John T. Edge, author of *Southern Belly: The Ultimate Food Lover's Companion to the South*

"It's hard to think of a sharper observer of the way we eat [than Roahen]."

—Todd Price, *Offbeat*

"*Gumbo Tales* is a before-and-after Katrina portrait of New Orleans foodways—a loving tribute to what endures—and a sad catalog of what has been lost."

—Robb Walsh, author of *The Tex-Mex Cookbook: A History in Recipes and Photos*

"By turns hilarious and heart-wrenching, Roahen's tales of how a Wisconsin-raised vegetarian came to adore the foods of New Orleans in the years before Katrina, and how they became a lifeline in the years that followed, are a reaffirmation of the bonds between cuisine and community."

—Matt Lee and Ted Lee, authors of *The Lee Bros. Southern Cookbook*

"If you're happy to be in New Orleans, this is the book to lead you, rejoicing, to your favorite restaurant, or fire up that kitchen stove to make a batch of gumbo for your mama 'n' dem. . . . This book is a joy to read, a pleasure to pass along, a book to treasure. It leaves you hungry in your body, satisfied in your soul."

—Susan Larson, *Times-Picayune* (New Orleans)

"Sara Roahen writes like a ravenous angel about her beloved and indomitable city and about the culinary culture that breathes life into it." —John Dufresne, author of *Louisiana Power & Light*

"[*Gumbo Tales*] is a passionate description of the rich, quirky food traditions and recipes that have set the Big Easy apart from the rest of the nation. . . . As much about loss, resilience, and change as it is about crawfish, red gravy, and Sazerac."

—Mary Bergin, *Capital Times* (Madison, WI)

"*Gumbo Tales* is food writing at its best, because it engages and informs and entertains—and it's about ever so much more than the food. I defy anyone to read any one of Sara Roahen's encounters and ruminations in *Gumbo Tales* and not be irresistibly drawn to another, and another. Think of it as eating a shrimp po-boy or a bowl of crawfish bisque: There's no way you're gonna push it aside unfinished." —John Egerton, author of *The Americanization of Dixie: The Southernization of America*

"A deeply informed and plainly heartfelt investigation into New Orleans' finest (and even its not-so-fine) food traditions taps into a cornucopia of cultural riches." —Bliss Broyard, *Elle*

GUMBO TALES

Finding My Place at the New Orleans Table

Sara Roahen

W. W. NORTON & COMPANY
NEW YORK LONDON

Printed in the United States of America
First published as a Norton paperback 2009

For information about special discounts for bulk purchases, please contact
W. W. Norton Special Sales at specialsales@wwnorton.com or 800-233-4830

Manufacturing by LSC Harrisonburg
Book design by Wesley Gott
Production manager: Anna Oler

Library of Congress Cataloging-in-Publication Data

Roahen, Sara.
Gumbo tales : finding my place at the New Orleans table / Sara Roahen. — 1st ed.
p. cm.
Includes bibliographical references and index.
ISBN 978-0-393-06167-3 (hardcover)
1. New Orleans (La.)—Folklore. 2. Food habits—Louisiana—New Orleans.
3. Drinking customs—Louisiana—New Orleans. 4. New Orleans (La.)—
Social life and customs. I. Title.
GR110.L5R63 2008
398.209763'35—dc22 2007039312

ISBN 978-0-393-33537-8 pbk.

W. W. Norton & Company, Inc.
500 Fifth Avenue, New York, N.Y. 10110
www.wwnorton.com

W. W. Norton & Company Ltd.
15 Carlisle Street, London W1D 3BS

7 8 9 0

For each of you who fed me,
for each of you who shared my table, and
for the city that brought us together.

Contents

Note

OCTOBER 2005

A flood can disappear neighborhoods, it can cause good-hearted police officers to commit suicide on duty, it can rust ten thousand perfectly seasoned cast-iron skillets, and it can banish a thriving Vietnamese community to refugee status, again. I'm going to suspend disbelief for the next sixteen chapters, however, and assume that a flood cannot destroy the most interesting and ingrained food culture in my country.

If my use of the past and present tenses is loose at times, it's not because I've overlooked the inconsistency. In a city where there never was an obvious delineation between the now and the then, disasters of nature and government blur the lines to the brink of invisibility.

GUMBO

A Higher Education

Not long after I moved to New Orleans, my younger sister, Stephanie, flew down from our home state of Wisconsin to evaluate the city as a prospective home. Exercising New Orleans' most persuasive means of seduction—dinner—I took her to the great neighborhood restaurant Liuzza's Restaurant & Bar and ordered like mad: Abita Amber beer in frosted schooners, fried green tomatoes with shrimp rémoulade, a stuffed artichoke, fried chicken, seafood gumbo.

"Ew," Stephanie said, inhaling, when the gumbo arrived. "It smells like Haumerson's Pond."

Her judgment hung over the table carpeted in algae, murk, and other scummy aquatic things we'd never dreamed of eating as little girls. Haumerson's Pond began where our paternal grandparents' front yard dropped off. We'd never so much as dipped a toe in it, but the pond had fired our childhood imaginations and filled our free time. We'd poked branches into the thick mud that surrounded its expanse and watched older boys slide hockey pucks across its frozen plane. We'd known absolutely that its depths contained hideous beasts: swamp monsters, alligators, quivering spiders, crayfish.

Stephanie went wan at the scent of Liuzza's gumbo, just like our mom does when she detects anything fishy. Its appearance couldn't have helped—the gloomy broth splashed up the bowl and ringed it with a chlorophyllous sediment. Without lifting her spoon, Stephanie pushed the soup brimming with shrimp, oysters, and several landlubber components to my side of the table. I passed her the fried chicken.

One of the best lines ever written about food is in *Eating Together*, the funny, touching book on which two friends with New Orleans ties, Peter Feibleman and Lillian Hellman, collaborated. "If you're having a pompous gourmet to dinner, gumbo, I think, is a good main dish," writes Feibleman, whose own humility is questionable at times.

It's true: gumbo is an event. In New Orleans–speak, you "have" a gumbo, like you have a barbecue or a picnic. I once attended a Fourth of July gumbo in the Seventh Ward; the hostess served us barbecued ribs, candied sweet potatoes, and stuffed fish on disposable plates, but she ladled her gumbo into pretty china bowls. Gumbo can be reason enough for . . . anything, really. It's not unthinkable that a person would decide to pack up a U-Haul and head south based on a single transcendent bowl of it. Stephanie wound up doing just that, but I still should have known to start her off with a seafood-free chicken and sausage gumbo instead.

Though Stephanie was born eighteen months after I was, she arrived with a head of raging purple-orange hair (I was still bald), an insatiable desire to be tickled (my nightmare), and a bright future as a forward on the varsity basketball team (I was asked to resign quietly from the junior varsity team after one season on the bench). In other words, I've spent most of my life trying to keep up with my younger sister. Finally, as an adult, I discovered food to be the one arena in which she could be out-toughed. After college, while Stephanie trained for marathons and learned to surf, I slugged it out in the testosterone-fueled community of line cooks. She learned to pitch a tent in a hailstorm; I learned to sauté and swear like a sweaty boy. She developed a taste for Clif Bars; I tasted everything in the walk-in for signs of spoilage. Now she was in New Orleans shopping Ph.D. programs, and I was pursuing a higher education in gumbo.

There is an elemental, forever landlocked part of me that reacts precisely the way Stephanie did when faced with the more aromatic qualities of seafood—a part of me that still fears eating the unknown as much as it fears, say, quivering spiders. Over time, however, I've learned to channel that anxiety into curiosity and even desire, which must be what enabled New Orleans' various gumbos—those of the swamp and those of the prairie—to snag me, first by the nose, then by the belly, and soon enough by the heart.

Gumbo is the most important dish in the Louisiana lexicon for its prevalence and dependability alone. It's difficult to come up with a single regional-leaning restaurant in New Orleans with a menu of any substance that doesn't serve some version of it at least once a week. Gumbo's pervasiveness does not, however, diminish the dish's mystique; just as its variations are infinite, so are gumbo's controversies and questions.

Every native can, and is dying to, describe her quintessential gumbo down to the final grain of rice, rice being the single constant among gumbos. Usually. There are at least as many definitive gumbos in Louisiana as there are accents, and like accents, definitive gumbos are established at home. It's an intensely esoteric topic, as personal as pie crust and pimento cheese: whatever style a person grows up eating tends to remain her ideal for eternity. If you disagree with that ideal, it's clearly because you're impaired in some sad, fundamental way.

My first inkling of native gumbo biases came courtesy of my friend Lolis Elie, a writer and skilled interlocutor of his city's food culture. When I once asked his gumbo preference, Lolis directed me to Fay's Take-Out (since closed) in Gretna, a town just across the Mississippi River from New Orleans. On Fridays, Fay Antoine served the only retail gumbo that lived up to a standard originally set by Lolis's late grandmother—a robust and briny seafood potage that was thinner than most New Orleans restaurant gumbos I'd tried but thick as a cypress swamp in flavor.

While participating in a panel discussion about gumbo in the food-geek area at the New Orleans Jazz and Heritage Festival (aka

Jazz Fest) some years later, Miss Fay explained that she "marinates" her seafood overnight and makes her stock with shrimp shells. "I like gumbo when I don't have to see an oyster, a shrimp, or a crab, but you know it's been there," she said.

I agreed with Lolis: Miss Fay's shellfish-imprinted gumbo was a lovely prelude to her husband Reyna's chocolate Honey Whip doughnuts and seasonal deep-fried doughnut king cakes. After my first foam quart container of it, I drove to their brown cement corner shop frequently. And yet when I failed to swear to Lolis that I had never tasted and would never, ever taste something that defined gumbo as truthfully as Miss Fay's fine gumbo did, Lolis pretty much stopped talking to me about gumbo.

And so it goes.

Shortly after I moved to New Orleans, the first southern city I'd ever inhabited, I lucked into the position of restaurant critic for *Gambit Weekly* newspaper. This hastened the need for some authority on the subject of gumbo, and I soon realized that while accumulating native friends would introduce me to a variety of gumbo styles, I possessed no vocabulary with which to break it all down. I needed a crash course, and so for a few weeks I set up shop in the cookbook shelves of the Nadine R. Vorhoff Library at Newcomb College Center for Research on Women. Words cannot replace the value of eating when you're aiming to understand a particular food, but they can illuminate where there is darkness, and in gumbo there is much darkness.

In the glossary to her cookbook *The Welcome Table: African-American Heritage Cooking*, the scholar and part-time New Orleanian Jessica Harris traces gumbo's ancestry: "This dish went from Africa to Louisiana with only a slight name change. *Quingombo* is the name for okra, gumbo's main ingredient, in one of the Bantu languages." Gumbo, she concludes, is based on the traditional African concept of a stew served over a starch.

There may not exist a more educated account of the word's origin, and the city's okra gumbos—like the ones I've tried at Willie Mae's Scotch House, Casamento's, and Café Reconcile—serve as testament to the dish's African lineage. But taking into account the amazement of gumbos that don't contain okra at all, and considering the congeries of nations whose cooks have contributed to Louisiana's foodways, I figured there must be more to the story.

In 1971, Time-Life Books turned out a comprehensive study of Creole and Cajun cooking in which the aforementioned Peter Feibleman imagines the rest of gumbo's story by merging Africa's okra with the French settlers' taste for bouillabaisse, the Spanish colonists' contribution of peppers, the Acadian way with shellfish, and the Native American tradition of grinding the leaves of the sassafras tree as a thickener and seasoning agent called filé. Whereas Ms. Harris's definition is limiting, Mr. Feibleman's is suspiciously inclusive and tidy, like the point in a musical when a believable story line is suddenly disrupted by every actor's having perfect pitch and knowing all the words. It works if your goal is to account for every historical possibility.

Because culinary scholastics depend on documentation, they often fall short of fully explaining the historical and cultural import of a food. In gumbo's case, it's the lack of information about the eating and cooking habits of Louisiana's Native Americans and early slaves (neither of which groups journaled much) that creates the most disappointing gulf in our knowledge.

A 1971 copy of *The Picayune Original Creole Cook Book*, an invaluable resource first published in 1900 as *The Picayune's Creole Cook Book*, wiggles around the question of gumbo's evolution by positing that gumbo didn't evolve at all but rather is "an original conception, a something sui generis in cooking, peculiar to this ancient Creole city alone." This possibly lazy and certainly dubious explanation is the one that comes closest to articulating my own thoughts on gumbo, which are at best imprecise. How to define a dish whose variations are infinite and whose full evolution is unknown and incomplete?

The differences between Willie Mae Seaton's summery shrimp and okra gumbo and Ken Smith's satiny duck and andouille gumbo at Upperline Restaurant are so vast that if New Orleans were to undergo an alien invasion, I can't imagine the new occupiers recognizing them as the same dish. Add to those the traditional Creole gumbo with fresh pork sausage (*chaurice*) at Pampy's Creole Kitchen, the seafood gumbo with oysters and shrimp cooked à la minute at Liuzza's by the Track (related to Liuzza's Restaurant & Bar in name only), and the Friday gumbo at Dunbar's Creole Cooking (closed since Katrina, though Celestine Dunbar, the owner, is running an adapted campus restaurant at Loyola University) that's thickened with okra, roux, *and* filé, and you've moved beyond one-dish territory and into the terrain of an entire cuisine.

One generalization does apply to all of them: no dish or drink is better than gumbo at transmitting New Orleans' character directly into the bloodstream. It didn't take this resident alien long to discover that.

No gumbo is extraordinary in its parts. Whatever the variation, the key to a gumbo's excellence is never included in its humdrum ingredients list: flour, fat, onion, celery, bell pepper, shrimp, chicken, sausage, water, to name some regular possibilities. The instructions are equally straightforward. One of New Orleans' earliest cookbooks, Lafcadio Hearn's *La Cuisine Creole*, reduces the process to a few lines:

Simple Okra Gombo

> Chop a pound of beef and half a pound of veal brisket into squares an inch thick; slice three dozen okra pods, one onion, a pod of red pepper, and fry all together. When brown, pour in half a gallon of water; add more as it boils away. Serve with rice as usual.

Even for someone with a habit of glorifying ancient recipes, this one's a bore. No era's gumbo recipes succeed in translating the dish's potential magnificence. Hearn seems to acknowledge this in his introduction, warning the reader that economy and simplicity govern his recipes, and that the book's savory dishes "are rendered palatable more as the result of care in their preparation, than any great skill or expensive outlay in the selection of materials."

"Magic" is on my hackneyed-word blacklist; I've promised myself never to denigrate food or New Orleans by applying it to either of them. And yet something like it—something not articulated in ingredients lists, recipe instructions, or words in any other combination—does occur inside the gumbo pot. Take, for example, the rabbit and andouille gumbo that Frank Brigtsen serves at Brigtsen's, the Riverbend-area restaurant he runs with his wife, Marna. One whiff of it stops the Earth's spinning. It smells something like the way fried chicken smells as it's pulled from the skillet, though chicken is not among the gumbo's ingredients. Tipping back the first spoonful besieges your tongue with a hundred impressions you want never to end: the sting of black and red peppers, the snap of celery, the essence of lemon, darkness, lightness, damp, heat, cloves. If the chef doesn't actually use cloves in his gumbo, it doesn't lessen that Christmassy tingle, and it doesn't matter. Best not to deconstruct a gumbo's mysterious conversation of flavors anyway; rather, sit back and marvel at how it renders even good words useless.

This burbling up of inexplicable flavors occurs in gumbos all over town. Another example: I swear I once tasted cumin in the highly seasoned broth at Liuzza's by the Track. But when I phoned to ask the restaurant's owner and gumbo chef, Billy Gruber, about it, he swore to me that I was wrong.

When sausage is added—and often it is—it's gumbo's wildest wild card, sausage being a mélange of unknown pieces and parts itself. Commercial seasoning blends are equally unpredictable and ever-present. Tony Chachere's (pronounced *Sa*-shree's, or sometimes *Sha*-she-ree's) Creole seasoning is as common in the New Orleans kitchen as salt. Do keep that on the down-low, though, as such culinary abhorrences could cause a pompous gourmet's gout-ridden big toe to spasm.

I would know. I'm a recovering pompous gourmet myself. How

else to explain the snooty note I jotted in my recipe diary—or the fact that I *keep* a recipe diary—the day I made my first gumbo, following one of Chef Paul Prudhomme's recipes? Beside the ingredient garlic powder, I wrote, "I never thought I would have *that* in my kitchen."

After exhausting the cookbook library's resources, and still harboring big questions about gumbo's omnipresence in New Orleans and why I can't seem to down enough of it, I faced the next step in my higher gumbo education: cooking. It was a petrifying thought, one that filled me with that nauseous tickle that curdles the stomach before a final exam. What if I burned my roux? What if my okra didn't slime? What if my gumbo tasted as bland as the recipe sounded? No wonder I'd never considered graduate school.

By eating in New Orleans, continually asking questions about eating in New Orleans, obsessively reading about eating in New Orleans, and writing a weekly column about eating in New Orleans, I had created a comfortable world in which it looked and felt as though I were really doing it—really becoming one of them, a New Orleanian. But my rusty cast-iron skillet told a difficult truth. I was like those expats who eat France out of Camembert and croissants but continue to read Sartre in English. In Louisiana, cooking is a foreign language. It was time to step up.

For my first lesson I chose a recipe for a thin, dark chicken and andouille gumbo, because my seafood-wary mom was visiting, and I chose it from *Chef Paul Prudhomme's Louisiana Kitchen* because it provides visual aids for making a roux. This would be my first stab ever at taking a roux beyond the creamy shade of résumé paper, and I needed any available props. What I didn't understand beforehand is that there's no time for rifling through a cookbook for pictures once your flour and fat start smoking; I've since committed Chef Paul's roux color chart to memory. That first roux did work out somehow, if you discount the black flecks that melted off my plastic whisk. Making a roux is a mind-over-matter endeavor during which you exercise internal rhetoric to convince yourself that you can do it. The flour and fat respond well to a confident hand.

It was Mardi Gras season, and I had quadrupled the gumbo recipe for a party, a none-too-swift move on the occasion of your first gumbo; the enterprise took me longer than an epic Endymion parade. Our postman at the time ducked in at around the halfway point and noted that "gumbo should take you thirty minutes." This man had a unique sense of time, as evidenced by the thirty seconds it took him to down a cold Abita beer huddled inside our front door.

My amateur rendition of Chef Paul's gumbo was an event to the degree that my husband, Matt, requested a repeat for his birthday the next year, and the next. Matt (full name Mathieu) is a Belgian by birth and by pleasure points; this particular gumbo hits the latter with four of his favorite tastes: toasted nuts, dark chocolate, bitter beer, and coffee. Naturally, it doesn't actually contain any of them. While Chef Paul's gumbo is different every time I make it—variables like stock strength, shifts in roux shade, and sausage ensure a measure of mystery—it's also always one of the most delicious things we can remember eating. I cannot explain why. The ingredients are ordinary and the instructions are straightforward. Sure, it's a time-consuming project, and I always break a sweat making the roux, but it's not magic or anything. And if it were, I guess I couldn't say it anyway.

Ask a Louisiana cook what kind of gumbo she makes and she'll likely answer with her thickener of choice: roux, okra, or filé. From a newcomer's perspective, this betrays a strange and subtle prejudice. For my first few years in New Orleans, the mode of thickening a gumbo seemed trifling compared to what kind of meat it contained (duck, chicken, hen, rabbit), what kind of sausage (smoked, hot, tight, fresh), what kind of fat (oil, lard, butter), and what role, if any, seafood played. But a gumbo might burst with all of the above plus dried shrimp and turkey gizzards, and if it also contains filé, often it's called simply filé gumbo. No subtitle. Okra can be similarly definitive.

Since passing Chef Paul's chicken and andouille test, I've experimented with a host of other gumbo recipes and begun to understand why cooks might stress the presence of a specific thickener. While roux, okra, and filé get most notice for their cohesive abilities, they also establish a gumbo's overall personality. For instance, I couldn't achieve the dark chocolatey nuttiness that Matt likes in gumbo without using a roux. Okra in any amount contributes a fresh, gardenlike quality that's wholly absent in gumbos that ignore it. And filé at once brightens a broth with its herbaceous tang and dampens it with a dark, mulchy character.

There are no hard-and-fast rules for when to use which of the three thickeners, and in what combination, but that doesn't stop Louisianians from making them. The *Picayune* cookbook asserts that okra and filé are not as a rule used together in making gumbo. I once asked a cook slouched against the wall outside Mother's Restaurant for his opinion. His answer sounded as grave and deliberate as if he were standing before a criminal court judge: "I believe that filé doesn't go with seafood and okra doesn't go with chicken. That's just what I believe, ma'am."

I broached the topic again while chatting with strangers in Cajun country, because gumbo, like hurricanes and coffee strength, is a topic everyone in Louisiana is champing to entertain. One of them gave me her policy: "If you're making a roux gumbo, you always use filé. If you're making an okra gumbo, you don't have to."

During the gumbo panel discussion at Jazz Fest when Fay Antoine spoke about her technique with seafood, Frank Brigtsen insisted that roux is a gumbo's "chief characteristic." Richard Stewart of the Gumbo Shop restaurant chimed in with a story about his mother's okra gumbo. She never used a roux.

Et cetera.

Within those unofficial rules are yet more rules, microrules, itty-bitty rules along the lines of whether you believe ketchup belongs on hot dogs or sugar in tomato sauce or walnuts in brownies. You know, the kinds of strictly personal, utterly subjective food rules that jeopardize friendships. For instance, everyone knows that filé powder must be added at the very end of cooking or your gumbo will have a ropy texture. Everyone, that is, except those cooks who add it at the beginning, as the seasoning vegetables are sautéing, and everyone who insists that it ought to be added at the table, by individuals, when they're also seasoning with hot sauce. (Lionel Key, one of the few people in Louisiana known to grind cured sassafras leaves by hand with a large mortar and pestle for retail sale, double-dips: he adds filé as a thickener while cooking his seasoning vegetables and then again just before eating for flavor.)

Cooks who agree on using a roux might argue over whether store-bought roux is acceptable, or over the ideal fat-to-flour proportion, or over which fat is superior, or over roux color. One of my friends learned from his Cajun grandmother that a proper roux attains the color of an old copper penny. Another friend has a friend whose mother begins saying a rosary when she starts her roux; the roux is finished when her prayers are. Frank Brigtsen told Jazz Festers that he takes his roux to the dark-brown shade of fudge. The Creole chef Leah Chase, who calls hers a "typical Seventh Ward roux," said that she joined the festival's panel discussion expressly to learn "how in the heck they get that roux so dark without burning it." Some cooks use their own skin as a guide. Sporting the pallor of béchamel sauce myself, I cannot emulate this technique.

Early on in my higher gumbo education someone told me that all Louisiana old-timers used lard in their roux, and I believed it because it sounded logical, and because it's human nature to grab hold of a truth when it presents itself. Then one day I opened old-timer Justin Wilson's Cajun cookbook, *Justin Wilson Looking Back*, published four years before he died, in 2001, and read that he preferred olive oil. Olive oil. That's when I knew that the gumbo lessons would never end, that there couldn't be a final exam, and I loved that.

The deal about how gumbo preferences are established at home does not apply when cookbooks account for the entirety of your domestic gumbo exposure. In other words, I cannot rightly claim to have learned to make gumbo at the hip of Paul Prudhomme. Alas, no amount of eating or cooking earns a nonnative membership in that society of Louisianians who were born with roux in their genes and weaned on shellfish stocks and sticky bits of okra. I continue to make Chef Paul's gumbo more than other styles, but that has to do with comfort level, not predisposition. There is, thankfully, a silver lining to never belonging: devoid of an inbred gumbo bias, I'm open to appreciating the full spectrum of gumbos without the hindrance of a gold standard. It's a great luxury in a town like this one.

Whereas cookbooks and natives help me identify gumbo's rules and the ways in which they're broken, and whereas cooking allows me to observe those rules playing out in a tactile reality, I still feel closest to the raw power of gumbo while conducting my fieldwork, which basically amounts to lunch. Within a couple of years of eating out, I developed my own outsider's system of gumbo classification, filing the varieties according to what I perceived as their most outstanding characteristics. Crossover is rampant, but the system nevertheless gives structure to my internal gumbo dialogue.

First, there's the primarily seasonal Okra Stew style, the strongest evidence of gumbo's African heritage, in which steely-colored okra seeds bob around like soft BBs—or, if you're okraphobic, like crab eyes. Tomato and tomato paste are common in Okra Stew gumbos, though as a general rule only in the city. Hartman LeJeune, a thoroughbred Cajun whose family has run LeJeune's Bakery in the country town of Jeanerette since 1884, breaks that rule by adding a can of Ro-tel tomatoes to his. I've never tasted Mr. LeJeune's gumbo, but he shared his recipe one night over dinner, and I considered it a tipping point when I produced a successful gumbo according to his spoken-word instructions, such as "Don't cook the okra to complete mush—there should still be a lot of slime in there."

Next up is the medium-dark, thin but not watery, seafood-and-usually-sausage gumbo variety that I call Homestyle Gumbo because New Orleanians of all colors and backgrounds say it reminds them of home. The seafood in Homestyle Gumbo often has been purposely overcooked into little pouches of sand, all of its flavor absorbed into the soup, and the broth tends to stain bowls and foam containers with the olive hue of an unpolished wedding band on its fiftieth anniversary. This is a broad category. Liuzza's and Fay Antoine's gumbos fall into it, as does the house gumbo at the Real Pie Man, a takeout operation catty-corner to Fay's in Gretna where the cashiers and clientele are so silent as to be disquieting. The only sound in the crowded waiting area on a recent visit came from a woman testing cell-phone ringtones. I always wind up either submitting in the corner or shoving my way to the counter with false confidence, neither of which methods is rewarded with speedier service. But the Real Pie Man's gumbo ultimately delivers, its oily broth leaning harder on the earth than on the sea, echoing citrus and thyme, and overcrowded with shrimp, chicken, smoked sausage, and crab shells.

While enjoying a bowl of Homestyle Gumbo at Mena's Palace in the French Quarter, the former restaurant critic and New Orleans native Gene Bourg helped me put a name to a third gumbo category: Restaurant Gumbo. This is the Guinness beer of gumbos, a corporal commitment, dark, thick, and tending toward bitter; it's a showpiece for extreme roux-making and a bottomless receptacle for pepper of all colors. From Gene's perspective, which extends back to the 1940s, Restaurant Gumbo is an aberration perpetrated on the city by higher-end, new-line, Creole-esque restaurants, many of which are run by branches of the Brennan family. Indeed, Paul Prudhomme believes that he introduced roux gumbo to Commander's Palace, a Brennan family restaurant, in the 1970s. In an interview for an oral history printed in the *Times-Picayune* in June 2005, Chef Paul called the gumbo he served at Commander's during that era "down and dirty Cajun."

Then there's what I've come to call Traditional Creole Gumbo, the fourth genre, identified by the presence of a single ingredient: the fresh hot pork sausage known as *chaurice*. Restaurants operated by black Creoles, or *gens de couleur*, like Dooky Chase Restaurant and Pampy's, are the most reliable places outside Creole homes for finding it.

Word of less familiar gumbos has come over the transom—squirrel gumbo, egg and potato gumbo, red bean gumbo, seven steak gumbo (made with a cut named for the shape of its bone)—but as none have entered my immediate sphere, I've happily avoided developing a category for them. It threw me when the Louisiana native Donald Link opened Cochon Restaurant in the spring of 2006 and introduced an unusual house gumbo that incorporates pork, black-eyed peas, and greens. Stickler New Orleanians mumble that the chef has committed gumbo sacrilege—all gumbos are stews, but not all stews are gumbos, even those made with roux, they say. But it is an exceptional creation, and it somehow tastes of gumbo without sounding anything like one.

If I've become partial to any single gumbo style, it's the lusty, oily, everything-but-the-sink sort that's ladled out at black-owned restaurants, often only on Fridays. I call this type Big Mama Gumbo in honor of the first one I ever tried, which was at the now-shuttered Inn Restaurant, a warped and welcoming lunch place near downtown's hospital district. On my first visit, the owner and chef, Lovie Williams, pulled up a chair to watch censoriously as I waded through a bowl of what her menu called Big Mama's Seafood Gumbo. We'd never met, and she didn't say much, and so I ate like I imagined a big mama would. Years later I learned that Miss Lovie's grandchildren called her Big Mama not for her stature, which was average with curves in all the right places, but for her station in their family—she literally was their big mama.

Miss Lovie's gumbo was a phenomenon, not in the least because it must have been the meatiest seafood gumbo available in New Orleans on Fridays during Lent. My portion that day surged with chicken, *chaurice,* shrimp, pig tails, and a crab exoskeleton oozing soft, marrowlike crabmeat, all wading in a broth of oil and brine. I finished it both because Big Mama was sitting at my table and because I couldn't stop. "You look tired," Miss Lovie said with a laugh when I finished, breaking her theatrical scowl. No doubt, that gumbo knocked me out for two solid hours as soon as I found my bed.

Miss Lovie lost her Inn Restaurant during a battle with cancer that took all her energy but, fortunately, not her life. I lost track of her after the storms of 2005, which flooded her Gentilly home. The legacy of her gumbo continues to thrive in my desire to eat more of its kind, which I do whenever I can afford to lose a Friday afternoon to digestion.

There's a life force in no-holds-barred Big Mama Gumbos that's comforting and electric, fantastical and intimidating, in the same way that the places in which I tend to find them can be intimidating. One of my Big Mama Gumbo standbys is Two Sisters Kitchen, a sweet community dining room whose community includes anyone with enough sense to enter. Two Sisters is classic New Orleans in that it's a black-owned and -frequented restaurant in the historic Treme neighborhood, where a white woman lunching alone looks totally out of place and feels totally welcome—like the fleet of green parrots, émigrés from South America, that somehow arrived in New Orleans around the 1970s, reproduced, and now rove the city sharing telephone lines with the native birds. Everyone looks twice when they spot one, sometimes they comment, and then they keep walking.

I always leave Two Sisters filled with as much hope as gumbo.

The restaurant's gumbo is different every time but generally follows a recipe of multiple sausages (sometimes *chaurice*), filé, and enough bones and shells to excite an archeologist. I like to imagine the meat from the bones in my gumbo flavoring someone else's. I once encountered okra in there too, but the chef-owner, Dorothy Finister, told me over the phone that it didn't belong; a renegade employee must have skimmed some of the vegetable from a nearby pot of stewed shrimp and okra and added it as a personal statement.

Perhaps the best argument for Two Sisters' Friday gumbo is the accompanying saucer of mostly mashed potato salad tarted up with pickle relish. You can manage this freebie in multiple ways: treat it as a dinner salad and eat it before the gumbo; eat it as you would any other side dish, snacking on it now and then to prolong the life of the main course; or dab your soupspoon into the potatoes before plunging it into the gumbo. What emerges then is a rendering of potatoes and gravy that makes sense only while you're eating it. At home, Matt and I are disciples of the potato-salad-and-gumbo pairing, which Paul Prudhomme also sanctions. We're not yet parents, but that doesn't keep Matt from acting like one; he never lets a guest move on with dinner unless she's at least tried one bite of the combination.

The steam table at Café Unique, which was the peerless Harbor Restaurant and Bar until the building was sold in 2002, also helps fill my Big Mama Gumbo quota, and it deserves additional mention for having exorcised my fears of turkey gizzards and eating alone in barrooms. One noon hour before the new owners tidied up with paint and light bulbs, the only source of light was a solid beam of sun angling in from an open corner door and illuminating the tavern's air with a pale, dusty glow. I took a table near a single man kept company by a fifth of Chivas Regal, a silver ice bucket, and a sweating highball glass. At a certain moment the man lifted a one-dollar bill from his card table and waved it in the air. The only other person in the room, a woman watching court television, retrieved the money and forced it into a jukebox pushed against a far wall. Soon Otis Redding's languorous "That's How Strong My Love Is" detonated sweetness into the room's darkest corners. The woman raised her arms and spun around and around, eyes closed, singing along. The man drank. I plunged my spoon into a ceramic bowl filled with turkey gizzards and other frightening, fantastic unknowns.

Just as it causes rifts, so can gumbo forge friendships, sometimes under the most unforeseen circumstances. As an intern in pediatrics at Louisiana State University, Matt met a father who knew just how to drive home his disapproval when his teenage son broke a wrist while fighting on a Friday after school. "You made me miss my favorite gumbo" were the only words the father wielded in the emergency room. Matt, who has never brought home flowers, brought me the man's phone number for future gumbo recommendations. We called and then found his favorite at Hank's Seafood, then a Ninth Ward drive-by for fried seafood po-boys, boiled crawfish and turkey necks, and $4.50 quarts of a woodsy-smelling filé gumbo that I would be put out at missing too.

Far to the east of Hank's, almost visible from I-10, is/was the kind of black-hole DMV in which hours disappear like cocktail peanuts. I learned from observing others how to make the stay in this purgatory more pleasant: first, stop by Stella's Family Restaurant next door for takeout. Smothered pork chops, smothered okra, stewed chicken, potato salad. One lunch convinced me to return for Friday's gumbo.

The hush in Stella's dining room made the Real Pie Man sound like a Metallica show in comparison, as everyone seemed to stop talking when I entered. I shook off my paranoia by doing my best green parrot impersonation, perching myself on a chair and acting like I'd always been there. It worked. A girl at the next table violated the heavy quiet by beginning to hum. About nine years old, she wore black soccer shorts, a white T-shirt pulled taut over her beetle-shell belly, and a head of black pigtails. She sat erect with one foot tucked between the chair and her shorts, the other seesawing beneath the table. Two women with her, her mother and her aunt, kept silent while the little girl's energy electrified our corner of the dining room. Her harmonic humming was so close to song that wordlike sounds escaped her lips when she chewed.

At a certain moment the girl raised her head and belted out, "Praise the Lord!"

"That's good to hear her say," said the aunt.

"It's in her." The mother nodded.

The little girl was meanwhile absorbed in her gumbo, picking out smoked sausage with her fingers and gyrating in her seat. Her humming exploded into full-blown singing, rousing gospel verses like "I'm high on you," "take me home," and "every day I wait." Her passion was pure, her singing nothing like the brittle tunes we used to lift from our Catholic missals up north.

I wondered what it must feel like in her belly, that communion of innocent faith and gumbo. Noticing that I hadn't been fed yet, the girl offered me an orange crab claw she had already excavated of its meat with a few powerful inhalations. Her mother scolded her for the impropriety and then, as if puzzling out her daughter's behavior, said to me, "She's been like this every day of her life. I really believe now that people have their own ministries, because if I try to sing like that, my voice gets all crackly."

Finally my own gumbo arrived, in a typically broad bowl sloshing with a tomato-stained broth and brimming with ingredients of the freestyle Big Mama Gumbo genre. As I ate, it became clear at the next table that the girl scarcely was able to communicate beyond her singing. She sang through the waitress's questions, sang through the iced tea refills, sang through the paying of the bill. Her mother's mood shifted from proud to exasperated when the girl sang herself right out into the parking lot as if in a trance. "Get back here and finish your sausage, girl!" the mother yelled.

The girl fell suddenly silent and inched back to the table. "I'm sorry, Mama, I'm sorry, I'm sorry," she whispered, wrapping her round brown arms around her mother's neck. Then she and I finished eating our sausage, at separate tables, together.

On my first post-Katrina trip to check on Stella's and the DMV, ten months after the storm, the restaurant's walls still stood but its front windows were blown out, cracked mud carpeted the floor, and the surrounding neighborhood was nonfunctioning. A pair of shoes aligned as if their owner had stepped out of them yesterday waited—for what?—in the parking lot outside Stella's door, next to a cordless telephone that could no longer ring.

I *do* know what it felt like deep inside that girl's belly. Now more than ever, gumbo is often the only thing that makes sense to me on Fridays too.

SAZERACS

I Take My Liquor Brown

In both my birth home, Wisconsin, and my adopted home, New Orleans, Fridays tend to make most sense after a cold one. My people drink too much, both geographical sets of them. I sometimes seem to be the only person in either place who understands this. I'm an incorrigible lightweight and a misbehaving drunk; I learned early, around the eleventh grade, that these traits make a destructive combination. Aside from the two years I spent in high school under the spell of a boy who drank Mad Dog 20/20 like soda, I've managed to maintain the status of soberest chump in the room. (If my friends remember otherwise, they were too gone themselves to judge.)

Alcoholic enlightenment comes with its burdens. I may as well have *DD*, for "designated driver," tattooed on my rear end, and I often wind up paying more than my fair share of the bill. But it also comes with a reward that I wouldn't trade for Hemingway's tolerance: as with food or friends or money, the less alcohol you have, the more you appreciate it, and I have a lover's appreciation of a good cocktail. More precisely, a good brown cocktail.

When in Wisconsin, I covet a regional variation of the old-fashioned, the brandy old-fashioned sweet—a tawny concoction of muddled fruit, brandy, Angostura bitters, sugar, and either 7 Up or soda, or, less common, water. In New Orleans, it's the promise of a Sazerac, a not altogether dissimilar regional drink now made with rye whiskey, that teases me through the days.

There's no single supreme bowl of gumbo in New Orleans, no gold standard against which locals agree to judge oyster po-boys, no definitive recipe for shrimp rémoulade. I do believe, however, that there exists a perfect Sazerac, and I first drank it on Lundi Gras 2003, in the bar at Clancy's Restaurant.

The perfect Sazerac is a foxy brown-red, the hue that rye whiskey attains when stained with a few dashes of Peychaud's bitters, a vital Sazerac ingredient first swallowed by New Orleanians in the early to mid-1800s. The perfect Sazerac is shaken or stirred to cool lightly and served up in an old-fashioned glass, a stout and comfortable shape for a stout and comfortable drink. Its raspy brown-liquor base smooths out like melted chocolate with a touch of sugar and a swirl around the glass of breathy, anise-flavored Herbsaint; Angostura bitters add a warm, quiet spiciness (though not every bartender uses it). A twist of lemon, its essential oils releasing as you drink, is the Sazerac's versatile mediator, brightening the whiskey, steadying the sugar, and matching the bitters with its own dull bitterness.

When I pulled out my notebook and asked Clancy's bartender for his technique, he shrugged. "Just luck, I guess. Don't ask me for another one." Of course I asked him for another one. I may be a one-and-a-half-cocktails-a-night kind of gal, but my people north and south always ask for another one. I am loyal to both.

When you consider that brown liquor defined my childhood as much as, say, snow days and sunburns did, my predilection for the Sazerac begins to look predestined. My barely postadolescent parents made me and Stephanie right about the time that their partying habits matured to include mixed drinks. Loving both, they determined that kids and cocktails were not mutually exclusive. They were correct. While the adults raged on Badger football Saturdays, Stephanie and I got to eat unlimited taco dip and monkey bread. Once, after I gorged myself sick on toffee bars, my aunt Nancy set me up with a stiff shot of peppermint schnapps—not to drink, but to place on my bedside table as an aromatherapy treatment.

Much of my parents' early partying went down at the hilltop home that Nancy shared with my uncle Larry, a man whose command of the brandy old-fashioned remains unparalleled, awing and intoxicating my mom's side of the family once a year at their Christmas party. Larry stirs his old-fashioneds with a cinnamon stick, which softens as you drink and slowly releases its spice. You're meant to leave the cinnamon stick in your glass to flavor the next one. Of course there's a next one.

No one but my kindergarten teacher flinched when at six years old I mentioned my desire to become a cocktail waitress when I grew up (an aspiration first borne out eleven years later, when I got a job carrying cocktails at a private country club). The early parties marked me in so many ways. I still have a stash of purple velveteen Crown Royal bags in my underwear drawer. I don't know what to use them for now that I no longer need a lightweight storage solution for Barbie clothes, but they hold too much sentimental weight to toss.

On either end of the Mississippi River, Wisconsin and Louisiana are in opposition, geographically and culturally. Whereas the former excels at giant muffins, the latter bastardizes batter baking and prefers croissants; midwesterners pass summers in basements, protected from the tornadoes that spin away entire towns, even as hurricane season keeps the Gulf Coast running for higher ground; whereas Wisconsin drove its Native Americans onto reservations, Louisiana gave them Houma and other integrated towns of their choosing. In spite of these differences, it was my brown-liquor-soaked Wisconsin upbringing that sensitized my booze antennae to the Sazerac's magnificence.

How else to account for my deliberate amnesia regarding any other drink imbibed on my first trip to New Orleans—the frozen White Russian daiquiris, Bourbon Street's neon shots served in test tubes, Pat O'Brien's Hurricanes? I flew down for a wedding, and my fellow twentysomething travelers and I partook of all varieties of New Orleans intoxication, including at Artist Café, where two sisters stripped and then tried to spank each other without blushing, and where the drinks were served in go-cups, ostensibly because no one stays very long. But my purest memory of drinking on that trip is reserved for the Sazerac.

It may be that I lucked out, first trying the cocktail at Commander's Palace, the revered house of Creole cooking old and new where the kitchen occasionally slips but the bartenders never do. More likely it was the drink's inherent righteousness that spoke to me. The Sazerac is a cocktail so classic that it has never suffered a coming of age or a fall from grace. And unlike the Wisconsin brandy old-fashioned, whose history is so undocumented that it seems to have sprung from some country well, the Sazerac's noble past is one of immigration, entrepreneurship, and regulated debauch. Something like the origins of New Orleans itself.

The Sazerac's muse, if not its sole inventor, was just a child when his family, plantation owners originally from France, fled the colony of Saint-Domingue (now Haiti) during that country's long and violent slave rebellions. Antoine Amédée Peychaud grew up to be an apothecary in New Orleans. In 1834 he opened a storefront on Royal Street where he ground roots and herbs, spices and barks, and administered his healing tonics to ailing customers. An empath like all good bartenders, Peychaud realized that a spoonful of liquor helps the medicine go down; the running story is that he dribbled his bitters into *coquetiers*, or hourglass-shaped eggcups that were the precursor to jiggers, filled with cognac. Thus one of America's first cocktails—and the French Quarter's first shots—was born.

Some histories, namely those of New Orleanian persuasion, contend that Peychaud mixed *the* first American cocktail. The proof, they say, is the word *cocktail* itself, an obvious bastardization of *coquetier*. There exist other convincing theories about the origin of the American cocktail, but as none directly involve the story of the Sazerac, I'll let them be.

In Peychaud's time a taste for brown drink was ubiquitous in this port city, including at the French Quarter's Sazerac Coffee House (long not in business), a namesake of the French brandy Sazerac de Forge et Fils, and the location that's acknowledged today as the birthplace of the first cocktails that New Orleanians called Sazeracs.

Eventually ingredients other than bitters and brandy entered the cocktail's mix; among them was French absinthe, that poetic, debilitating, naturally anise-flavored spirit that was banned worldwide by the early twentieth century—but not before New Orleans established itself as a grand place to lose a few days.

Absinthe was outlawed because of its reliance on the plant wormwood, a bitter herb with debatable psychoactive properties. A demand for absinthe was so strong in Europe and New Orleans at the time that producers soon improvised by making wormwood-free, anise-flavored pastis such as the New Orleans native Legendre Herbsaint. Originally produced and bottled here, Herbsaint now comes from a distillery in Kentucky. I prefer it in Sazeracs to other popular pastis brands (such as Pernod and Ricard) for its local roots, its more aggressive herbaceous overtones, and its pretty olive-amber shimmer.

As of fairly recently, you can purchase quasi-local, wormwood-inclusive absinthe again, and while its production is still illegal in the United States, you may drink it here. The Louisiana native and environmental chemist Ted Breaux produces three artisanal varieties of absinthe in France, in a distillery designed in the 1800s by Gustave Eiffel. He sells them legally, via the Internet, for a mint. In the summer of 2006, Breaux spoke about his absinthe production at a drinks summit in New Orleans called "Tales of the Cocktail," explaining that wormwood is a historical scapegoat, not a satanic herb, and that drinking absinthe in moderation is as safe as drinking any other liqueur. He circulated samples of his absinthes, and also of the herbs he sources from French growers to make them. Placing a single leafy fleck from a bag of wormwood (*Artemisia absinthium*) on my tongue confirmed that absinthe's definitive ingredient *invented* bitter—it pained my soft palate as it brushed down my throat, and the hurt intensified over time. Breaux's absinthe, on the other hand, went down just as he promised it would: "like perfume." I could detect the wormwood's bitterness without actually tasting it in the liqueur's pure, minty, anise flavor and its powdery finish. Most other alcohols taste far less legal.

Before Breaux's tasting, I believed that the modern Sazerac

missed nothing by lacking absinthe; I know now that pastis (which, Breaux explained, is made with licorice root and Chinese star anise rather than straight herbs) is a poor approximation of the real deal. Nothing to be done about that, though, until domestic production of absinthe makes it affordable again.

In the meantime, while Herbsaint is preferable, the brand of pastis is not as important as using it is. A Sazerac is no Sazerac without that trace of anise, a hauntingly irresistible bluish flavor to the black-licorice-inclined and a fatal repellent to all others. In a collection of her short stories, the New Orleans writer Poppy Z. Brite speaks for the world's Sazerac-averse through a character whose father "would give me a sip of his Sazerac to teach me not to be an alcoholic." The character, John Rickey, describes Herbsaint as "like the black jelly bean if you took the sugar out and replaced it with bug spray."

I'm fond of this description because it's dead on, whether you love Sazeracs or despise them. Mr. Rickey's parental wisdom is more dubious. Our parents used to let Stephanie and me gnaw on their brandy-logged cinnamon sticks during the weekend-long parties of our childhood. Neither of us is an alcoholic today, but Stephanie holds her wine like a flask, and I'm so enamored of brown drink that I can't stop writing about it.

Recipe writers are divided on whether Sazeracs ought to include Angostura as well as Peychaud's bitters. Stanley Clisby Arthur, who wrote *Famous New Orleans Drinks and How to Mix 'Em*, included Angostura in his as far back as 1937. I follow his lead, and I don't doubt that it's because Angostura's warm, barky, cinnamonlike qualities remind me of home. In comparison, there's a more medicinal anise edge and a black pepper duskiness to Peychaud's Shirley Temple–red tonic. The two bitters complement each other in a Sazerac, adding dimension without confusion, like the way you might fill out a gumbo with both powdered red pepper and liquid Tabasco.

At some point rye whiskey became New Orleans' brown liquor of choice, replacing brandy—perhaps around the time of the Civil War, when importing from France grew cost-prohibitive. In *Famous New Orleans Drinks*, Clisby Arthur submits that exactly when the switch occurred is moot: "American rye whiskey was substituted for the cognac to please the tastes of Americans who preferred 'red likker' to any pale-faced brandy." The red-likker preference stuck fast in New Orleans: to the best of my knowledge, I've never been served a brandy Sazerac without asking for it. A few class-conscious bartenders around town do ditch the rye for high-end, woody, burnt-sugar bourbons, but these are too robust and wind up drowning the Sazerac's harmonious convolution of flavors. An economical Wild Turkey rye does just fine. Ordinary bourbon works in a pinch.

Martin Sawyer, an octogenarian who tended bar at the Rib Room in the Omni Royal Orleans Hotel for about thirty-four years (and for three decades prior to that in other French Quarter bars), paid homage to former and contemporary tastes by stirring brandy *and* rye into his Sazeracs. I wish I had tasted one. While he has reinhabited his flooded New Orleans East home, Mr. Sawyer retired after Katrina.

I can't explain why brandy has enjoyed more longevity in Wisconsin, where residents consume more Korbel brandy per capita than people in any other state. Nor can I explain why brandy didn't make a significant comeback in New Orleans in later years, when the United States began to produce loads of it. Coming to know the Sazerac has, however, led me to formulate an unorthodox theory about the evolution of Wisconsin's brandy old-fashioned—a theory with holes but also intrigue. It begins with a Mississippi riverboat captain who took his Sazerac habit upriver but ran out of absinthe along the way (as anyone would). My Northern European ancestors, who would have received the captain, were an industrious people. I imagine they made do by adding a bit more sugar to his punch, a cinnamon stick for spice, and perhaps some canned fruit for color if the captain had drained his Peychaud's bitters. True to their Protestant temperance, they would have lengthened the drink with water, and later with soda. Voilà: the first Wisconsin brandy old-fashioned.

My fairy-tale history would have Wisconsinites and New Orleanians communing over brown drink not long after the pirate antihero Jean Lafitte (for whom one of New Orleans' oldest bars is named) was dealing in slaves and helping save Louisiana from English rule. It certainly would spice up the history lessons in my home state, which when I was in school leaned heavily on my ancestors' angelic involvement in the underground railroad and their mastery of milk production.

No one has corroborated my upriver cocktail theory. I once cornered William Grimes, who wrote the terrific cocktail history book *Straight Up or On the Rocks*, at a literary festival in New Orleans, during which he enlightened the crowd with the following observation: "You can tell by looking at the paintings of the French impressionists what the absinthe era was really like—someone looking paralyzed, sitting in the corner of a café." Having listened to my theory/fantasy on the connection between Sazeracs and brandy old-fashioned sweets, he replied, "Unlikely." I took it with a grain of optimism. It wasn't a no.

I've since run the idea by other students of the cocktail, though more casually than I did with Mr. Grimes. Now I pretend that I'm mostly joking, and I don't work up the courage for that until cocktails have been served. "Unlikely" turned out to be generous—other people just numbly nod. Sometimes even I ask myself why I persist in forcing connections between my two peoples. I found a home in New Orleans. I built a life here and discovered a cocktail to love. So why all the looking back, all the comparisons?

I suppose it's because the depth with which I felt instantly at home in New Orleans has never seemed entirely serendipitous. The tastes, the people, the places that touch me—on the surface they're exotic, different from anything I'd tasted or met or experienced before. But I often wonder whether they're wholly new or whether what resonates for me most deeply in New Orleans is the sense of home I had growing up, just in a warmer, more colorful disguise.

Is this is why I find it additionally heartening to note that New Orleans' first cold cocktails were chilled with ice harvested from northern lakes (including the Great Lakes around Wisconsin), packed in sawdust, and either paddled down the great river or sailed down the East Coast from New York and into the Gulf of Mexico?

The transport and, later, production of ice forever changed the Sazerac, which like all early cocktails was first drunk warm. Some drinks makers, such as those at Galatoire's Restaurant, still revel in the luxury of ice by lavishing their Sazeracs with cubes of it. One never scoffs openly at anything frozen in the subtropics, but I don't prefer rocks in mine. Too much cold dulls a Sazerac's thrilling points of flavor.

If it seems counterintuitive that a lightweight would find such an obsession in cocktails, consider the first drink—or rather, the second drink. Aside from its ritualistic pleasures, isn't the second drink always a letdown? It's like the second kiss, or the second time in New York City, or the second breath after you've been underwater too long. All the warm fuzzies of intoxication and none of its evils are concentrated in that first drink, above all the first sip. There's a soft melancholy in drinking liquor, which I experience most strongly drinking the brown kind, which settles at once into the bones, a complete benign passivity. Long before drunkenness takes over, drinking offers the release of the final sob following some deep misery, when your body just can't cry anymore.

It's natural, then, that drinking became emotional first aid following Katrina, when tears fixed nothing. Matt and I were visiting his mother and stepfather in Manhattan on the day of the hurricane; we didn't get to use our return plane tickets for a month. During those long days and nights in New York, I naturally yearned for a Sazerac. Because of the drink's claim on me, coupled with my lousy tolerance, I basically had given up drinking anything else in New Orleans. But even on the evening we visited one of those fashionable Manhattan bars where the "mixologists" specialize in resurrecting classic American cocktails—and account heartily for inflation when ringing up your tab—I couldn't bring myself to order one. Though my affair with the Sazerac had stifled my cocktail curiosity and biased my palate, it made no more sense to drink one outside New Orleans than to eat a po-boy. The French refer to *terroir* when speaking of the effects of a specific grape-growing region's climate and geography on the character of its wine. It's not the best association, as no Sazerac ingredient grows in New Orleans soil, but there is a sort of emotional *terroir* that can unite certain tastes to specific places. During our Katrina displacement in New York, I took up with the manhattan.

Matt and I eventually used our return tickets before we were technically allowed back into New Orleans. His hospital ID was enough to convince a peach-fuzzed National Guardsman to wave us over the Orleans Parish line. Before heading to our home in a sliver of Uptown that hadn't flooded, we checked on a few of our favorite food places. The vintage neon sign at Angelo Brocato Ice Cream & Confectionery had smashed to its Mid-City sidewalk; flies darkened the water-ruined ice cream parlor's windows from the inside. There was no movement, or turtle soup, at sodden Mandina's Restaurant around the corner. We rejoiced to see a few dirty men brushing themselves off outside Port of Call, a French Quarter burger joint—they told us that they would resume grilling burgers as soon as gas and electricity were restored.

Our own block was silent—no kids, no cars, no electrical buzz, no birds—but for the small man who stamped down the street and asked for our credentials. Mr. Leo had been staying at his brother's (our neighbor's) house since warlike chaos at the Superdome "shelter" had driven him upriver. For the first few days after the hurricane, before the cavalry arrived, he performed boat rescue missions as far out as the Jefferson Parish line; he pushed Pedialyte in shopping carts ("borrowing" both supplies and cart from our officially closed neighborhood supermarket) to the dehydrated babies stranded downtown; he donated a generator to a nearby police station; he watched the gas tanks of every vehicle on our block get punctured and drained by a man desperate to escape the city; he cooked for hungry stragglers before he gave away the generator; he slept on his brother's porch, armed; and he mowed all of our lawns so they would look pretty when we returned. Mr. Leo told impossible stories. Over time, many of them checked out.

After he made sure, by checking our IDs, that we belonged to the house for which we had keys, Mr. Leo asked if we had thought to import some cold beer. Dang. Only momentarily disappointed, he offered to share the ice and juice a relief agency brought by his place every morning if we would bust out some of the spirited mixers in our liquor cabinet (he correctly assumed that we had a liquor cabinet). Then, cocktail in hand, he helped us clean the maggots out of our refrigerator, patch our wind-damaged roof, and feel at home again.

Of all the American things most New Orleanians in the city could not do for months following Katrina and the ensuing flood—make a phone call, take a warm shower, surf the Web, heat a can of beans, shop at Wal-Mart, go to work—catching a buzz was not among them. The everyday movement of the city had all but stopped, but the drinking never did. Mr. Leo had hit upon a six-pack of his favorite beer, Natural Ice, while browsing in the dark, unstaffed supermarket and had considered it a gift from God.

Once residents began to repopulate New Orleans, drinking calmed frazzled thoughts and fried emotions. Friends and neighbors toasted the relief at seeing each other again, and they toasted the sadness of innocence—and more than 1,500 people—lost. Our house sustained the sort of wind-related damage you expect from a strong hurricane: shredded roof, torn siding, a downed pecan tree crushing the backyard fence. We had no right to complain, given the hell others struggled to endure, but after a day of minor inconveniences—waiting with other heartsick people for an hour at the grocery store, arguing with insurance adjusters, breathing plaster dust, triaging curbside debris into tree remains, construction trash, and household garbage—Matt proclaimed that cold booze was more sanitizing than a shower.

I didn't notice a subsidence of alcohol consumption among my friends and neighbors as everyday conveniences began to return, because the storm lingered. (New Orleanians use *the storm* and *Katrina* not only to indicate the primary meteorological incident, a hurricane; the terms additionally encompass the levee breaches, the ensuing flood, the resulting deaths, the rescue efforts, the governmental blunders, our extended—sometimes permanent—stays in the diaspora, the near-death of our city, Hurricane Rita, which arrived three weeks after Katrina, and in many cases every single day that has passed since August 29, 2005. For the hardest hit, *the storm* and *Katrina* continue to define everyday life.) Depression and ways of coping with it, like drinking, became casual conversation topics. In June 2006, nine months after the hurricane, a cabdriver taking me to the airport commented apropos of nothing—other than that we both were living in post-Katrina New Orleans—that he used to be a social drinker. "Now, I can't even eat until I've had a couple of beers," he told me. The following week, the *New York Times* published an article about the alarming suicide rate in our town. Overdrinking sounded like a responsible alternative.

In first devising this book, before Katrina, I vowed to resist mentioning some of the obvious New Orleans clichés: *laissez les bon temps roulez*, "the Big Easy," Goldschlager shots from a drive-through daiquiri shed, that kind of thing. At the time they seemed lazy and unoriginal, evoking an image of life in New Orleans that the city should perhaps try to shed. Now I long for lightheartedness to define us again one day. Certainly there were New Orleanians who drank to fill a void before the storm; I worry that now most of us do. Which is not the same as saying that we're a city of stumbling drunks. Most nights end soberly.

My northern people are good-times drinkers. My dad (birth name David) has been called Fud since childhood—a good-time name if ever there was one. Thirty-six years of marriage haven't stopped my mom, Marcie, from laughing with (or at) him. As far back as my memory reaches, I've been envious of my parents' ability to cut completely loose. As when they were raising me, their partying now appears to be pure enjoyment. And yet ever since Katrina did to me at thirty-five what I did to them in their twenties—turned me into an adult—I do wonder.

. . .

I still don't have much of a tolerance. Good for my liver, but too bad because there are so many other New Orleans cocktails to drink. The Ramos gin fizz (gin, egg white, cream, orange flower water, soda), Herbsaint frappés, whiskey old-fashioneds, obituary cocktails (gin, vermouth, pastis), Pimm's Cups at Napoleon House, monsoons (rum punch) at Port of Call, anything at the Columns Hotel. The mint julep isn't indigenous to New Orleans, but it is possible here, and it is brown. So is brandy milk punch, a sweet cocktail that might taste like after-dinner but is more often drunk after church. Once as I entered a private Sunday brunch party at Commander's Palace, a server handed me a slender shot of brandy milk punch before directing me to my seat. It was 11 A.M., and I had to ask for coffee. I recognized this as a natural progression, owing to the tradition on my dad's side of the family of kicking off holiday feasts with a few rounds of brandy Alexanders, because any drink made with heavy cream and crème de cocoa (which we pronounce "cream de coke") is an obvious apéritif.

There's one major catch to being a lightweight who loves brown liquor, though, especially when said lightweight is a restaurant critic or otherwise keeps company with the food police (other critics, food writers, chefs, sommeliers, and nonprofessional but opinionated gourmets). I can stretch one and a half Sazeracs over the course of the most extravagant meal with delight, but rarely do I possess the physiological wherewithal for one and a half Sazeracs *and* wine. Fine food without fine wine? No, ma'am. Anybody who takes food seriously takes it with her fist clenched around a glass of fermented grape juice.

The food police run Western Europe. Try ordering a Jack and Coke at a café or a trattoria. The soda will be warm, the Jack scarce, and the ice cubes on the side—or some other combination of those nouns and adjectives. Whenever we return from visiting Matt's Belgian family, my first indulgence (after waxy American chocolate) is a cocktail. Any cocktail.

I do enjoy wine; I just enjoy liquor more. And yet I can't pretend that Sazeracs drink well with food. Authors of cocktail books often file the Sazerac under apéritifs, with reason. They're too stormy, too sweet, like the town that birthed them. Even a martini cooperates better with a meal; white liquors sting and then disappear like a pinprick, whereas brown ones punch and then continue to smart like a black eye. Tequila, an in-between spirit, just generally hurts. Me, anyway.

What to say in my own defense, then, other than that I don't care?

One evening a couple of years ago, my friend Brett Anderson and I had a mutual desire for oysters. At the time he and I wrote restaurant reviews for separate New Orleans newspapers. As his was the daily and mine a weekly, his expense account covered the wine list while mine covered one drink. Consequently, he had grown increasingly knowledgeable about wine and extravagant in his selections, and I had committed myself body and soul to a cocktail.

We both began with Sazeracs that night (Brett, a Minnesotan by birth, was an aspiring New Orleanian too), and we drank them while chitchatting over saltines and crusty bread. Then he ordered a bottle of Champagne—if memory serves, a nonvintage Roederer Brut.

"I'll have another Sazerac," I told the waiter.

"*Really*. With raw oysters?" Brett asked.

The question sounded more like an accusation, though he claims not to have meant it that way. Brett is everybody's most libertarian friend, so I'm inclined to believe him. My own conscience must have inserted the italics; it knows it's wrong to drink a Sazerac with raw oysters when there's Roederer Brut on the table. It's as wrong as wearing perfume on the evening you plan to order the tasting menu at Alain Ducasse. It just *feels* so right (the Sazerac, not the perfume—I'd never do that).

When the waiter returned with our drinks and oysters, I submitted and asked him to pour me a glass of Champagne as well. It bubbled demurely beside my new, sweating Sazerac, slenderness and poise beside bravado and brown. Two drinks, one for show and the other—or at least half of it—for sipping.

SNO-BALLS

The Bittersweet of Summertime

Before Katrina forced everyone into high gear and eradicated the customary downshifting into weekends, New Orleans was the ideal town for an underachiever, a place where whiling away Saturdays on the stoop or on projects so underproductive they wouldn't count as hobbies in other cities was the norm. This environment suited me and other people who, like me, wanted to appear more industrious than average without doing much work. The town's lighthearted languor was (and, I hope, will be again) more frustrating for born gunners like Matt, who for most of our dating years I couldn't imagine marrying because the instant morning light brushed his eyelids he was upright, springing about the bedroom, the Beastie Boys at full tilt. Before coffee. Including on weekends.

We moved to New Orleans so that Matt could attend medical school at Tulane University. I'm not sure which wore him down first, the city, medical school, or me, but by our third summer of living here Matt began passing his free time at a music stand he had commandeered for an easel, squeezing acrylic paints onto salvaged cardboard and listening to National Public Radio. In general I thanked Fortuna for Matt's unexpected mellowness, but one Saturday art project rankled worse than "Brass Monkey" at sunup: it took him three hours to mix the perfect brown background for a sign advertising Ernest's Own Root Beer, a dreamy syrup flavor at Hansen's Sno-Bliz, where we would present the sign once it dried. The problem was that Hansen's would close by seven o'clock, if it hadn't already, and I couldn't be held accountable if I didn't get a sno-ball that day. I have hypoglycemic tendencies, and New Orleans' sno-ball culture both aids and fuels my sugar dependence. Matt understands me. By six o'clock we were both blowing on the paint.

Ernest Hansen set to building his original Sno-Bliz machine out of wood in 1933 to make sno-balls for his first son, Ernest Hansen, Jr., who is now a physician in Thibodaux, Louisiana. According to Ernest's family members, at the time of his invention vendors pushed carts through the streets of New Orleans rasping ice by hand with the sorts of planing tools that woodworkers use to level doors. A machinist by trade who could make anything out of metal, Ernest found this method neither sanitary nor elegant. He patented his homemade, motor-driven, clean ice-grinding apparatus in 1939. He later made a larger machine from steel, still used at Hansen's today, which must be disassembled periodically for maintenance but otherwise doesn't budge. From the beginning, the fineness of his shaved ice appeared to be in direct proportion to the bulk of the Sno-Bliz machine itself.

Ernest's wife, Mary, saw a business model in his sno-balls and soon took them to the sidewalk, setting up shop beneath a chinaball tree (New Orleans–speak for chinaberry tree). She developed recipes for syrups that, when poured over the ice, transformed it into something New Orleanians seem to enjoy in the summertime more than ice cream and candy combined. Back then they charged two cents for a scoop, a scoop being a shapeless syrup-drenched snowdrift served on a cardboard tray. Those first sno-balls came without silverware, forcing customers to lap at them as you would an ice cream cone. Only a Hansen's sno-ball doesn't resist your tongue like ice cream does, and I imagine it didn't back then, either; the feathery ice vanishes the moment your breath touches it, leaving the rapture of sweet, ice-cold syrup in its wake.

Two cents was double the price that other shaved-ice vendors were charging during the Depression, and many people couldn't afford the markup. Family members say that Mary gave away more sno-balls than she sold in those early years, even while she traded her own family's meat rations for sugar in order to keep the business going. Her charity, frankness, and disregard for segregation—not to mention the quality sno-balls—earned her and Ernest a loyal following as they moved the operation around town, from the sidewalk on St. Ann Street to a shop on Valmont Street and finally to a boxy cinderblock building on the uptown autobahn known as Tchoupitoulas Street.

That's where Matt and I found them when we moved to the neighborhood in 1999. By then the sno-balls had long been served in paper-towel-wrapped cups, and they came stuck like pincushions with plastic spoons and straws. The smallest cost seventy-five cents. Ernest had been plowing ice into snow as downy as the Rockies on a powder day and Mary had been dousing it with sweetened color for sixty years. They were eighty-nine and ninety years old, respectively, and they were beginning to serve their fourth generation of customers.

With a dime-size dent in his forehead (an aneurism memento) and glasses that made his eyes appear extraordinarily large, Ernest gripped his noisy apparatus of steel and saw like other men his age clenched their walkers. Though his traveling days were long over by the time Matt and I met him, Ernest told stories of off-season travels to Australia and Sicily as if they happened last year. He sometimes recited and handed out original poetry, odes to his two greatest loves: Mary and God.

Mary wore skirts to work in her later years, and she complimented nearly every customer on his or her individual beauty. She seemed never to stop smiling, though certain occasions brought out the feisty side that her family knew well—like the time when a favorite customer offended her rigorous sanitation standards by grabbing a syrup bottle from the counter to sniff at its contents. Mary threw him out of the shop.

Sno-ball is a common regional spelling of *snowball,* and an endearment. For the record, New Orleans sno-balls are not snow cones, those unfortunate, chippy, enamel-eroding horrors that I grew up eating and that replicate the icy pain of northern winters. No, a New Orleans sno-ball is an artisan product. While Hansen's shaved ice is by leagues the softest I've eaten, even the lowest-grade New Orleans sno-balls shame their counterparts elsewhere. To elucidate:

> snow cone : sno-ball :: squeeze-bottle supermarket honey : Sardinian corbezzolo honey, harvested from the blossoms of the rare evergreen strawberry tree

If Ernest's shaved ice appeared more meteorological than man-made in its fineness, its capacity for absorbing flavored simple syrups defied all branches of science. Handed a cup of Ernest's freshly plowed snow, Mary would tip one of her syrup bottles on its head, allowing it to spill its contents until the airy ice drift sank beneath the weight of the liquid to disappear below the lip of the cup. Then she would hand the cup back to Ernest, he would shave another mound on top and hand it back, and Mary would repeat her work. Then they would do the dance again, three times total per sno-ball—one for the Father, one for the Son, and one for the Holy Spirit. The family credits this shave-syrup-shave-syrup-shave-syrup technique as much as they credit the Sno-Bliz machine for the supremacy of the finished product.

Technically a Hansen's sno-ball is called a Sno-Bliz (short for "snow blizzard"), as in *Let's stop by Hansen's for a wild cherry Sno-Bliz*. But if anyone speaks this way anymore, they're too old-school to be hanging out with me. In my experience, Hansen's fans—and even often the Hansens themselves—discriminate between other New Orleans sno-balls and a Hansen's Sno-Bliz simply by making sure always to use the family name, as in *The first Hansen's sno-ball I ever had was cream of nectar.*

. . .

The first Hansen's sno-ball I ever had was cream of nectar, a soft vanilla-almond flavor similar to Strawberry Quik that's always dyed some shade of little-girl pink. Natives associate the flavor with soda jerks, drive-in hamburger stands, and the nectar cream sodas they used to drink at the aggressively purple, no-longer-in-business K&B drugstores. The nectar flavor is said to have been invented in the late nineteenth century by a New Orleans pharmacist and inveterate recipe maker, but the story doesn't end there. Nectar is the kind of mythical entity that inspires rumors about hidden recipes and secret formulas throughout the city.

Ashley Hansen, Ernest and Mary's granddaughter and the Sno-Bliz heiress, told me that they run through three gallons of their secret-recipe nectar cream a day at the shop. She framed the flavor's mystique this way: "When you grow up in New Orleans, that's the flavor that makes it all real. That's the flavor that makes you remember your childhood. It's fluffy, it's pink." With such an endorsement, and with the primary dictionary definition of nectar being something like "the drink of the Greek and Roman gods," you do wonder why anyone orders another syrup.

Except that at Hansen's there are so many exceptional ones (around twenty-two all told) and so few days in which to try them. Despite the near year-round swelter in New Orleans, the Hansens have upheld conservative parameters for summertime during our time here—parameters adopted by Sno-Bliz loyalists, who consider the stand's seasonal opening as the unofficial but absolute declaration that summer has arrived, whenever said opening may occur. If you set your calendar to Hansen's time, as April heats up you cruise past the shop often. Finally one day you note with a skipped heartbeat that the red number painted on an exposed side of the cinderblock building has increased by one. In 2006, the number jumped from 66 to 67, indicating that Hansen's was on the brink of opening for its sixty-seventh year (Ernest and Mary started keeping tally when they moved to Valmont Street in 1939).

Before the painted number can dry, Hansen's opening date begins to circulate as word-of-mouth breaking news that's usually grounded in pure rumor. I worked briefly with Ashley when I moved to town, at a catering gig, before I understood the significance of her lineage. I consequently had her home number when I later began writing a food news column for *Gambit Weekly* and thereby was able to inform my readers of Hansen's real projected opening date (which was still only more or less accurate—you never knew for sure until a line formed outside). A few weeks into each season, I used the column again to report on my inaugural Hansen's sno-ball, usually cream of nectar for nostalgia's sake. A month or so after that I wrote about discovering some new flavor combination; a drizzle of tart lemonade over root beer was one epiphany. Near the end of every August, I warned my readers that Hansen's sno-ball season peters out around Labor Day. Eventually the newspaper's managing editor suggested that maybe I was overdoing it. Something about objective journalism.

No matter how unadvertised its opening, Hansen's is mobbed that first day and every sunny Thursday through Sunday that follows, or thereabouts (Hansen's opening days and hours have been fickle in our time here; it's best to think of the sno-balls as a privilege, not a right). It's also crowded when it rains, but as the line shoves through the screen door rather than snaking around outside as usual, the wait appears less intimidating. Either way, satisfying a yearning for a Hansen's sno-ball tends to dissolve other afternoon plans.

Inside the shop, a yellow line repainted annually on top of a powdery red cement floor travels from the screen door along the interior Tchoupitoulas Street wall and then makes a sharp right turn down toward an ordering counter. The line designates a path through the musty room, the sticky fan-blown air, that's impossible not to follow; you obey it if you're the first customer of the day or the last, never, ever taking a short cut diagonally across the hard red expanse. The yellow-line shuffle is as much a part of the Hansen's experience as the low, motorized putter of the Sno-Bliz machine, and the balloon-colored syrups, and the molasses shifting of damp bodies.

Slow as it goes, important things happen while you stand, shuffle, sweat, and yearn to mainline the ice-cold sugar. For instance, this is when you debate which flavor you'll choose—sweet and refreshing (blueberry, spearmint, grape), sweet and rich (cream of chocolate, cream of coffee, cream of peach), sweet and sour (lemonade, orangeade), or some combination of the three. People with the kinds of dispositions that enable them to file their taxes on time never waver in their selections, but for me the internal flavor debate is perennially as conflicted as the sweet-or-salty breakfast quandary—pancakes or omelet? Sweet roll or huevos rancheros? Pain perdu or eggs Sardou? It always boils down to mood and impulse, which fight each other as I play tightrope along the line.

Another major sno-ball-ordering decision, portion size, never seems to be up to me. Hansen's choices run from kiddie cup to garbage pail, or Atkins loyalist to future diabetic, with an extra-large popcorn tub in between. Whatever my appetite, and whatever my intention at the start of the line, I cannot resist ordering the signature plastic cup printed with colored drawings of Ernest and Mary looking young, happy, and more colorful than life. Beneath them is stamped their motto: "There Are *NO* Shortcuts to Quality." Fortunately, this cup is the size of a Jr. Atomic, the most decadent creation at Hansen's, which with characteristic humor Ernest named for its resemblance to the mushroom cloud that follows an atomic bomb. The Jr. Atomic is a standard sno-ball topped with canned cream topped with crushed pineapple topped with marshmallow fluff topped with a scoop of vanilla ice cream topped off with a cherry. Exposed to the ice, the marshmallow fluff stiffens into a chewy, pliable goo; as you spoon into the mushroom cloud of ice cream, cream, and shaved ice, the marshmallow stretches through the exhilarating whole like a ribbon of taffy. The Jr. Atomic is an insanely immature thing for a thirty-five-year-old woman to order, and yet I feel like the most enlightened person in the room every time I do.

An accidental function of the yellow-line wait is that it turns you into a scholar of Hansen's wall hangings. Nearly every inch of available space is devoted to some piece of the shop's history: decades of media clippings, children's art projects, hand-lettered signs ("Air

Condition Your Tummy"; "There are STILL no shortcuts to Quality"), and faded photographs of customers, of Ernest and Mary throughout their lives, and of Ashley when she was a child, not yet the heir apparent. It's like a hanging photo album of the Hansens' extended family. I imagine it makes you feel like royalty to see yourself up there.

Three summers into our Hansen's routine, Matt and I still hadn't made it onto the wall. We had tried. We visited the stand most weekends, sampling every flavor; one day we went twice. Matt introduced Ashley to his favorite refresher, spearmint plus lemonade (or at least she graciously let us believe she'd never thought of it herself), which she then introduced to some neighborhood kids. We brought friends, and friends of friends. We even stood behind a couple while they posed for the camera and tried to get our own heads in the shot. Eventually Matt painted the root beer sign. If our faces couldn't be on the wall, our intentions would be.

Walking the line. Penance for gluttony. Reparation for summer's sloth. Proof of loyalty. A study of painted toenails, flip-flops, tennis skirts, sweat marks, cornrows. That guy always gets almond with canned cream. She hasn't been here since her auntie brought her in 1965. That other lady remembers when the kiddie cup was a quarter. What's your favorite flavor? Purple. Are we almost there, Daddy? Almost—look at the pictures.

On the last Sno-Bliz day one year, before Hansen's closed for the season, I stood behind a woman and her toddler.

"Mommy, how much longer?"

"The wait makes the sno-ball taste better, sweetie."

The travel time from screen door to counter depends on several variables, such as the decisiveness—or not—of those in line before you and how many sno-balls they order. Kids sometimes hobble out of the shop balancing drippy cups for the entire neighborhood in their arms. (While employees at other sno-ball stands press funnels down upon the shaved ice, forming tidy ice pyramids with planed sides, a Hansen's sno-ball is free-form, cumulous, and messy.) Almost every order requires the syrup pourer to dash to a white refrigerator in a back kitchen for at least one of the cream syrups that could spoil if kept at the scalding room temperature. From the beginning, Mary was so concerned about the integrity of her product that she made the syrups daily, including her signature invention, Mary's Own Sno-Bliz, which looks like it could be wild cherry but tastes like a SweeTart. It's a painstaking process for a product that involves such simple ingredients as sugar and water.

Periodically the entire room pauses to watch the Sno-Bliz machine operator refill his ice supply by reaching down into a chest freezer behind him for a fresh loaf and then loading it into the machine. When Ashley began working at the shop full-time, in 1997, her grandparents still traveled to New Orleans East to hand-pick their ice at an ice house, where they competed with shrimpers for the cleanest, clearest blocks. They transported their several-hundred-pound purchase in the rear of a Jeep; back at the shop, family members chipped it with ice picks into machine-ready pieces, a five-hour process. Against her grandparents' will, Ashley "modernized" by hiring a traveling iceman to deliver roughly twelve hundred pounds to the shop once a week. He custom-cuts it on the premises using an electric chainsaw.

Everything about Hansen's feels old-fashioned. It's a business that operates only at the height of New Orleans' sticky summers, and it's not even air-conditioned. It nevertheless was astonishing to learn that the rectangular logs of ice fed into the Sno-Bliz machine have such primitive origins. I'd always imagined that they came from oversized ice cube trays.

I've found it difficult to convince the unindoctrinated (that is, those who have never lived through a New Orleans summer) that sno-balls are a significant part of the city's food culture. Perhaps not as weighty as gumbo or oysters, but certainly up there with the Sazerac and spaghetti. Sno-ball stands loom along country highways and come into focus as you drive through thickly residential neighborhoods. A walk-up window sawed from the flank of a po-boy shop.

The shed that used to back up against the parking lot of my dentist's office. The clover-green cottage trailer towed to the edge of Audubon Park. Depending on the stand, you might order your sno-ball "stuffed," with a scoop of ice cream hidden at the center (at Hansen's, this is called a Hot Rod); topped with whipped cream, sweetened condensed milk, or evaporated milk (the Hansens call the latter "canned cream" and use it often); decorated with gummy candies, candied sprinkles, crushed pineapple, or cherries; soaked in flavors that have nothing to do with their names, like Tiger's Blood and Ninja Turtle; sprayed with a substance whose sour quotient exceeds straight lemon juice by a factor of about two million; or drenched in a sugar-free syrup (at Hansen's, a no-sugar-added option is Martinelli's apple juice).

Given Hansen's short season, I do sometimes boost my blood sugar with a heathen sno-ball elsewhere, such as at SnoWizard, another institution. My fall-back flavor is straight orange plus cream of ice cream—both are New Orleans standards, and the combo makes a creamsicle. That is, unless I'm at Plum Street Snowball, another stalwart in Uptown, to which a friend once dragged me for a violet-colored orchid vanilla cream sno-ball topped with sweetened condensed milk. The orchid syrup tasted similar to supermarket birthday-cake buttercream, which by my estimation is the baking world's tackiest and most marvelous achievement.

Shaved and sugared ice sold from sheds and cinderblock bunkers at odd hours part of the year isn't as low-profile as frozen treats get in New Orleans. Within the city's neighborhood culture there thrives a black market for huckabuck frozen cups: Kool-Aid frozen in Dixie cups and sold from porch and patio. Linda Green, who is known around town as the Ya-Ka-Mein Lady, has been making huckabucks for decades; she brought them out of the proverbial closet and sold them to the masses at Jazz Fest in 2005. I enjoyed a lip-staining cherry one shot through with fruit cocktail. On Sunday evenings at Hansen's, the leftover syrups are frozen into similar treats, more commonly called "icebergs." Eventually they either give the improvised popsicles away to neighborhood kids or sell them for pocket change.

Flavored ices are no more unique to New Orleans than beans and rice are, or mayonnaise-slathered sandwiches, or fried pies. Mexico has *raspado*, Hawaii has shave ice, Italy has granita, Philadelphia has water ice. Way back, the ancient Romans sweetened mountain snow with fruit and honey. Once, on vacation in the giant steamroom known as Bangkok and lost for the third time in as many hours, Matt and I ducked into a back alley café dying for some iced coffee. Inside, businessmen squeezed around low wooden tables, each one waiting for the labor-intensive house specialty: white toast torn to pieces, placed in a shallow bowl, covered with freshly shaved ice, drenched with a nonspecifically sweet hot-pink syrup, and then drenched again with sweetened condensed milk. Suddenly we weren't so lost.

South Louisiana's taste for sweet cold things probably originated with the first human sensation in these North American subtropics. Four hundred miles east of New Orleans, in Apalachicola, Florida, John Gorrie patented his now-famous artificial ice machine in the 1850s, at which time a substantial ice trade ran between the region and ice harvesters in the north. We know for sure that icy treats predate 1900's *The Picayune's Creole Cook Book*, which contains recipes for sherbet (sorbet), slushy frozen fruits (*fruits glacés*), and fruit and nut syrups (*sirops*). Beneath "Sirops" it reads:

"Under this heading are classed those delightful beverages of fruits or nuts, served by the Creole housewives during the summer season. Of a hot, sultry day, if you enter a well-regulated Creole household, the first thing Madame will do will be to regale you with a glass of Lemonade, or 'Iced Orgeat,' or 'Iced Pineapple,' etc. The syrups are often put up and bottled by Madame herself, or purchased commercially, but are always at hand."

In comparison, one of my fondest memories of my home state in August—a month when the Wisconsin air is so damp that pushing a vacuum through carpeting is aerobic exercise—is of the steamy afternoon when my aunt Judy greeted me on her porch with a sweating glass of ice water. No lemon. No mint. The epitome of appropriateness. It was too hot, and our people too practical, to drink lemonade, or iced orgeat, or even Diet Coke.

My two peoples tend to consume sugar differently. Whereas Louisianians seem to prefer it by the liquid shot (a shot over ice, or a frozen shot, is still a shot), Wisconsinites are masters of the baked sugars: butterhorns, banana bread, brownies, bran muffins, kringle, snickerdoodles. Our cultural weakness for a good cookie notwithstanding, we do enjoy frozen sweets. As long as they're ice cream. At the supermarket where I worked during high school, the ice cream selection consumes an aisle of freezers so long you need mittens to browse comfortably. My job was to close down the bakery department, which meant eating the day-old crullers and Danish. I settled for this job with its polyester vest and red-billed cap after I didn't make the cut across the street, at Frosty Freeze, a retro-pink ice cream stand where the cheerleaders and pompom girls worked. I was on the swim team.

To this day, my parents drive through Frosty Freeze even more often than I go to Hansen's in the summertime, and it's been almost twenty years now since high school, but I'm still bitter about my rejected application. Over the years, as Ashley Hansen's grandparents aged, my affection for Hansen's Sno-Bliz became increasingly tied up in my affection for Ashley, and not in the least because she could beat the khaki pants off any Frosty Freeze girl.

When she's not slinging simple syrup, Ashley makes her living as a professional cook who sharpens her own knives. In her early thirties, she still has a girlish look about her—small stature, freckled nose, chipmunk cheeks, eyes that squint when she smiles, which is always—except that she's strong as steel, inside and out.

An interloper in the city's food culture, I wondered for a long time whether my esteem for Ashley and her family's sno-ball stand was overblown, a result of my desperation to belong here. But then I met Bebe Ryan and Dean Charbonnet, high school pals and native New Orleanians of roughly Ashley's age. My little fascination had nothing on their lifelong obsessions. Time hasn't lessened the flavor debate for Bebe, who likens her plight to Sophie's in William Styron's *Sophie's Choice*. One flavor in particular, though, always appears when it's supposed to. Before the close of each Hansen's season, someone in Bebe's family buys a ten-dollar cream of chocolate sno-ball, which is stored in the freezer until Thanksgiving, at which time it is microwaved at half power and divvied up among family members. The Hansens condone this treatment of their handiwork, also noting that a frozen-solid, ice-cream-stuffed Hot Rod makes an attractive sliced dessert.

Dean ups Bebe's ante by keeping a 150-pound ice-shaving machine in his living room, enthroned on a table customized with a hole through which the drip pan drains. Ice and syrups were a fascination throughout Dean's childhood and youth: the teachers who poured "real snowball syrups" over crushed ice at Newcomb Nursery; the neighbors' Snoopy Sno-Cone Machine; the mini Hawaiian ice shaver he took with him to college in Atlanta. Eventually returning to New Orleans as an adult, Dean decided it was time to invest. He shopped around, visiting a local manufacturer who keeps a small museum of sno-ball machines, including one similar to how the family describes Ernest's original, wooden Sno-Bliz apparatus. Dean likes to spend "time in the laboratory" developing his own syrup recipes (mint chocolate cream is a prized original invention). But while he's proud of his own sno-balls, he hasn't forsaken his Tchoupitoulas Street muse: "I still patronize Hansen's. Nothing compares to the real deal."

I first met Dean at a party where he and Bebe were on a Hansen's tear; they held court on their passion for the subject until closing time. Just a few months later, desperate to connect with New Orleanians from my Katrina exile in New York, I e-mailed them both. Bebe replied: "This year, 2005, was the only year in the history of my life that I did not get a Hansen's sno-ball all season, and I fear that as a result, our city's fate was sealed."

We grieved together through a virtual reality, for the city in general and the Hansens in particular. Mary Hansen had passed away. She had been hospitalized at Touro Infirmary before Katrina and had died after being airlifted to a hospital in Alexandria and then transferred to Thibodaux during the poststorm pandemonium. Ernest had stayed by her side during the hurricane, but as he was not technically a patient at Touro, and wasn't ill, he was evacuated in a van. It was the first time since Ernest had retired from his day job in 1976 that the couple had been apart for more than a few hours. Family members say that they didn't go to the drugstore without each other.

New Orleans was a ghost town when Mary passed; it was too soon after Katrina for a burial here, so the spot they had prepared for themselves in this city went unused. She was buried instead in the tomb in Thibodaux that her eldest son, Ernest Jr., had prepared for himself and his wife. Ernest joined Mary there just a few months later, in March 2006, after dying of cancer. Ernest Jr. ensured that the town would always know its gain by inscribing the tomb with a clarification that here lies *the* Ernest Hansen, inventor of the famous Sno-Bliz machine.

I had my own remorse, which was not as superstitious as Bebe's but was haunting. Matt and I lived just eight blocks from Hansen's, and the shop was at the tail end of its season when Katrina hit, and yet I could count the number of Hansen's sno-balls I'd eaten that summer on one hand. I tried to tell myself that I simply had been too full for sno-balls, that the lines had been too long, the hours too erratic, my fear of diabetes out of control. But reality was that, whereas during previous summers in New Orleans the promise of a Saturday afternoon sno-ball had gotten me out of bed, going to Hansen's had begun to make me feel sad and guilty. I had been avoiding it without processing why.

Analyzing my shaky loyalty at a distance, I first presumed that my sadness and guilt had been dread in disguise, that watching Ernest and Mary grow elderly and weak had brought me too close for comfort to my own mortality. Ashley and her father, Ernest and Mary's second son, Gerard, a judge in the magistrate section of the Orleans Parish Criminal District Court, had progressively taken over running the business. Ernest and Mary still came to work in the summer of 2005, though Ernest could no longer operate his Sno-Bliz machine and they both needed to take long rests away from the crowds. That must have saddened me more than I had recognized.

But such a theory didn't correlate with the inspiration that Ernest and Mary's consistent presence at the shop had actually been for me, right up until the end. I've always marveled at the way older New Orleanians weave into the city's common culture—the Uncle Lionel Batistes (bass drummer for the Treme Brass Band), the Marie Fagots (Saint Joseph altar builder), the Dot Domilises (of Domilise's po-boy shop), the blind man on Magazine Street who reaches toward the sky with his cane to catch Carnival beads during the Toth parade, the porch sitters, the streetcar riders, the Morning Call Coffee Stand regulars, the Hansens . . .

No, on further examination I realized that it wasn't Ernest and Mary who had kept me from the sno-ball shop that summer. It was Ashley.

Before my maternal grandmother became a teetotaler (that one glass of wine a day is for health and so doesn't count), she used to pour shamrock-green crème de menthe over her vanilla ice cream in the evenings, a delicacy connected in my memory with viewings of *The Lawrence Welk Show*. My memories of her and my other grandparents and elderly relatives are all like that—sentimental images that well from my heart as I crunch through a spearmint sno-ball, or catch a whiff of some stranger's Old Spice, or read a notice in a newspaper about a bridge club meeting at a local church. They are snapshots from the best of times, from holidays, family reunions, and quick trips back home, and together they compose a dear album in my mind's eye. But my grandparents are not a tangible part of my day-to-day existence, because I moved away from home seventeen years ago; because I have chosen this town, and others before it, over my hometown; because I am not managing the family sno-ball stand, so to speak.

By assuming her family's legacy with such quiet and appropriate charm—painting each year's new number on the side of the building, driving her grandparents to and from their sno-ball stand nearly every workday, learning how to make Mary's syrups by peeking over her shoulder—Ashley had become an unwelcome reminder of all the ways in which I am an absent granddaughter, daughter, niece, cousin, sister.

As long as I've known her, there has been a cult of Ashley Hansen. As the new-school guardian of colored syrups and a vision of sweetness herself, she was bound to develop a substantial fan base. On my weekends of medical widowhood, and before the realities of post-Katrina job prospects moved him and his family to Chicago, Michael Tisserand, the editor of *Gambit Weekly*, often walked Hansen's yellow line with me. After our audience with Ashley, we would sit on a metal-surfaced bench outside, lean our backs against the building's warm cinderblocks, and fend off an assault of ants as we spooned through cups of sugary slush and his kids danced away their sugar rush. If we didn't connect at Hansen's, Michael would call me on Mondays with his weekend report. It always included four news bytes: how Ernest and Mary had looked; what flavor he had chosen; how finely plowed the ice had been (or not); and how terrific Ashley is. I used to tease Michael, a medical widower himself, for harboring an Ashley Hansen fetish, though I knew his appreciation for her was, like mine, more complicated than that. Most of her followers do not want to date Ashley Hansen. We want to *be* her.

In the spring of 2006, a few of us fans got a backstage look at Ashley's life when we gathered at the sno-ball stand to help her get it in order for its first post-Katrina season (all over town, New Orleanians continue to pitch in elbow grease to help their favorite food businesses reopen). Losing both of her grandparents and nearly her town in the space of a few months had broken Ashley's heart but not her will. A new number was painted on the cinderblocks, the lawn was mowed, a backyard fence was erected, and all the old photographs and media clippings were retaped to the interior walls once they'd gotten a good wipe-down. I helped organize a back storage room, filing a stack of old papers that included phone numbers, thank-you cards, newspaper articles, and a poem that Ernest had written for Mary.

Ashley stood at the sink in the shop's narrow back kitchen washing out some of the recycled liquor bottles that Mary had used for her syrups for decades. I offered to help, but she declined. Like her grandmother before her, Ashley doesn't like anyone touching her syrup bottles. Whereas Mary was concerned about germs, Ashley worries about breakage, for each precious bottle is labeled with Ernest's handpainted white lettering: CREAM OF COCONUT, CREAM OF STRAWBERRY, BUBBLE GUM, ICE CREAM . . . Beside her, ready for action on top of an electric range, sat the stainless steel stockpot in which Mary had mixed her syrups since before Ashley was born. It shone like new.

As Hurricane Katrina was bearing down on the Gulf Coast the previous August, the mayor had called a mandatory evacuation of Orleans Parish, and Ashley had complied. Not, however, before disassembling the Sno-Bliz machine and hiding all the parts in different places so that no thief could make sense of them. Once she and her father returned to the city, they faced reconstructing the machine for the first time ever without Ernest's guidance. Their memories of annually watching him put it back together prevailed as one of Ernest's favorite sayings drove their spirits: "If you say you can't do it, you mean you don't want to do it. There's nothing you can't do." They did it, and New Orleanians thanked them by packing the house, as usual, all summer long.

When I asked Ashley whether she'd ever considered a life besides the sno-ball stand, she said that one winter in Chicago had been enough to keep her in New Orleans, devoted to her grandparents and their business: "There are too many benefits, there are too many memories, there are too many smells and scents that I couldn't live without in that place. There are too many friends we've made, there are too many customers, there are too many kids growing up that I can't wait to see every day."

RED GRAVY

Pray for Us

The last time Ernest Hansen left his bed, before surrendering to cancer twenty days later, was to visit the Saint Joseph altar at St. Joseph Co-Cathedral in Thibodaux. His wife, Mary, had been a Gemelli, of Sicilian heritage; for their first date, Ernest had taken Mary to Louis Prima's birthday party. As the couple had done together every March 19 since as far back as their family members can recall, Ernest paid his respects in 2006 to the patron saint of confectioners, dying people, and Sicily. He made a small deposit on the altar's donation plate in exchange for a few brown-paper goodie bags, which he distributed to his sons and to a dying friend. He also kept one for himself. At that point Ernest was too weak to stand; his younger son, Gerard, had to lift him from his bed to a wheelchair and then back again after the outing.

Before opening the small brown sacks, the recipients knew what they would find inside them, because no matter which altar to Saint Joseph you visit in and around New Orleans, the goodie bags contain more or less the same items every year. There's always a prayer card, sometimes a small medal imprinted with the image of the saint holding a child in his arms, and usually a couple of firm Italian cookies sprinkled with sesame seeds, flavored with almond extract, or filled with fig paste.

A dried brown fava bean knocks around the bottom of each bag as a reminder that Saint Joseph saved Sicilians from a drought during the Middle Ages by ensuring that the fava beans they had planted for their livestock survived to sustain the human population. Many New Orleanians carry these "lucky beans" in their wallets and pocketbooks under the superstition (or belief) that a blessed bean will keep them in money, and thereby food, throughout the year. I recently attended a panel discussion about New Orleans food during which the topic of St. Joseph's Day arose. The speaker asked who in the audience kept a dried fava bean with them. You could hear handbags unzipping, change purses unsnapping, and coins jangling in pockets; soon enough half the room was waving smooth brown beans in the air. I was in that number.

The goodie bags also contain pieces of blessed bread, which both devout and superstitious New Orleanians store in their freezers until hurricane season. When a storm brews, they throw the bread into the wind, an active prayer for the bad weather to abate. Saint Joseph is the patron saint of, among more than eighty other things, people in doubt. Given the number of stale bread pieces that must have been tossed into the air when Hurricane Katrina was nigh, New Orleanians needed Saint Joseph more than usual the year that Ernest Hansen was taken away.

The patron saint of immigrants

Pre-Katrina census figures reported around a quarter-million Americans of Italian descent in Louisiana. The vast majority of those in the greater New Orleans area were descended from the Sicilian immigrants who arrived en masse around the turn of the last century, fleeing social and economic unrest in their homeland. According to Joel Denker's *The World on a Plate: A Tour Through the History of America's Ethnic Cuisine*, 50,000 Sicilians passed through the Port of New Orleans between 1880 and 1910. They found employment on the riverfront, in farming, on sugar plantations, and in the French Market, often with bosses of Italian ancestry (Italians had been growing roots in New Orleans since its founding; Louisiana already had America's largest Italian population by 1850, according to Denker). Early in the twentieth century the French

Quarter was a residential neighborhood for the working poor; at one point Sicilians accounted for 80 to 90 percent of its residents, and also for the Quarter's nickname, Little Palermo.

The dominant population dictated commerce in the area: the French Market was Italian; macaroni producers flourished, including the maker of Bologna & Taormina Liberty Brand pasta on Chartres Street; and in 1905 the young Angelo Brocato from Palermo opened a Sicilian bakery and gelato shop on Decatur Street, just off Ursulines. In the 1980s Angelo's descendants moved the shop to a location in Mid-City, where they continue to do a steady trade in gelato, filled-to-order cannoli, spumoni, and the firm, two-bite cookies that supply Saint Joseph altars every March 19 and sweeten coffee breaks throughout the year.

While much of the French Quarter's housing stock has been transformed from multifamily tenements to second-home condominiums over the past hundred years, almost entirely pushing out the working man, contemporary New Orleans remains an Italian/Sicilian stronghold. In some pockets of the city before Katrina, the concentration of Italian descendants was so solid, their vaguely Brooklynesque accents so rich, and their mark on New Orleans culture so certain that it sometimes felt as if these were the truest New Orleanians. (By the way, it's impossible to guess a New Orleanian's ancestry simply by listening to her accent. The melting-pot effect has natives of all genetics and backgrounds—Italian, Irish, German, African—sounding like stereotypes, sometimes like the Sopranos, sometimes like Archie Bunker, sometimes like the guys on the radio program *Car Talk,* and sometimes like a fusion of all three with some marbles added to the mouth for entertainment.) Italian culinary traditions have bled into all corners and kitchens of the metro area. There must be as many recipes for red sauce as there are for red beans. The smell of simmering tomatoes and garlic crosses all boundaries—geographic, economic, racial. If you don't care for spaghetti and meatballs, you ought to pack your own lunch on Tuesdays and Wednesdays, when it's the special at casual lunch joints, takeout stands, and black-owned restaurants that also specialize in

Big Mama–style gumbos. Emeril Lagasse included a spaghetti and meatballs recipe in his cookbook *Emeril's New New Orleans*, and I imagine I would have thought he was filling space if I hadn't lived here long enough to know better.

The Italian impact on New Orleans culinary traditions was so strong in the early 1970s when Richard Collin wrote *The New Orleans Underground Gourmet* that he divided his restaurant guide into two main parts, New Orleans cuisine and ethnic and specialty restaurants, and filed his twenty-three Italian restaurant reviews beneath the first heading. "Italian food is one of the two dominant cuisines in New Orleans, second only to the Creole," he wrote.

It requires an open mind for people who have learned to eat Italian food elsewhere (such as Italy) to acclimate to its New Orleans treatments. The Sicilian influence may be new, for one, and accepting red sauce is paramount. Also, since the integration of Italian/Sicilian cooking into New Orleans cooking at large is as complete as the integration of the people who brought it here, many casual neighborhood restaurants offer crossbred menus that confuse diners who are unaccustomed to eating gumbo as a precursor to veal Parmesan. At places like Liuzza's Restaurant & Bar, Casamento's, Pascal's Manale, Fury's, R&O's, and Mandina's—all high on a chowhound's to-do list—you might find boiled crawfish and lasagna on the same table, or oyster po-boys and daube with red gravy, or fried chicken and chicken Parmesan.

When Brett Anderson interviewed Tommy Mandina about Italian cooking for the *Times-Picayune* in April 2005, the latter, whose grandfather immigrated from Sicily, said that his restaurant, Mandina's, isn't Italian "by any stretch." This was news to me, because I'm like a homing pigeon for Mandina's Italian sausage and red gravy over spaghetti. Mandina's was originally a corner store and opened at a time when Italians dominated New Orleans' corner-store culture. In spite of a complete post-Katrina gutting and renovation, it remains steeped in its Italian heritage: waiters dressed in formal shirts and bow ties, garlic galore, veal Parmesan on Thursdays. Then again, taking Tommy's side, Mandina's turtle soup and trout amandine are iconic Creole dishes. Corned beef and cabbage is a regular special, and the house cocktail is an all-American whiskey old-fashioned.

This common overlapping of cooking traditions spawned the popular classification "Creole-Italian," which writers employ in guidebooks and restaurant reviews and at other times when it's necessary to qualify the cultural amalgamation with brevity. I prefer to use the term "New Orleans Italian" (implied in which is New Orleans Sicilian), because it encompasses all New Orleans–specific Italian cooking, including those dishes untouched by Creole manipulations. The muffuletta sandwich, for example.

The patron saint of laborers and pioneers

Salvatore Lupo, a twenty-seven-year-old immigrant from Sicily, opened Central Grocery as just that—a central grocery—in 1906 in the heart of Little Palermo. He stocked casks of olive oil, barrels of olives, pastas, dried beans, anchovies, cold cuts, cheeses—European imports all, tastes of home for the neighborhood folks. The store became a meeting place for Sicilian truck farmers who sold their harvests at the French Market. The farmers composed antipasto lunches from Salvatore's wares; they sat on crates and barrels in the store and balanced drippy trays on their knees as they ate. Eventually Salvatore thought to consolidate the meats, cheeses, and marinated things between halves of round, flat "muffuletta" loaves. Thus was the eponymous, and righteous, sandwich born.

That's the neatly packaged story as told by Salvatore's daughter, Marie Lupo Tusa, in her cookbook *Marie's Melting Pot*, anyway, and I've rarely heard the lore disputed. (In *The World on a Plate*, Denker attributes the sandwich's invention to Progress Grocery, which operated beside Central Grocery for decades. Also, the similarly constructed Roma sandwich at the former Montalbano's Delicatessen on St. Philip Street may have preceded Central's muffuletta.)

Alighting on a stool in the rear of Central Grocery, after having traveled a Hansen's Sno-Bliz-length line, I find it absurd to imagine that the muffuletta evolved from the desire for a tidier lunch. Oil seeps through the sandwich's white paper wrapping during the course of your five-step walk from the ordering counter to the eating one, and even the daintiest eater cannot avoid the emerald bath that pumps from the sandwich with each depression of finger and tooth. Mortadella, salami, ham, Emmentaler cheese, and the grocery's own olive salad striate between the stiff, bland, perfect-for-its-purpose, sesame-sprinkled bread that gives the sandwich its name. (Most muffuletta sandwiches are made with milder, Italian cheeses, such as provolone. In her cookbook, Marie Tusa describes Central Grocery's sandwiches as being made with "Swiss" cheese; when I asked an employee at the grocery for a description, he said they use Emmentaler, a variety of Swiss cheese.)

Old-timers complain that Central's muffulettas are skimpier than they used to be and that they're no longer made to order, though the last time I checked, a whole one still weighed just slightly less than a discus, and one quarter still delivered a sucker punch of green oil and garlic that turned me to wondering whether the critics hadn't become desensitized to excess. I suppose this can happen in a town where po-boys, the other favorite sandwich, are considered deficient if they're not "overstuffed."

I admit to having favored other muffulettas in the past—the bigger ones at Nor-Joe Importing in Old Metairie, the cheaper grab-and-go ones at Zara's Supermarket in Uptown, the ones with more olive salad at Dimartino's across the river. But there's no stand-in for a muffuletta from Central Grocery, because there's no stand-in for Central Grocery. Dried fava beans in burlap sacks, fig cookies in cellophane bags, salt cod in wooden slide boxes, olive oil in gallon tins, sherry vinegar on unreachable shelves, tomatoes from San Marzano, truffle oil from Umbria, anchovies in jars, halva in cans, vacuum-packed semolina, marinated octopus, white cheeses, hanging salamis, green coffee beans . . . Some of the grocery's products are so unfamiliar that walking among them transports you to a foreign place, and some of their labels are so dusty and faded the goods appear to be relics stocked by Salvatore Lupo himself.

It's in such well-preserved French Quarter institutions that you still can feel the original heartbeat of a neighborhood that's become so polluted with novelty shops blaring washboard music and daiquiri shops pumping techno that you sometimes can't hear yourself sigh with disgust: in its century-old restaurants, like Antoine's and Tujague's; in the coffee and chicory at Café Du Monde; in the miniatures at the recently—and tragically—shuttered Le Petit Soldier Shop; in the vetivert and tea olive sprays at Hové Parfumeur; in the antique barbells at the New Orleans Athletic Club; in the obituary cocktail at Lafitte's Blacksmith Shop Bar, the Pimm's Cup at Napoleon House, the Sazerac at Galatoire's. It's the greatest of ironies that if ever you forget why you live in this city, an afternoon of making handpicked stops in the tourism-warped French Quarter can bring it all home.

Within a month of returning from my Katrina-dictated exile in New York, I drove downtown one afternoon, parked on Esplanade Avenue, wandered up the punk end of Decatur Street (where I overheard a transient Goth teenager asking another, "Didn't you used to have fangs?"), and into the twenty-minute line at Central Grocery for a ceremonial poststorm muffuletta. Two acquaintances I had not seen since the storm lined up behind me. They had come for the same reason: to resolve dual hungers, one physiological and the other emotional.

The New Orleans citizenry, in the city and in the diaspora, has two lives now: before the storm and after the storm. We're constantly noting, aloud and to ourselves, during which life we did what. Because the storm turned us into such different people, the clarification is compulsory: we need to reconfirm everything we once knew with our new identities. If I hadn't been to Central Grocery for a post-Katrina muffuletta, in a way it would feel as though I'd never had one at all during this lifetime.

It was life-affirming to note on that day that the storm hadn't changed the business style of Salvatore Lupo's heirs. While running the restaurant equivalent of a living history museum, they contribute to the grocery's Old World charm by acting the part of grumpy old butchers. If an audience with Ashley Hansen is like a teddy bear hug, meeting the Tusas is like getting your ears boxed (the grocery's lineage passed through Salvatore's daughter, Marie, who married a Tusa). The men who take your money don't pretend to be interested in anything besides taking your money, which works for me because all I want from them anymore is a muffuletta. I used to want more, when it was my job to call the grocery to update its listing in *Gambit Weekly*'s restaurant guide. But questions are met at Central Grocery with the sort of aggressive brevity ("Our hours haven't changed in thirty years," *click*) that makes journalists miserable and customers think they've stumbled onto something extra-special. And of course they have.

The defining ingredient on a muffuletta, the one that prevents barbarians like Matt from crossing Central's threshold and the one that separates muffulettas from other Italian cold-cut sandwiches, is olive salad, an aggressive entity itself. Olive salad acts like a relish on the muffuletta, cutting the heft of the cheeses and meats with its piquant, pickled edge. Central Grocery's name-brand mix, sold at the store in quart jars, contains a rainbow blend of imported garlic, large green olives, bug-eyed capers, pepperoncini, celery, carrot, cauliflower, and mentholated oregano leaves. No matter how much olive salad the kitchen piles onto a muffuletta, it's never enough for those of us who name the olive as our favorite fruit.

Olive salad served over iceberg lettuce as a salad is a lesser-known, and underrated, New Orleans delicacy. Often called "Italian salad" on menus, it's prevalent in the kinds of restaurants that are patronized by locals who appreciate the not-so-freshness-focused forms a salad may assume. The same friend from Los Angeles who balked at learning that Mandina's vegetable soup is constructed around beef brisket also considered ordering the Italian salad there. I told her she could have a bite of mine, knowing that's all she would want from my wondrous bowl of iceberg lettuce, green olives, whole cocktail onions, artichoke hearts, unripe tomato wedges, hard-boiled egg, and limp asparagus spears, all overlaid with crisscrossed anchovy fillets. (The Angeleno, by the way, ordered French fries.)

In regional vernacular, the proper (albeit improper) name for Italian salad is "wop salad," and so it was called at the hungry man's restaurant Rocky & Carlo's in Chalmette, where the glossy salad contained so much minced garlic you could see it as clearly as the other ingredients; I thought it was grated Parmesan at first glance. Iceberg, purple cabbage, celery, green olives, and apple-sweet onion marinated in an acidic vinaigrette that blazed a cool fire from the palate to the scalp.

Rocky & Carlo's was one of the innumerable places trapped in time and wood paneling that Katrina's flood had no right to ruin. In so doing, it declared to a community that what it cherished most was disposable: stuffed bell peppers, baked cheddar macaroni smothered in red gravy, chicken fried to order, Dylan on the jukebox, a nonagenarian owner who fussed in Italian, the town of Chalmette itself, and too many of its citizens whose lives the water claimed.

When I drove out to Rocky & Carlo's a full year after the storm, expecting to find rot and gloom, the restaurant's interior was bare to the studs and the side door stood open, inviting me to peek inside and see that some new plywood had been erected where I used to order my wop salads. I detected no garlic sting in the air, but there was a blissful smell of sawdust. The restaurant has since reopened; Chalmette is in olives again.

Wop is a pejorative term for people of Italian descent, except in and around New Orleans, where it's what people of Italian descent fondly call their olive and iceberg salads. The term is out of vogue in most restaurants even here, particularly those restaurants on the tourist map. In my time I've eaten salads called wop at Sid-Mar's on the lakefront (which washed away during Katrina), Tessie's Place in Metairie, and Rocky & Carlo's in "da parish," the Yat name for St. Bernard Parish, where the Chalmatians live.

Natives all over the metro area speak in a regional parlance known as Yat. The name apparently derived from the popular greeting among Yats of "Where y'at?," the proper response to which is "Awrite" (or some other version of "Okay"). The staple-bound paperback booklet *New Orleans Talkin'*, which I picked up at Borders for $5.95, calls Yat "the Cockney of Noo Awlins" and compares its sounds to the vernacular of Brooklyn, but with southern drawled vowels. Yats are a proud people; the other day while grocery shopping, I saw a man wearing a T-shirt that read, "God Is a Yat." I mention the Yat dialect during this discussion of olives and wop salads because it's dominant among New Orleanians of Italian descent, who pronounce *muffuletta* "moof-uh-*lot*-uh," *purse* "poiss," and *Catholic* "cat lick"; also because eavesdropping on Yats is half the fun of being at Rocky & Carlo's for someone with *Fargo*esque speech patterns like myself.

The patron saint of social justice and working people

A good century after the Sicilians' mass arrival, you'd never guess from the complete integration that their early years in the city were marked by racism so brutal that it fueled the largest mass lynching in American history. That was in 1891. Innocent men died. It was a horrific event, by no stretch justifiable, worse prejudice than I hope we'll ever know again.

I sometimes wonder whether the stuffed artichoke had anything to do with it.

The restaurant critic Richard Collin found stuffed artichokes so insulting that he crowned them the height of perversity in his restaurant guide (in 1970, he wouldn't have met the turducken yet). "In New Orleans the artichoke is virtually raped," he wrote in describing the culinary melodrama of stuffing the innocent vegetable to vulgar dimensions with garlic and breadcrumbs.

The first time I ordered Nonna's Italian Stuffed Artichoke at Liuzza's Restaurant & Bar, years ago, it looked to me like a turtle napping on a bed of lettuce. Breadcrumb stuffing that had been pushed beyond capacity into the crevices between the artichoke's leaves had blossomed during cooking so that a grayish breadcrumb shell completely camouflaged the spiny, delicate-tasting vegetable. The lumpy, monochromatic composition appeared to be no more complex than your average mushroom-soup casserole, and yet my waitress disclosed, "Only grandmothers make those. They're very time-consuming." I didn't understand until I prepared the dish myself that by "time-consuming" my waitress meant as in darning socks.

To stuff artichokes à la New Orleans, you first trim the vegetables of their spiny parts, tough stems, and prickly chokes. If you were making artichokes à la California, you would stop here, steam them, grab the aïoli, and have yourself an austere little dinner. But instead you boil, peel, and chop the artichoke stems to add to your other stuffing ingredients, of which breadcrumbs, garlic, and olive oil are essential. The most basic stuffed artichokes contain little else. Liuzza's stuffing also tasted of lemon and an elusive brininess that the waitress attributed to anchovies and cured black olives. Parsley, dried herbs, cayenne pepper, green onions, canned artichoke hearts, bacon bits, and Parmesan, Romano, and Swiss cheeses are other common additives. Frequently a lemon slice decorates the top of the whole shebang, a sunny seal that imparts a bold citrus-rind flavor once the artichoke has been cooked.

Having assembled the stuffing for a batch, you pry apart the artichokes' leaves and spread your breadcrumb mixture on each one, continuing either until you run out of stuffing or until the artichokes attain the look of pinecones in need of liposuction. The final step is baking or steaming until the leaves are tender and the stuffing is warm. Both methods have drawbacks. If not arranged carefully in a pan, the artichokes may tip and take on water during steaming; baking risks dehydration. Some cooks avoid both hazards by using a microwave, but I still have too much pompous gourmet in me to recommend that.

It's serious work, and judging from their commercial pervasiveness, stuffed artichokes aren't in the weekly rotation for most home cooks. My neighbor, a grandmother, is one exception. Once I saw her sweeping her sidewalk and thought to ask whether she ever made them; she answered by presenting me with an artichoke she happened to have stuffed the previous evening. You often run into plastic-wrapped stuffed artichokes on the deli counters of large supermarkets, near the cash register at independent groceries (including, sometimes, at Central Grocery), and in neighborhood restaurants with an Italian bent. One afternoon someone had chalked "stuffed artichokes" onto the sidewalk sandwich board propped outside Franky & Johnny's, along with "chicken-fried steak" and "boiled shrimp." I took the closest parking space, ducked inside the wood-paneled bar-restaurant, where the ambiance derives from checkered oilcloths and the aroma of cigarettes from the night before, and bought one to take home for dinner. For kicks I drove it to Whole Foods Market a few blocks down Arabella Street first and set it on a produce scale: one and a third pounds. Is it ladylike to admit that I had no problem finishing it?

To eat a stuffed artichoke, you may excavate the stuffing with a fork and then go to work on the vegetable itself. But that technique misses the point and disrespects whatever cook so fastidiously paved every leaf. To honor the stuffed artichoke and its maker, you pull the leaves from their breadcrumb bush one by one and scrape them clean of their garlicky stuffing and artichokiness all at once, with your front teeth. This technique may not win you etiquette points anyplace else, but it is what's been done down here for maybe a century, and down here precedence rules.

Artichokes flourish in Sicily's hot sun and volcanic ash–cut soil, and a common assumption is that Sicilians brought the vegetable to New Orleans when they immigrated. But while the Sicilians could be responsible for deifying the breadcrumb stuffing recipe, it was earlier settlers—either the Italians or the French, the latter originally having learned about artichokes from neighboring Italy—who instilled a preference for the vegetable in the New Orleanian diet. In 1753, a century and a half before the Sicilian influx, Jean Charles Pradel, a French officer turned farmer, began growing artichokes on his West Bank plantation and selling them at the city's markets. *The Picayune's Creole Cook Book* already contained artichoke recipes in 1901, including one for "*artichauts farcis à la barigoule*," which involves garlic, ham, and mushrooms but no breadcrumbs.

The exact evolution of the massively stuffed artichoke eaten in contemporary New Orleans is a mystery. While researching an article in 2003, I called a few of the city's Italian chefs to ask whether the dish had a place on the authentic Italian table. No, said Irene DiPietro, the Sicilian-born proprietor of Irene's Cuisine. She grew up eating artichokes like bananas in Sicily but didn't learn to stuff them until she moved to New Orleans. "They're like meatballs, which you don't find much in Italy either," she said.

Christian Rossit, a chef from Venice then working at La Riviera Restaurant, concurred. He was raised on baby artichokes stuffed with Fontina cheese and deep-fried but knew nothing of the breadcrumb bombs until he moved here.

"I grew up with my mother stuffing them like they do here," countered Andrea Apuzzo, a native of Capri and the proprietor of Andrea's Restaurant in Metairie. He told me that his family still cultivates artichokes on his home island.

In 2005, Liz Williams, the director of the Southern Food and Beverage Museum in New Orleans, toured Sicily, her ancestral homeland. There she saw round loaves of seeded bread called muffuletta and ate fried rice balls (*arancini*) just like the ones her grandmother used to make. She also recognized New Orleans in the various breadcrumb-stuffed vegetables she encountered; nearly every available vegetable received the breadcrumb treatment, Liz said, *except* the artichokes.

Liz's New Orleans upbringing was so Sicilian that she remembers watching her grandmother, who emigrated from Palermo at age eighteen, beat round steaks with the bottom of a full red wine bottle. Having sufficiently tenderized and flattened the meat, she would overlay it with a garlicky breadcrumb stuffing, roll it up with long strips of carrot and whole hard-boiled eggs, and smother the meat roll in tomato sauce. Liz calls the dish "broo-shah-*loh*-nee." When I asked her for the spelling, she answered, "Kitchen wasn't a written language in my house."

New Orleanians seem to agree never to spell *broo-shah*-loh-*nee* the same way twice, and certainly never to spell it like it sounds or to pronounce it the way it looks. In her cookbook, Marie Tusa of Central Grocery spells it *bracioline* and suggests making it with veal sirloin tip roast. On his Web site, John Folse spells it *braciolini* and calls for pork loin. At Mandina's it's veal *bruccialone* and stuffed with spinach and egg as a Thursday special. It's *broccolini* at Rocky & Carlo's, and while the word looks as though it belongs to a hybrid green vegetable, the actual dish is a ground meat sculpture concealing a buried egg treasure. The *bracialoni* at Vincent's Italian Cuisine is a beef dish redolent of bacon, the size of a small roast, and served with a "side" of pasta that alone fills up a standard takeout container. At Venezia, a Mid-City dining room that lost its burgundy-painted ceiling during a post-Katrina gutting and renovation, it was *brocilone* when I tried it and made with veal top round that the kitchen tenderized to meat shavings and lumped around a nutmeg-scented breadcrumb stuffing pebbled with pine nuts.

The variations in spelling and the form of the dish itself (a lump of brown lolling in tomato sauce) point to the Italian *braciole*, which according to the Italian cookbook author Marcella Hazan is a center-cut steak of the top or bottom round. *Braciolone* is a big *braciole*. Even New Orleans' odd pronunciation of the dish varies; sometimes it incorporates a soft *g* sound and stretches the *o*: broo-jah-*loo*-nee. Intentional or not, the spelling and pronunciation vagaries act as cultural preservation tools—they keep outsiders from getting a handle on the dish. When you can't pronounce it, you order the spaghetti instead. Perhaps this explains why broo-shah-*loh*-nee is such a sleeper specialty in New Orleans Italian restaurants, the kinds of places where the artichokes are stuffed, where the veal is panéed, and where the manicotti and lasagna entrees come with sides of red-sauced pasta; where the ladies tuck napkins into their blouses before tucking into their lunches, and where the waitstaff could karaoke any Dean Martin song. Often there's a statue of Saint Joseph on a shelf in such restaurants, or a print of him holding a small child tacked to the wall, possibly beside a map of Sicily or an Italian flag.

One major exception is Lilette, a sexy corner restaurant set in a former pharmacy building smack on Magazine Street's boutique row. Lilette's chef-owner, John Harris, cooks practically nothing derivative of the traditional New Orleans kitchen—any traditional New Orleans kitchen. White truffle and marrow toasts, boudin noir, skordalia, heart of palm salads, oysters from Washington, and halibut from Alaska fill out a French-inspired menu with Italian twists that, like the restaurant's lethal designer cocktails, makes you forget where you are. Almost. The chef's main course braciola is a curl of tender veal, prosciutto, pine nuts, and warm spices, all collapsing in a bath of San Marzano tomato sauce. Even with its regionally unfamiliar soft polenta accompaniment, it tastes like home.

While broo-shah-*loh*-nee is unknown to heaps of New Orleanians—the imports, the strict spaghetti eaters, and the anti–red sauce snobs—New Orleans Italians are fervent about it. One morning while workers put the finishing touches on the reconstruction of his family's Katrina-flooded ice cream parlor, the frenzied Arthur Brocato had no time for the interview I had pressured him into scheduling. But his eyes softened and his spirits perked when I asked him about the dish, a Sunday staple when he was growing up in a Sicilian household in New Orleans. Arthur also drew a blank when I asked him to spell it, but he insisted that I write down that difficult-to-procure full-cut veal rounds (versus the more common short-cut ones) are essential for making the real deal. He recalled how his aunt brushed her veal with lard before stuffing it, trussed the roulade into a tight cylinder, browned it in a skillet, and then "dropped it in the red gravy to cook the rest of the way."

I adore that term, *red gravy*, because it implies that tomato sauces can attain a homespun, pour-over-anything likability, and that jibes with my feeling about most of them—especially those tomato sauces that are poured over homely lumps of meat pounded to tender smithereens and stuffed with savory riches. Once, after I used *red gravy* in a restaurant review in a flourish of localism, an anonymous reader of Italian heritage who hadn't taken it as a compliment called to berate me. Red gravy, he bellowed into my voicemail, does injustice to Italian tomato *sauces*, which aren't gravies at all!

He kind of had a point. *The New Food Lover's Companion* defines gravy as "a sauce made from meat juices, usually combined with a liquid such as chicken or beef broth, wine or milk and thickened with flour, cornstarch or some other thickening agent. A gravy may also be the simple juices left in the pan after meat, poultry or fish has been cooked." But though this definition would preclude meatless Italian tomato sauces, neither my careful reader nor the handy reference book accounts for the less technical and more emotional characteristics of a good gravy, whatever its color. For instance, the characteristic that overwhelms you with a feeling of well-being as you sop up the dregs with the butt end of an Italian bread loaf. Many of the city's less sugary tomato sauces possess this gravylike characteristic: the one at Fausto's in Metairie, where the kitchen uses garlic like salt; at Adolfo's, a treehouse of a restaurant run by a Spaniard in the Faubourg Marigny, where bay leaves and sweaty spices suspend in a thick brew; and at R&O's, by the lake, where the meatballs yield to a spoon and the sauce is dark and beefy.

One local tomato sauce that would qualify as a gravy even to the literalists is the oily, adhesive, brick-red sauce blessed with sweet smokiness and garlic that causes the chicken cacciatore at Mosca's to resemble an Arizona landscape. According to published recipes, Mosca's sauce attains its depth of color and flavor when the kitchen adds a straightforward tomato sauce to the hot pans in which butchered chickens have fried, thereby frying the tomato sauce and marrying it with the chicken's pan juices (and some wine). I'm overwhelmed with a feeling of well-being every time I eat Mosca's chicken cacciatore, which is every time I'm there, and I always use the braided sesame bread to mop up any leftover sauce. Oops, I mean gravy.

The patron saint of travelers

Mosca's is just the sort of family-run restaurant that New Orleanians tend to covet: it's creaky, set in its ways, and no picnic to find. Three generations of Moscas have staffed it without ever bothering to produce a cookbook. Because time scarcely touches the restaurant, everything has been said, chewed over, savored, digested, and said again; one could recite the fairy tale of oysters Mosca (oysters and garlic cooked au gratin, beneath oil-soaked breadcrumbs) without ever having driven over the river and through the woods to Avondale.

Which would be sad, because driving over the river is an essential ingredient in my Mosca's experience. While it's possible to get there from New Orleans by crossing the steely, sturdy Crescent City Connection instead, my cadre of Mosca's regulars prefers the Huey P. Long Bridge, an overused toothpick in comparison. The Huey P. is also made of steel, but when both of its train tracks and all four of its nine-foot-wide, shoulderless lanes are occupied, the ride begins to resemble that of a rickety wooden roller coaster, not because the bridge actually sways (I think) but because so much motion in such close quarters suspended so far above the barges and muddy river ripples makes a driver dizzy. I've had passengers in my car scream. Somewhere around the bridge's apex is when Avondale's bounty takes on weighted importance. You really don't want to die *before* dinner; Mosca's is a last-supper kind of place.

The restaurant, which I always think of as a clapboard lean-to even though it's a solid white-sided structure, is less than fifteen miles from our house in Uptown and a zip from the base of the Huey P., and yet it's so far removed from anything urban, or even suburban, that on our last visit my friends saw a wild boar in the backyard while I was refueling at the bar. I regret having missed the boar, but at Mosca's there are priorities, and one of mine is a whiskey cocktail, preferably prepared by Johnny Mosca, a welcoming man of heavy-lidded countenance who slides an insect-shaped ashtray around the bar. He explained to me once, in the husky, tired voice you want from the proprietor of a roadside Italian supper club in the boonies where some nights limos fill the gravel-and-grass parking lot, that *mosca* (which he pronounces with a long *o*) means "fly" in Italian. I can't pinpoint why it sounded so fitting; I know only that I wouldn't mention it here if Mosca had meant "horse," or "armchair," or "woodland nymph."

The Moscas don't take reservations for dinner on Saturdays. As at

Hansen's Sno-Bliz and Central Grocery, the wait at Mosca's factors into the pleasure of being there as much as the Louis Prima–stacked jukebox does, and the shoals of garlic in each dish, and the restaurant's possibly mythical mob connections. During a telephone interview, I once asked Mary Jo Mosca, Johnny's wife and the restaurant's chef, whether such rumors were fact or fiction. "I can't give you the correct data on that," she said after a dramatic pause.

Six is the magic number. Four people can't order enough, and eight are too many for sharing the Italian salad (iceberg and crabmeat tossed with olive salad), one of just three appetizers. Six rollicking friends—rollicking because they survived the Huey P. and celebrated by downing several juice glasses of Chianti—can manage the salad plus five of the colossal main courses and two sides of pasta. Every dish is served family-style, meaning that diners serve themselves from common platters. Such camaraderie grows out of all the passing and sharing that you wonder why we don't always eat out together this way.

Besides the cacciatore and the oysters, we order the chicken à la Grande (similar to the cacciatore but flooded with olive oil and garlic instead of tomato sauce); the pepper-spiked house-made sausage with soft, savory roasted potatoes; and the shell-on garlicky shrimp, which remain snappish despite the deluge of olive oil that engulfs them. Usually the kitchen is out of sausage, in response to which we order another bowl of the spaghetti and tangerine-sized meatballs. The other pasta preparation, spaghetti bordelaise, follows an odd but prevalent local interpretation of the classic French wine-and-demi sauce called bordelaise; in New Orleans, *bordelaise* translates to as much butter, oil, and garlic as your body can process without suffering a systemic failure.

For dessert, pineapple fluff, tart cheesecake, and espresso served in a dinged-up drip pot. And you've just eaten 80 percent of Mosca's menu.

Everything about Mosca's contradicts its revered status—the location, the window cooling units, the dented serving trays. And it's fundamentally different from other New Orleans Italian restaurants: while dependent on red sauce and garlic, the menu lacks stuffed artichokes, panéed veal, and broo-sha-*loh*-nee; its lineage is not Sicilian. The late Provino and Lisa Mosca, who once ran a restaurant of the same name in the Chicago area (mythology says it was near Al Capone's headquarters), opened the Avondale restaurant practically as is in 1946. The spiritual source of the family's never-changing recipes lies with their ancestors in the central Italian coastal town of San Benedetto del Tronto. Mosca's is nevertheless fiercely New Orleans.

After the storm, I wondered what had become of the Moscas, and what would become of us if the family didn't return and rebuild the business. Telephones were an unreliable means of communication at the time, so I drove to Avondale on a spring afternoon to take stock of the wind-damaged building and found a woman chasing swamp cats in the parking lot. She assured me that a reopening was imminent. By the time that day finally rolled around, most of my usual Mosca's crew no longer lived in New Orleans, Katrina-related attrition having more than halved the city's population. One member had lost her apartment and her cat in the storm and had taken a job in Georgia. Another had moved to Chicago, a third to Philadelphia. We stragglers planned a Saturday evening reunion around the schedule of yet another friend, who had moved to Atlanta but who drove back home for the weekend and the chicken à la Grande. The six of us who survived the Huey P. that night felt giddy at finding Mosca's repaired and updated but its core character unscathed. We waited two hours for a table, and the kitchen ran out of sausage before we could claim an order. I cherish the photo a stranger snapped of us as we posed beneath Mosca's new, beautifully banal black-and-white sign, smiling, our hands wrapped around juice glasses of Chianti. I hadn't realized before the shutter clicked that we were still capable of looking so happy.

An elderly woman who sits, and sometimes sleeps, in a chair near the entrance has become a fixture at Mosca's in the years I've known it. She's Mary Jo's mother, and she lives with the couple and other family members in a home beside the restaurant. It's a common stereotype of Italians that multiple generations of one family live together, and loudly, in one house. This is not just stereotype but true of many New Orleans families, Italian and otherwise. In this city, aunties raise nephews, *parrains* (French for "godfathers") raise their godchildren, and grandparents get supper for everyone.

While the traditional American nuclear family structure prevails even in this city, I've noticed little social pressure to follow it. A more-the-merrier attitude seems to extend across the board, from street life (second-line parades), to social life (crawfish boils), to communal family living. One part-Italian family in New Orleans, the Fagots, taught me all about the benefits of the latter. They also taught me about the more spiritual underpinnings of New Orleans Italian cooking traditions by allowing me into their Saint Joseph altar-building ritual.

The patron saint of engineers, unborn children, families, fathers, house hunters, carpenters, and married people

Marie Fagot's shih tzu, Poochie, beat her to the front door. It was March 17, and icicle lights still dangled along the low roof of her Lakeview home. Across Orleans Avenue, seagulls perched on a high levee wall. Beyond the levee stretched a cobalt-blue sky and the Orleans Avenue Canal.

After two rings of the bell, Marie appeared in the doorway, her pale cheeks and nose rouged pink, her hair jet-black to the roots. Marie's petite stature and bowed spine require her to twist a little and look upward to meet most people eye-to-eye. She twisted and looked up at me. "You look good," she said, as she often says, to everyone, somehow never diluting the expression's kindness. I always leave Marie's presence feeling better about myself.

She turned to lead me through the house, holding her left wrist with her right hand behind her back. In the front sitting room, a small shelf held a collection of statuettes—miniature saints. Marie pointed to a portrait farther down the wall. It was her grandson,

Christian, wearing a tuxedo jacket and a red bow tie. Handsome, with brown hair and big, almond-shaped eyes. "You'd never know there was anything wrong," Marie said to me.

She passed through a doorway into a kitchen that was dark and totally quiet despite an overwhelming smell of cooking garlic. Just beyond the kitchen were the silhouettes of a television, an ironing board, and a sofa piled with folded laundry. The house felt sleepy.

Then Marie reached a closed door and pushed it open. White light, a chorus of voices, and a more pungent garlic aroma gushed over the threshold as if a seal had been broken. "Welcome to my dungeon," she said, grinning playfully.

In 1997 the Fagots (pronounced fah-*goes*) built the "dungeon"—actually a cheery annex—on the rear of their house for one reason: St. Joseph's Day. The add-on room was white from floor to ceiling, with a full kitchen and a wall of windows that overlooked a pretty backyard. Each year the family built a large raised altar at the far end of the room. On this day it consisted of just three latticework arches and some pink tulle.

It was midmorning, and a dozen of Marie's friends worked at a dozen different tasks. Thanks to their devotion, to Marie and to Saint Joseph, in only forty-eight hours the altar would brim with fresh orchids and lilies, a small model church gilded with royal icing, and bowls of dried fava beans to remind worshippers of the saint's munificence. There would be wine bottles to symbolize the miracle at Cana, breads molded into fish to symbolize the Last Supper, sheet cakes shaped like the Bible and frosted with the mantra "St. Joseph Pray for Us," a whole baked redfish decorated with olives and boiled crawfish, lamb-shaped cakes covered in coconut, and breadcrumbs to represent the sawdust of Joseph the carpenter, the earthly father of Jesus and the husband of Mary. At the center of it all would stand a painted statue of Saint Joseph holding a small child, three lilies tucked between his arm and his robe.

Eventually the altar would have three tiers, one for the Father, one for the Son, and one for the Holy Spirit. Between softly painted statues of the Blessed Mother and other saints, Marie and her workers would squeeze cannoli, pignolatti (fried pebbles of dough stuck together with melted sugar and molded to resemble pinecones, the toys of Baby Jesus), platters of wreath-shaped fig cakes painted in pastels and stacked into pyramids, and citrus fruits. The belief is that a single woman who succeeds in stealing a lemon from the altar will be married within the year.

In the backyard, around an in-ground swimming pool, more than four hundred friends and strangers would sit down to a traditional Sicilian St. Joseph's Day feast (*la festa di San Giuseppe*). Volunteers wearing red aprons and Italian-flag jewelry would serve them stuffed artichokes, fried cardoons (*carduna*), vegetable omelets (*froschias*), olive salad, string bean and artichoke casseroles, seeded bread, and meatless pasta Milanese aromatic with fennel and anchovy and sprinkled with more of the carpenter's breadcrumbs. Beneath his carport across a back alleyway, beside a sign that read PARKING FOR ITALIANS, a neighbor would keep huge pots of spaghetti roiling over a propane burner.

Some of the guests would come just to eat lunch or dinner, some to get a new lucky bean, some to give Marie and her daughters their annual hug, and some to write prayer petitions to the saint. I would write one that year asking Saint Joseph to watch over Matt's father, Louk, who had been diagnosed with cancer. Later that night, once everyone had left, the Fagots would burn all the petitions without reading them. Everyone who stopped by would remark on how this year's altar was even more beautiful than last year's, and on how fabulous the food was. Both pleasantries would be true.

But March 19 was still two days away. Today was casserole day, and there was a lot to do. For starters, no one could remember how many casseroles they had prepared last year, to use as a guide. What's more, there was no more room in the icebox. Donna Gauthier, Marie's oldest daughter, was supposed to be conducting the casserole production, but she was at the doctor's with a scratched eyeball; she had nicked it while crawling beneath the altar. All around the group, frustration mounted.

Too many chiefs, not enough Indians

Marie's team was tired. They had begun preparing for the altar six weeks before, ahead of Mardi Gras. First they had baked and decorated more than 15,000 cookies—fig cakes, sesame cakes, round almond biscotti—which were now sealed tight in shiny metal garbage cans in a back room. At the beginning they had worked weekdays. Now, as the saint's day drew closer, some were logging overtime at night and on weekends. This is not your usual retiree's schedule, and it was beginning to show.

Marie doesn't reveal her age. "I'll tell you how much I weigh, I'll tell you I dye my hair, but not that," she told me once. So it seemed unfair to ask any of the other women. The years were marked in other ways—for instance, in the photo album of altars past that Marie liked to pull out. The photos dated to her very first altar, in 1984, when the annex was still a garage prone to flooding during heavy rains. Almost every page pictured someone who had since passed away busy icing cookies, arranging flowers, or serving dinners.

He used to help every year.

She had cancer.

We offer up the altar in memory of everyone who isn't with us anymore.

Neither her age nor her physical limitations kept Marie from taking charge. "All right, we had ten casserole pans last year," she suddenly snapped. Marie used the same high-pitched, crackly voice when she was irritated and when she was amused. This time, she was irritated. "The pans are bigger this year. Six is enough!"

With the casseroles declared finished, the group dispersed on autopilot to the next chores. The noise level resumed as the tension broke and all dozen friends vied for airtime to talk and tease. Marie's husband, Mr. Caryl, who kept tabs on morale and expenses and who took charge of the Milanese sauce on St. Joseph's Day, walked into the workroom leaning on his cane. "It sounds like the French Market in here!" he joked.

When those women talk, give aspirin a headache.

One thing about these ladies, as much as they talk, that's how much they work.

New Orleans didn't invent the Saint Joseph altar-making tradition. The inception occurred so long ago, in fact, that multiple theories attempt to explain the when, where, and why (the Sicilian drought is the dominant mythology here), and all of them predate reliable documentation. Suffice it to say that in modern American history, New Orleans is considered to be a focal point of the tradition. In the days leading up to March 19, the *Times-Picayune* runs notices in the classifieds that announce the locations of private and church-sponsored altars. Before an acquaintance introduced me to Marie's altar, I used to spend St. Joseph's Day driving around town collecting goodie bags. The Fagots never advertised their altar in the paper, as each year word of mouth sent them more visitors than they could count. Whereas some altars are funded by sponsors, the Fagots mostly paid out of pocket. Contributions to the altar's donation plate covered a portion of their expenses.

Altar builders and visitors aren't required, or even expected, to have Italian blood or worship a particular god—altar traditions also thrive among the city's Irish Catholics (who already are in saint mode, having just celebrated St. Patrick's Day) and in Black Spiritual churches. There was, however, a certain status to being Italian in the Fagot annex. Marie and Donna, Marie's daughter from her first marriage, are pure-blooded and proud of it. In comparison, Marie deadpans, her husband, Mr. Caryl, and the daughter they made together, just plain Caryl, form a "league of nations." Mr. Caryl describes himself as half Cajun, half Metairie.

Like heritage, religion was a regular topic around the annex's production tables.

I'm worried about the pope. He didn't look good last Sunday.

My grandchildren think I'm so holy, one of them asked me to pray that she would pass her history test.

I gave up popcorn for Lent. We pop a bag every night, so it's a real sacrifice.

Mr. Caryl was confirmed Catholic more than fifty-five years ago in order to marry Marie, then a young widow, in the Church. Marie is devout, and while the social intensity of building the altar also seemed to drive her, the main reason for her annual devotion was to thank Saint Joseph for answering her prayers and to ask him to continue doing so. Marie dedicated her altar work to Christian, the young man in the portrait she had pointed out to me in her home's front room. Christian, Caryl's son, is mentally retarded. He communicates well with his loved ones—he gave Marie's dog the name Poochie and is highly tuned to the family's movements and moods—but his motor skills have deteriorated since childhood. "Christian's condition could be so much worse," Marie told me. She attributed his relatively good heath and humor to Saint Joseph.

Everyone who worked on the altar told me stories about how "JoJo" had helped them or how they hoped he would help. Family members had recovered from illnesses. Empty parking spaces had appeared when they were most needed. In 2005 one altar worker sent a box of cookies to her grandson who was stationed in Baghdad. She told me that he had four children and that he carried a Saint Joseph prayer card in his breast pocket for protection.

Finishing this story, the woman asked me softly, "Do you have any children?" The question took me so off-guard that I didn't think to mask my disappointment when I answered no. She promised to bring me a prayer to Saint Joseph that would take care of my problem too.

. . .

The plated food is as integral to celebrating St. Joseph's Day as the altar food is, and Marie was an exacting cook. She eyeballed how much almond extract to pour into her biscotti dough, and she always got it right. She inspected all 180 artichokes to make sure every leaf was stuffed. Caryl told me that she rarely eats at Italian restaurants because none of them live up to her mother's cooking, especially not the red gravy. "She never uses a roux, not even in her gumbo. That's French—she's Italian," Caryl explained.

Christian was always the first to eat on St. Joseph's Day, along with Jesus, Mary, and the angels, parts played by children dressed in robes and halos. By tradition, this miniature Holy Family commences the feast with a tupa-tupa ("knock-knock") ceremony, recreating the Biblical story of Mary and Joseph knocking on the doors of Bethlehem asking for food and shelter. At the Fagot altar, different children played the other characters every year but Christian was always Joseph.

Marie never stopped moving, not while in altar-preparation mode nor on St. Joseph's Day itself, except during the moments immediately following the tupa-tupa, when she would sit beside Christian and help him eat. She became suddenly oblivious of the crowds that had gathered around tables in the backyard, waiting to be served, and of the restless children pilfering cookies from the altar. For a few sweet moments her world grew small and quiet. She would wipe Christian's mouth, point out the many visitors he knew from altars past, and talk to him while looking directly into his eyes.

The Fagot altar originally belonged to another Italian descendant, the late Miss Foto, who had lived next door and who had honored Saint Joseph every year for more than fifty years for saving her three young children from a house fire. In 1956, Miss Foto taught Marie to make her first fig cakes. That was the beginning. Miss Foto died at the age of eighty-six. "Next thing you know, here come her children with wheelbarrows," Marie recalled. They delivered their mother's statues, including the yard-high Blessed Mother statue draped in blue and holding Baby Jesus that sat on Miss Foto's very first altar.

"I had no intention of taking this altar, but like Miss Foto used to say, 'If you put your hand in here to make something for Saint Joseph, watch out.'" The saint's devotees believe that once you get involved in altar making, Saint Joseph claims you for life.

My hands were buried in string bean casserole when Marie said this. She could have been talking directly about me. I had originally shown up at the Fagot residence with a mind toward observing the preparations and writing about them for *Gambit Weekly* (which I did). Almost immediately, though, I enjoyed my notebook less than I enjoyed getting my hands dirty. In 2005, I took almost no notes at all. On my first workday that year, Marie let me glaze some of the wreath-shaped fig cakes that would decorate the altar (as opposed to the square ones that go in the goodie bags). Violet, robin's egg blue, Barbie pink, canary yellow, navel orange. Stuck to the edge of my cookie tray was a yellow paper with the number *74* written on it, meaning that they had finished glazing seventy-three trays before I arrived.

None of Miss Foto's children or grandchildren had wanted to take on her altar, a sentiment that seemed to resonate with Marie's daughters when I talked to them about it that year. Both of them took a whole week's vacation from their full-time jobs leading up to St. Joseph's Day to help with production, to make sure the staff meal was hot by lunchtime, to get wine for the night crew, and to decorate the yard with fresh flowers on the morning of. It was a lot of time and effort for working women, professionals and providers, to give. "I think the altar is going to die here," Donna told me. "This is her project, her passion. She's very devoted and she does it for a reason. As family, you need to embrace it."

As far as I could tell, the members of this family embraced everything about one another. Caryl and Christian shared a home with Marie and Mr. Caryl. Donna lived next door, in a house they planned would be Christian's eventually, once the rest of the family was gone. When I asked the sisters, who are best friends, to whom they devoted their altar work, Caryl stopped cracking eggs. She poked Donna in the ribs and smiled. "To her," they said in unison, meaning their mother.

Marie is blessed with those two girls.

Marie had a life before the altar, but during the first three years that I was getting to know her, once as an altar visitor and twice as a helper, no one seemed able to recall it. The entire year's momentum flowed toward the saint's day. During February and March, the Fagot annex was home for the entire family, while the main house held their other lives in suspension. There was no time even for taking down the icicle lights. Everyone assumed that Marie would maintain her devotion until sickness or death took her from it. Hurricane Katrina got there first.

Orleans Avenue was a priority destination the first time Matt and I made it back into the city after the storm. Knowing that the flood had ravaged the neighborhood did nothing to prepare me for what I saw. The Fagots' front door stood open, revealing blackness. I could see shapes of overturned furniture and heaps of what I guessed was clothing or drapery or . . . All the things the Fagots had acquired during their decades together in that house, all the daily physical reminders that they were a family who shared a home life, had been devoured by a damp, sinister blackness.

I couldn't locate the spray-painted diagram on the building's exterior that in other sections of the city indicated the date when a house had been searched for survivors, the organization that had searched, and how many people had been found dead inside. I learned later that rescue teams had floated by in boats at a level that required them to inscribe this information on the roof.

I left a note in the mailbox and later sent a letter, hoping it would be forwarded to wherever the family had gone. For months, no word. I assumed they had all left before the storm, but were they all together as usual? Had they remembered to pack Mr. Caryl's medications? Had there been space for Poochie in the car? Did Christian miss his dedicated caretaker? What about Miss Foto's seventy-five-year-old Blessed Mother statue?

In talking about the post-Katrina deaths of her grandparents and about what drove her to reopen their sno-ball stand so soon, Ashley Hansen explained to me, "We've lost so much in New Orleans. We've lost a generation of people, and it's just nice to hold on to a few things that haven't changed." The thought of how much had changed for the oldest generation of Fagots, of how little would be left to hold on to, was nearly too much for this heart to consider.

I had forgotten about the mulish permanence of family.

Caryl and I finally got in touch by e-mail. I learned from her that after a multistep evacuation, the family had rented a house in LaPlace, Louisiana, about thirty miles from New Orleans. Caryl's job had temporarily relocated to Houston, so she was commuting on weekends. Knowing that it would be years, if ever, before they could safely rebuild in Lakeview, Donna had purchased a house in Metairie, but she was spending most of her nonworking hours with her parents and Christian; when they were there together, the sisters had to share a bedroom. The family had found Christian's caretaker, who had been displaced to Baton Rouge, and he was spending time with her again. The Fagots were sad and exhausted but together, and that was exquisite to know.

Understandably, there would be no Fagot altar on the first post-Katrina St. Joseph's Day. The annex was a clutter of refrigerators and muck. The yard and swimming pool appeared to have been bombed. The neighbors were gone. The Fagots' friends had scattered to other towns in Louisiana and Texas; they hadn't heard from all of them yet. Eventually they did recover the saints' statues from the blackness in the house, but it was unclear whether they could be restored. Human survival was still the top priority.

Nevertheless, there would be a St. Joseph's Day on March 19, and Marie, Caryl, and I decided to spend it together at Cabrini Catholic High School in Mid-City, where volunteers had pulled together a heroic display. After viewing the altar, watching the tupa-tupa, and claiming our goodie bags, we sat down for lunch. Pasta Milanese, artichoke stuffing, garlicky casserole, seeded bread, olive salad. So the portions were a little skimpy. So the red gravy was a tad weaker than Mr. Caryl's. So the cookies weren't Marie's. Of importance that day was not what we ate, exactly, but that we ate it together, filled with a sense of well-being; that Saint Joseph still had his hooks in us; that we, travelers and immigrants in our broken city, still had something to thank him for.

STUFFED, SMOTHERED, Z'HERBES

Vegetables, a New Religion

> "A foreign critic once described America as a country which had one sauce and twenty different religions. Evidently he did not reach New Orleans in his travels, or else he would have discovered that its gravies are even more varied than its theology, and that good cooking is one of its religions."
>
> —Dorothy Dix, *Famous Drinks and Foods from the Carnival City (New Orleans)*

Like born-agains of any denomination—Christian, Buddhist, Weight Watchers—New Orleans converts tend to exhibit a more innocent, rose-colored zeal for their church than the flocks who've yawned through the motions all their lives. This is how quixotic, goateed hipsters wind up sitting knee to knee with strawberry-nosed lifers in the city's grittiest barrooms, like the Ninth Ward's Saturn Bar and Uptown's Brothers Three Lounge, regarding them as palaces of culture. It's what moved Massachusetts-reared Emeril Lagasse to turn cayenne pepper into a sound effect. And it's how I wound up taking fourteen pounds of mirliton, eight pounds of eggplant, and two refrigerators' worth of greens into my kitchen over the course of a single month.

Years into my conversion, I'm still getting a handle on the New Orleanian relationship to vegetables. A casually studious approach—observing in restaurants, perusing recipes, cooking the occasional okra gumbo—wasn't conclusive; I still fumble over questions like *Is stuffed eggplant a main course or a side dish?* The topic arose just recently during a dinner-planning session with my college friend and food ally Sarah Todd Olivier, a lucky Miami girl who married into a local family of white Creoles. Momentarily stumped, Sarah asked what I planned to stuff the eggplant with. My recipe called for shrimp and ham. "Well, then, I believe it's a side dish," Sarah decided. She made a beef daube to round out the meal.

Where shrimp and ham are thrown into vegetable preparations as afterthoughts, even a northern transplant familiar with obscurities like cushaw (a crookneck squash grown to obscene lengths and shapes) is bound to lose her way in the produce department. I first learned to eat from a midwestern plate upon which eggplant, shrimp, and ham never, ever touched. It was the 1970s. Vegetables were little punishments, prepared to look and taste like themselves and served in amounts guaranteed to make children strong. The dinner table was like boot camp or a surgical residency: the big guns never let us off easy; we suffered as they had suffered. It may have built character, but it created not a single degree of warmth for boiled Brussels sprouts, steamed spaghetti squash, or TV-dinner peas.

In time I grew into a big gun with midwestern hangups and, on regressive days, scorn for the lack of fresh produce in the New Orleans diet. I was backed by a loud chorus of fellow transplants who, like me, had made peace with vegetables as adults in places like San Francisco, New York City, and even Madison, Wisconsin, places where farmers' markets and seasonal-produce-driven menus overflow with heirloom tomatoes, forest mushrooms, chioggia beets, organic spring mixes—vegetables we find infinitely superior to the ones we ate as kids, possibly only because we weren't forced to eat them as kids.

Down in New Orleans' supermarkets we again face the enemy, in terrifying amounts: bell peppers, green beans, cabbage, celery, iceberg lettuce—vegetables so short on star power we're surprised they're still in production. We also meet new vegetables like okra, mirliton, and stiff greens, but because we don't understand them or know how to turn them into salads, they don't make it onto our grocery lists. On the late autumn day in 2002 when Whole Foods Market opened in Uptown's old Arabella Bus Barn, selling California pea shoots and organic avocados, those of us newcomers who shared a superior vegetable worldview began to see a lot more of each other. (The "whole foods" concept had been in New Orleans since the 1970s but in a hippie-dippier way; the bus barn's stunning transformation, impressive dimensions, and central location marked the city's introduction to the orgasmic potential of modern organics.)

Clarification: the vehemence of my New Orleans conversion hasn't kept me from falling off the wagon in the vegetable aisle and groping for, say, radicchio; in moments of weakness I still believe that it's New Orleans, not me, that needs to broaden its horizons. It's a never-ending conflict. New Orleans usually wins. Case in point: the last time I asked a waiter at Galatoire's for à la carte advice, he recommended the broccoli hollandaise, a creation that went out of style with the smoking jacket in most of civilization. Yet, fashions aside, when was the last time broccoli tasted better? Honestly? Up north, broccoli was allowed palatability just once a year, on Christmas Eve, when cheesy chicken-broccoli casserole kept Stephanie and me from hunger-striking against our aunt's other holiday tradition, oyster stew.

New Orleanians show their vegetables more consistent love. The ultimate in vegetal affection is called smothering down here, as in smothered string beans. Merriam-Webster's fourth definition of "to smother" gives the basic idea: "to cook in a covered pan or pot with little liquid over low heat." But while the definition more or less describes the technical process by which you might smother something—a seven steak, turnips, crawfish tails (crawfish étouffée is French for "smothered crawfish")—it doesn't account for the amour tasted in dishes like the smothered rabbit and caramelized onion gravy at New Orleans Food and Spirits, the smothered okra and shrimp at Dunbar's Creole Cooking, or the cabbage smothered in ham broth in any self-respecting southern kitchen. Nor does it account for the coffee can of bacon fat beside the stove of master smotherers. The technique is as emotive as it is practical: to smother a vegetable is to play upon its most lovable attributes, like smothering a sweetheart in kisses.

One of the city's most overall succulent dishes is the smothered mustard greens at Ms. Hyster's Bar-B-Que, which, having been violated with pork and cooked to Olympian flexibility, manage to overshadow the barbecue ribs even while looking like pond dredgings. One afternoon while I was interviewing Virginia Johnson, Ms. Hyster's owner, for a story about barbecue, the restaurant's front door swung open to admit the swooshing sound of a city bus barreling down South Claiborne Avenue and two customers, their dusty work clothes draped over strong frames. Miss Virginia half rose to greet them with the bad news: "No greens today. The truck should be here in about an hour. Come back tomorrow, all right?"

"Aw," one of the men teased, pushing his partner back out into the hot afternoon. "He's been crying all day for them, too."

Soon a farmer from rural Lutcher, Louisiana, arrived with a truckload of freshly harvested mustards, naturally crumpled, warm and windblown from the ride downriver. Miss Virginia had already explained that it takes her staff two full days to pull, clean, and cook the once-a-week delivery; it nevertheless awed me to see that her wet, murky, pork-infused specialty really does originate as raw greenery.

Ms. Hyster's greens were a turning point. There wasn't a vegetable I wouldn't eat, and I'd come to fetishize some, but I'd never so closely witnessed the culinary emancipation that allows southern cooks to take a leaf so rich with nutrients it glows and manipulate it in a way that prompts red-blooded men to choose it over smoked pork. Before seeing the workers' disappointment, hearing about Miss Virginia's long preparation method, and watching that truck pull in from Lutcher, the latent wound-tight northerner in me had been unconsciously interpreting this region's typical vegetable treatments—smothering and stuffing, for example—as manifestations of aversion. Why would you work so hard to disguise something you liked? On this day I finally understood smothering's most outstanding characteristic: it's an endearment. It's about tenderness, after all.

Gumbo z'herbes (a contraction in Creole dialect of *gumbo aux herbes*), or green gumbo, is the ultimate in green vegetable manipulation. Recipes call for between five and fifteen different greens—anything from scallions to chard, carrot tops to cabbage, arugula to peppergrass (a spicy weed that urban Creoles are said to pick from neutral grounds, New Orleans–speak for boulevard medians). I mention gumbo z'herbes in this chapter and not in the chapter about gumbo because the only ways in which gumbo z'herbes resembles more common meat and seafood gumbos are that it's eaten with a spoon, often crammed with sausage, and thickened with a roux—and the latter only sometimes. In preparation, gumbo z'herbes is a multiplicity of smothered greens united in a communal pot likker. Its flavor and its origins are more mysterious: no two bites, or theories, are the same.

My seventeenth-edition copy of Caroline Merrick Jones's *Gourmet's Guide to New Orleans*, first published in 1933, suggests that gumbo z'herbes originated in Africa and was modified by our country's Native Americans, who had a "rudimentary knowledge of medicinal or 'pot' herbs." Jessica Harris, the scholar and cookbook author, thinks it could be a cousin of *sauce feuille*, African leaf sauce. Others compare it, along with other gumbos, to the Afro-Caribbean dish callaloo. In his encyclopedia of Cajun and Creole cuisine, the chef John Folse provides a convincing argument that the German Catholics who began settling in Louisiana around 1720 and took to farming immediately inspired Louisiana's gumbo z'herbes recipe with a traditional seven-herb soup they ate on Holy Thursday.

In New Orleans today, green gumbo is an established Lenten dish, sometimes prepared without meat. A Holy Thursday gumbo z'herbes is an event at Dooky Chase Restaurant (which was out of commission due to flooding in 2006 but received guests for gumbo on Holy Thursday 2007), attended by many who could explain the Eucharist no better than driving in a blizzard. The octogenarian Creole queen Leah Chase has feasted on gumbo z'herbes once a year since her childhood in Madisonville, on the north shore of Lake Pontchartrain, when anyone older than seven ate nothing before noon on Good Friday and very little after. In preparation for the fast, they bulked up on the rich gumbo the day before.

In keeping with local vegetable treatments and a rather New Orleanian interpretation of Catholic rule, Mrs. Chase makes her version with roughly as many meats as greens, including hot sausage, smoked sausage, andouille, beef stew meat, chicken, and ham two ways. While she passes the greens and seasoning vegetables through a meat grinder to produce a smooth, deep-green soup, she keeps her meats in bite-sized chunks. "Creoles don't like to see their seasonings, but they have to see their meat," Mrs. Chase told me once.

Mrs. Chase believes that green gumbo ought to remain Lent-specific. "Leave things be special," she said to me. Although in 2006 she granted John Folse special dispensation to make and market a frozen version of her gumbo labeled with her name and image, I would argue that as she isn't standing over the pots herself, she continues to leave things be special.

Disobeying, I made my first gumbo z'herbes at home during my vegetable-obsessed month, just prior to Lent and during the Mardi Gras parade season, which also happens to be high season for greens and cheap beer (the only other item that would fit into the refrigerator). Like Mrs. Chase's, mine was mulchy, bitter, strangely sweet, zinging with cayenne pepper, meatier than an NFL locker room, and inordinately refreshing. Some bites were breathy with anise, for no logical reason, and others held all the sensations of an Easter dinner, any Easter dinner.

I had followed a recipe from Mrs. Chase's cookbook and was pleased, but the depth and the complexity of flavors in mine didn't touch the one that she made in my kitchen two weeks later for eighteen judges of the James Beard Foundation Awards, who were meeting in New Orleans and needed lunch (we used my kitchen because the FEMA trailer where she was living with her husband, Edgar "Dooky" Chase, across from their flooded restaurant couldn't accommodate another body, much less a backyard garden's worth of produce). Her chief arsenal, even more than the greens and the sausage, turned out to be ham. Directly upon entering my kitchen, she filled a pot with two ham shanks and water and set it over a flame to simmer into stock.

Gumbo z'herbes is not a precision project; it doesn't matter if the bunch of turnip greens you buy in Salt Lake City is half or double the size of mine. Every batch is unique, dynamic in its own way. Mrs. Chase didn't glance at the weights of the meats she bought when we shopped together, she pushing the cart, I standing aside as a parade of other customers rushed to kiss a smooth cheek, touch a caramel hand, and ask when her restaurant would reopen. She didn't measure the flour or fat for her roux. She didn't even count her greens. Most every gumbo z'herbes recipe (including the one in Mrs. Chase's biography) commands that for luck's sake you must use an odd number of greens; according to the adage, the cook will acquire one new friend for each variety. I was such a faithful dilettante that when I accidentally burned all the beet greens to the charred tone of a campfire for my solo batch at Mardi Gras, I ran to the grocery store at 11 P.M. to buy more rather than using only ten varieties. Later, when I busted Mrs. Chase acting blasé in the produce section and settling for an even number, she rolled her eyes and put on her low, bossy voice: "Go ahead, throw a bunch of collards in the cart."

Mrs. Chase was busy on the day of the James Beard luncheon, so I served the gumbo in her stead at a downtown hotel where the judges, who had flown in from all across the country, were meeting. Cursing was the most common reaction, as in the writer-editor Pete Wells's "This is the best gosh-darn thing I've ever put in my mouth!" (That's my whitewashed version of Pete's reaction. I don't have a policy against swearing in print, but I'd have a lifetime of Hail Marys to pay if I took the Lord's name in vain in a section about Leah Chase.) When I reported to her that the gumbo had reduced the judges to expletives, Mrs. Chase responded, "Well, you don't need to curse at gumbo."

She wasn't up for a Beard Award that year, but it's always nice to wow a group accustomed to the best. Most gratifying, though, was the army-ant-like procession of New Orleanians—bellhops, managers, cooks, waiters—who hauled up to the twenty-third floor once word got out that I was giving away Mrs. Chase's leftovers. I walked into the kitchen to overhear a maintenance worker in a blue jumpsuit on the phone with his wife: "Baby, this is the best gumbo I ever had . . . and it's green."

When I asked Mrs. Chase for her thoughts about the easy relationship between New Orleanians and their vegetables, she cited the state's continuous growing season and the fact that so many people in south Louisiana grew up like she did, eating only what their parents raised. Vegetables were main courses not by design but by necessity. "Meat was unheard of during the week," she remembered. "We'd have string beans and rice, eggplant and rice," with meat only on Sundays or around the winter hog killing. "And all that dried stuff y'all think is so fancy, we did that ourselves." Sun-dried tomatoes, okra, shrimp, strawberries . . .

Urban grocery shopping in New Orleans today allows even most families on a tight budget pickle meat, chicken thighs, turkey necks, and sausage. Regional tastes plus modern economics equals a surfeit of deliciousness and often a deficit of nutritional value. If vegetables aren't cooked down with pork fat, then they're stuffed with oil-laden breadcrumbs, bulked up with cheese and cream, or fried clean of every possible health benefit. Surely health-conscious native cooks exist, just as there are New Orleans children who despise stuffed eggplant as much as I loathed steamed broccoli, but neither cookbooks nor restaurant cooking represent them in any magnitude.

It used to be that if you sat 'round the horseshoe-shaped bar at Ye Olde College Inn at noon, you'd be in the company of men, some of them manly enough to order a collection of vegetable side dishes for lunch. And no wonder; when I joined them once, the selection included okra stewed softly with tomato and ham, thin caramel-colored sweet potato fries, ham nubs stuck like thumbtacks into a casserole of yellow squash and breadcrumbs, and noodles engorged with a sea of orange cream. Down here, macaroni and cheese counts as a vegetable. Potato salad is salad. Sadly, Ye Olde College Inn was inundated by Katrina, and its relatively new owner, John Blancher, reopened in a space next door; good-bye, horseshoe bar. At the time of this writing, the vegetable plate is history too.

No, New Orleanians generally don't complain about having to eat their vegetables. I wouldn't either, not now that I've been liberated, except for this persistent inbred sense that if vegetables don't require some amount of getting used to, if they cause you to fret over gastric reflux and cholesterol, if they give you as much pleasure as barbecue does, well, then they might as well be pizza. If vegetables can't help compensate, physiologically and morally, for the croissant I ate for breakfast, the muffuletta I ate for lunch, and the Sazerac I'm planning for 7 P.M., what exactly is my life expectancy? Where is my self-respect?

Among the reasons that I choose New Orleans is that its cultural mores don't accommodate this sort of culinary self-flagellation. I'm almost certain that if I had attended college at Tulane or the University of New Orleans, I wouldn't have sunk into the masochistic period of pseudo-vegetarianism that darkened my early twenties. The overriding theme of my first year at St. John's College, where the great books of Western civilization dictate the only curriculum, was *what is the soul?* I denounced meat midway through first semester, after a short course on dissection, and by Christmas I had talked the school psychologist into excusing me from the mandatory cafeteria plan, ostensibly on account of its reliance on animal proteins. I persisted in a life of meatlessness for the next half-decade, more as an exercise of will and of a young woman's food neuroses as time wore on than because of some deeper Aristotelian dialectic. Of course I ate seafood; everyone knows that fish don't have souls.

That chapter of my life never seemed so buried as on the evening when I served hollowed-out eggplant skins stuffed with shrimp and ham—you chop the shrimp and grind the ham and mix them with fresh breadcrumbs and the eggplant's sautéed innards—alongside Sarah's beef daube. It's a trinity that was meant to touch: fragrant, garlicky, reminiscent of the smokehouse and of the sea. Since our dinner-planning session, I had learned that most New Orleanians treat stuffed eggplant as a main course (eggplant stuffing, the same thing only without the skins, is a side dish), which meant that the daube technically was overkill. Any disappointment in getting the local formula wrong was offset by the thrill of beating New Orleans at a game of excess. We also used the opportunity to indulge in a heretofore undocumented version of wilted lettuce that Sarah's father-in-law remembers his Creole mother serving. Olivier wilted lettuce is made by ladling gravy over iceberg.

I cannot give up the food pyramid entirely. I've eaten gumbo for breakfast only once, and when I make the old-school specialty called soaked salad (you toss iceberg lettuce and half-ripe tomatoes with vinaigrette and then let it soak for hours), I count it as a white. But I have made progress. My favorite vegetable vendor at the farmers' market in New Orleans is Jim Core, because he grows heirloom eggplant and sweet salad turnips as well as all the unglamorous greens for gumbo z'herbes. And my favorite vegetable chef is Corbin Evans, currently at Savvy Gourmet, because he favors ingredients like oyster mushrooms and broccoli sprouts *and* he keeps a can of bacon grease by his stove.

I'd just left my car in Metairie because the floor was leaking (in a floodplain you have to worry about leaking from the bottom up), and a man who lived in New Orleans East was driving me home in the dealership's sedan shuttle. Before Katrina, New Orleans East was immense and primarily residential, and thus basically unknown to those of us who didn't live or work there. I began milking the driver for eating recommendations in his neighborhood, for places that served Big Mama–style gumbo and Vietnamese po-boys. Then I asked him where he liked to eat in Metairie, a more restaurant-oriented suburb, when he got off work. Bennigan's and Outback Steakhouse, he said. It always distresses me to see the parking lots of generic chain restaurants packed in a town with its own rich food culture. I prefer family-run restaurants, I told him, places where the food is homemade. "Why don't you just eat at home, then?" he asked.

As much as I'd glommed on to New Orleans' foodways, left to my instincts, my own home cooking rarely reflected it during my first half-decade living here. It was like swimming upstream to enter the Sav-A-Center supermarket up my street, where the most prominent display as I write is a mountain of purple, green, and yellow soda cases arranged to spell out "Happy Mardi Gras."

But when it took the Whole Foods in Uptown five months to repair and reopen after the storm, I developed an unexpected allegiance to my neighborhood superstore, whose aisles I'm almost positive have never hosted a chioggia beet. Shopping and cooking like a local, and eating like one at home, began to feel more natural out of necessity. I had always been studious, cooking red beans with pickle meat and smothering okra by the gallon, because I knew it would help me become the person I wanted to be, a devout New Orleanian. But intellect and instinct finally merged for an extended period, which is what brought about that month-long vegetable spree. I'm still not ready for Outback, but I sure do know my way around a mirliton.

Of the mirliton's various other appellations—chayote, custard marrow, and christophene among them—vegetable pear is the one that best encapsulates its dual character: it's not your typical fruit, and it's not officially a vegetable. Uncut and upright, a commercially grown mirliton looks like a pear with extra-wide hips, and it shares a palette of greens with the Granny Smith apple. A ripe one is heavy for its size, and its unpeeled skin feels thick, something like a mango's but tauter and more leathery. The skin meets at a stem on one end while a puckery crease runs lengthwise at the other, a toothless grimace. *Mirliton* is French for a small, kazoo-type flute. Neither looking at the subtropical squash nor cooking it explains the connection.

A raw mirliton crunches like potato; it tastes like very green cucumber, and a little like zucchini. Sautéed, it smells like starchy apples; boiled and fried, its translucent green flesh suggests what a honeydew melon would look, feel, and taste like if honeydew melon were a vegetable. When you peel a mirliton, its flesh sweats a dewy substance that sticks to your hands and dries quickly into a second skin, similar to what remains after you've manhandled a butternut squash. Homegrown mirlitons may break any and all of these rules, reaching the size of pomelos, developing bumps on the skin, appearing more yellow than green, and tasting more robustly squashlike. The vines overtake New Orleans' backyard gardens and the backyards of former New Orleanians. Leah Chase's brother produced so many in his garden in Southern California one year that he FedExed her two boxes full. She stuffed them with shrimp and ham.

The mirliton's white inner seed, or pit, which transforms into something slimy when cooked, is a delicacy eaten raw, like a skinned almond crossed with a water chestnut. Most recipes call for removing the seed (thanks to the Mexican cooking expert Diana Kennedy for outing this secret luxury to me in one of her cookbooks). By all accounts the mirliton was cultivated in pre-Columbian Mexico, and it still factors widely in that country's cooking practices. Most Americans know it by the Spanish name chayote, if they know it at all. My 1,136-page edition of *The All New, All Purpose Joy of Cooking* devotes just half a page to the chayote, and only one recipe—for Louisiana-style chayote, which everyone in New Orleans calls stuffed mirliton.

Forever drawn to the underdog—in love, automobiles, sports, and vegetables—I never pass up a chance to order mirliton in a restaurant: Restaurant Cuvée's fried mirliton and shrimp rémoulade stack (a take on the more common preparation of fried green tomatoes with shrimp rémoulade); the delicate, milky shrimp and mirliton bisque at the late Lee Circle Restaurant; pickled mirliton at Taqueros-Coyoacan, an ambitious Mexican outfit; mirliton fritters with crabcakes at Irene's Cuisine; mirliton-corn relish at Brigtsen's; and any number of mirliton slaws, ragouts, and side dishes prepared by LaCôte Brasserie's Louisiana native son Chuck Subra, whose menus rarely exclude the vegetable pear. When Randy Barlow, an early Paul Prudhomme protégé, was running the kitchen at Gretna's Red Maple Restaurant, he served a lunch special that involved a plank of deep-fried mirliton crowded with shrimp, oysters, and andouille sausage, all bound by a garlicky lemon-butter sauce. In local parlance, this was a mirliton pirogue, named after the dugout canoes favored by Cajuns.

The preceding examples are not the greatest hits of my restaurant mirliton eating; it's a comprehensive list, culled over more than six years. Its brevity does not reflect the importance of the vegetable pear to New Orleans' food culture. For the most part, mirliton is something that people who might eat at Outback cook at home. And so did I, every night for a week.

Mirliton Week discovery number one: not everyone uses the vaguely French-sounding vernacular *mel-lee-tawn*. I had been practicing this pronunciation to myself as long as I'd consciously been replacing *trolley* with *streetcar*. When I tried it out on the produce stocker at Sav-A-Center, he cocked his head. "Oh, the mir-le-tuns," he said phonetically. "They're over there, by the okry."

Unless you're shopping in season at the farmers' market or from the bed of a produce truck, Louisiana's mirlitons come from the subtropics farther south. The eighth pound of my marathon week was from a deep-green Mexican batch. Geography didn't diminish their local clout. "Those are some beautiful mel-lee-tawns," the cashier at Langenstein's, a locally owned supermarket, noted. "You making dressing?"

In New Orleans–speak, dressing is synonymous with stuffing, a dish that's served exclusively during the holidays up north where I'm from and that comes in approximately one flavor there: Stove Top. As with the eggplant variety, mirliton stuffing differs from stuffed mirliton in that it's baked in a casserole dish, not in its hollowed-out skins. All some shade of brown or cream, soft enough to swallow without chewing, and incalculably tastier than they look, dressings down here may be constructed around dozens of different ingredients—vegetables, seafood, sausage, rice, cornbread—and while they know no seasonal limitations, they do appear in droves around the holidays. I've spent just one Thanksgiving in New Orleans, at a home in the Gentilly neighborhood, where I was paid to warm up catered food for a modest family dinner. The family had ordered four different dressings, two with eggplant, one with oysters, and one with mirliton. On purpose.

Mirliton Week discovery number two: the best and most prolific sources of mirliton recipes tend to be the spiral-bound community cookbooks that rely heavily, no matter what community produces them, on canned cream of mushroom soup. The spiral-bound work most useful to my mirliton mania was, aptly, *Mirliton and Other Neighborhood Favorites*, produced by the Bywater Neighborhood Association. This group throws an annual Mirliton Festival, an event so legitimate it has a beer sponsor. Forty in all, the book's mirliton recipes span every chapter but two, candy and beverages.

To compare, other influential local cookbooks pay homage with just a few. The Junior League of Baton Rouge includes three mirliton recipes (for baked, cold, and stuffed) in its *River Road Recipes*, a prodigy that enjoyed its forty-fifth printing in 1977, the year my copy was published. *The Dooky Chase Cookbook* contains four. There are two in Mary Moore Bremer's red-spiral-bound *New Orleans Recipes*, copyright 1932, including one for sweet mirliton glacé. I'm sure she meant well.

Mirliton Week discovery number three: the mirliton is a vegetable at heart.

It rarely tastes correct to me when vegetables (or vegetable-like fruits) are sweetened and passed off as savory dishes. Candied sweet potatoes, glazed carrots, and sweet tomato aspic, for instance, are abominations on the dinner table, and no amount of cultural submersion will convince me otherwise. To prepare the glacé, Bremer's cookbook has you bake sliced mirliton with brown sugar, allspice, ginger, nutmeg, cinnamon, and cloves—enough of each spice to anesthetize the tongue in one bite. Just before serving, you accomplish the glacé, or candying, by running the dish beneath the broiler. The finished product tastes like mulled squash, the sugar accentuating the mirliton's most vegetal qualities. I enjoyed no more success in serving sweetened mirliton for dessert: the only redeeming feature of my mirliton pie was its meringue.

Mirliton Week discovery number four: dairy, of course.

I've felt a soul connection with the mirliton since our first meeting, an intimate and conspiratorial bond that's different from the intellectual and cultural curiosity that at first drove me to cook and eat New Orleans' other favorite vegetable obscurities. Okra may be the bigger underdog, what with its never-ending production of slime; within seconds of reaching a simmer, a pot of sliced okra and water thickens into a barely stirrable bog. "Mucilaginous" is the polite description adopted by dictionaries and academic texts. But Mother Nature gave okra physical beauty: symmetrically ribbed pods, perfectly round seeds, a blunt tip on one end, a proper cap on the other, and a mossy carpet of green in between. The okra pod is the ubiquitous symbol of all things good and southern. Give it eyes and a smile and it almost looks human. Set beside okra, a mirliton is a shapeless lump, camouflaged by its own plainness. It's how I imagine my milk-scrubbed, feathered-haired Wisconsin self would have appeared as a teenager on the society page of New Orleans debutantes.

How fitting, then, to discover that dairy actualizes the totality of a mirliton's potential. Three nights in a row I cooked six of them into a gratin with butter, cream, and Havarti cheese, riffing on a recipe from the mirliton cookbook. New Orleanians are so fond of gratins that crabmeat au gratin is a popular restaurant main course. No side salad, no chaser—just a burbling dish of crab, cream, and cheese, and more of each than anyone probably ought to admit consuming in one sitting. My mirliton gratin was like that, thicker than a Colorado snowstorm, richer than an offshore bank account. In this savory context, the mirliton itself tasted sweet and fruitlike, tender bites of dew. Several of my guests one night burned the roofs of their mouths by digging in too soon. It was just like pizza.

. . .

Some people are born with religion, some are reborn, and some die faithless. I'm in the middle group, having found religion in my thirties as an imperfect New Orleanian. Whether by free will or intelligent design, during that post-Katrina phase when shopping and cooking like a local began to feel more natural, I attended mass for the first time ever by myself, at St. Augustine Church in the Treme neighborhood. And then I went again, and again.

I was baptized Catholic as an infant and confirmed as a teenager, and while no one technically forced me into the latter, it didn't exactly arise from my own desire. My friends were doing it, I supposed that my family wanted me to do it, and it seemed harmless and logical—what, other than a sacramental graduation, had been the purpose of ten years of catechism classes anyway? Directly after my confirmation I stopped going to church. I loathe getting out of bed on Sundays.

The storm further attenuated my relationship with the God I had grown up studying. At the risk of stretching a metaphor, for me the Church's post-Katrina magnetism had less to do with doctrine than with vegetables, or at least with the freedom of spirit that compels New Orleanians to smother their green beans in bacon fat, to stuff their eggplants with shrimp and ham, to glory in bingeing before fasting—and to jump up clapping in midsermon. A bowl of gumbo z'herbes is no penance, and neither is a jazz mass conducted by Ellis Marsalis, during which Father Jerome LeDoux takes the floor, leaving his altar to a guitar, a trombone, two saxophones, a standing bass, a piano, an organ, a tambourine, a drum set, and a choir that grows during the nearly three-hour service, presumably as its members wake up. Such was the beatitude of my first visit to St. Augustine.

I ate vegetables for thirty years in the same way that I attended catechism. I believed both were good for me; occasionally I even suspected (or tasted) a higher power at work. But neither had ever impelled me to spring up from sitting, grab my neighbor's hand, belt out a choral version of the Lord's Prayer, and think, *God, I love this town!*

I knew all the words, could recite even the priest's lines by memory, but mass was so different this time around. Because I was choosing it, because I needed it. New Orleanians needed pampering after Katrina. We needed to hug and be hugged, to sing and be sung to, to cook and be cooked for. We needed to feel ourselves, our city, each other. At St. Augustine, when it was time to share the sign of peace, people I'd never seen before danced clear across the room to shake my hand.

Church wasn't the only place of worship. Drum circles, second lines, book readings, meditation sessions, yoga practices, prayer groups, neighborhood meetings, protests, trash pickups, rallies, porch talks, dinner—participating in almost anything communal during that period in New Orleans felt purposeful and sacred.

Sarah Olivier and I served our stuffed eggplant and beef daube dinner on the compact rectangular table that she and her husband, David, had purchased at Ikea to replace the spectacular round antique oak dining table that had been in David's family for generations but whose base had rotted in the floodwaters that had besieged their home in Uptown after the levees broke. During the ensuing fourteen months, which they also spent nurturing their two daughters, meeting with contractors, paying rent *and* mortgage, and bellying through the insurance process in order to rebuild their home, Sarah and David created a sanctuary in their temporary, cramped living quarters by extending an open invitation for friends to have dinner and share a cocktail with them there. One friend helped Sarah begin to replace her ruined cookbook collection by giving her Richard Collin's classic *New Orleans Cookbook*; I brought over a spare copy of the Time-Life book on Creole and Acadian cooking that had inspired my stuffed eggplant recipe. It was a new kind of prayer for us to cook and eat from them together.

PO-BOYS

Not in California Anymore

Of all the follies I committed en route to becoming a New Orleanian—pronouncing Burgundy Street like the wine (in New Orleans–speak, the emphasis is on *gun*), locking my mountain bike on the front porch (once, before it disappeared), agreeing to work on Fat Tuesday—the most egregious was disrespecting the po-boy. Just a submarine sandwich, I'd sneer as another month passed without trying one. But po-boys are as unavoidable in New Orleans as mousling cockroaches are, and in time the determination of both broke me. I don't scream anymore when I see the cockroaches limboing beneath the doorsill, and curiosity eventually drove me up Magazine Street to Guy's Po-Boys.

Turkey, roast beef, hamburger, fried shrimp, BLT—Guy's sandwich selection seemed less inspired than the restaurant's décor, the centerpiece of which was a rotating fan that blew dust with the room's hot, deep-fried air. One option appealed to me, though, possibly a symptom of my allergy to the era's low-carb mania: a fried potato po-boy. If anything could restore balance to the protein-weighted universe, French fries on white bread was it.

"You want that dressed, baby?" the cashier asked. Dressed. Dressed? I had already embarrassed myself so many times by then, by requesting clarification for local vernacular. "Erl," I now knew, is oil, "berl" is boil, and "hawt" is short for *sweetheart,* but those lessons had been hard-earned. My northerner's ear was a personal torture device in the catering kitchen staffed with natives where I landed my first job in the city; I panicked every time the most foreign-tongued of them addressed me. At Guy's, the line behind me grew. Sure, dressed, I caved, not learning until I freed the sandwich of its white butcher-paper wrapping at home that by ordering your po-boy dressed, you agree to the addition of shredded iceberg lettuce, sliced tomato, pickle chips, and mayonnaise, a condiment that had been triggering my gag reflex since birth. Fortunately, I had also agreed to a dousing of roast beef gravy, the cashier's suggestion. Gravy can cover almost any culinary evil.

At the time of this writing, Guy's "small" fried potato po-boy costs $2.50. Neither its advertised size nor its eensy price speaks frankly to the experience of finishing it, an act so intimidating that I never doubted the po-boy again. I remember slipping from my chair down to our hardwood dining room floor and stretching flat on my back, in which position at least I could breathe. The world went dark and quiet, and as this was not a regular happening for me yet (I grew used to it), I could only guess that digestion had usurped all available energies. I didn't know how much time had passed once I roused—feeling fantastic, incidentally—but one thing was clear: I was not in California anymore.

I lived in San Francisco for just one year (during the dot-com boom, this was ample time for a line cook to wear out her savings and her one pair of work shoes), but I cooked and ate under the influence of California for most of my twenties. During the late 1990s, I made enough beet, nut, and cheese salads in restaurants across Wisconsin, California, and Wyoming to stain my nailbeds a permanent fuchsia. However did I pass the hours before there were fresh fava beans to be shelled and then blanched and then peeled? A new muscle in my back seared for every baby artichoke scaled, but who was counting? When Alice Waters spoke, American cooks with a conscience listened, and her sermons still reverberated on my palate when I landed in New Orleans and began to consider the po-boy.

To understand my initial snubbing of the sandwich, consider

what the cult of California cooking would have to say about the combination of white bread made with bleached flour, unwashed iceberg lettuce, pink November tomatoes, mayonnaise (*not* aïoli) scooped from a gallon jug, pickles the false color of a tree frog, and potato spears dumped into the fryer from a frozen bag. Then imagine the cult at Guy's. Tickles, doesn't it?

At the turn of the twenty-first century, everyday New Orleans eating remained largely untouched by the simpler-is-better, farm-to-table food movement that Alice Waters and friends launched at Berkeley's Chez Panisse restaurant in the 1970s. There was a wonderful network of farmers' markets in the metropolitan area, and support for purveyors of small-batch hot sauces, stone-ground grits, organic produce, and free-range chickens, but more often than not what happened to those products under the tutelage of local cooking traditions could not be described as typical of anything modern, simple, or even American. Recall the stuffed eggplant. I rest my case.

Modernity did (and does) have a presence in New Orleans' fashionable new-line restaurants, where chefs of all backgrounds played with beets, goat cheese, and bizarre greens like butter lettuce. (In fact, California cuisine has now asserted itself in an official way: following Katrina, while leaders and educators struggled to conceive of better public schools for Orleans Parish, the Samuel J. Green Charter School in Uptown became the second incubator school for Alice Waters's inspired Edible Schoolyard curriculum.) But there's never been enough California in New Orleans for Californians, and Matt and I have suffered for it. The first blow came from Los Angeles, with his sister, Maëlle. For three days we fed her our favorite—some might say outrageous—things: white, peppery rabbit sausage, an appetizer at Gabrielle; "barbecue" shrimp gurgling in garlic butter (or is it margarine?) at Pascal's Manale; gumbo, red beans, and muffulettas, all in one whacking meal at home. On her fourth evening here, just as our waiter at Clancy's Restaurant presented the climax of the food tour—deep-fried oysters beneath a pashmina of melted Brie cheese—Maëlle asked, "Isn't there anywhere in this town that's just American, where you can go and order a big salad and be happy?"

We had been related for two years, not long enough to retaliate without a fair trial, so I passed the oysters and mentioned that I did know at least one such place. "So there's a salad there with, say, a goat cheese crouton?" I didn't write in my notes of that night that Matt squeezed my hand under the table, but that's how I remember it. We were on the same team, and we knew approximately what was coming next. "I mean, where is the fusion, the ethnic food?" Maëlle continued. "We eat Thai at least once a week at home, we love Korean barbecue." While New Orleanians also enjoy international restaurants like Thai and Korean, we tend not to take our visitors to them because we have our own ethnic cooking to showcase. I tried to explain to my sister-in-law that New Orleans food is all about fusion and the merging of ethnicities. The French settled the city, the Spanish ruled it, Native Americans predated both, African descendants command restaurant kitchens, Paul Prudhomme brought Acadiana within the city limits, and new influences continue to shape what we eat.

When the waiter returned for our dinner order, Maëlle constructed a big, off-the-menu salad of mixed greens, bleu cheese, and Italian dressing.

Like any Belgian worthy of the passport, Maëlle can eat me under the table, and with the class of a thousand gianduja bonbons. During one of our first meals together, back in San Francisco, I threw in all my chips for the grilled salmon and pasta while she swallowed a dozen raw oysters and dug the marrow from roasted beef bones. Fair is fair; nearly everyone who visits us in New Orleans reacts as she did to the unctuous, uncompromising food. They try cutting Casamento's bulbous Gulf oysters with a knife; they order the vegetable soup at Mandina's, ignorant that it's constructed around a slab of beef brisket; and they cry uncle when, before they've recovered from dinner the night before, we drag them out for a grillades-and-grits brunch kicked off with cocktails.

I've been there too, but not for a long time. It's a point of pride now that I can finish a small fried potato po-boy from Guy's, dressed and gravied, and move forward with the afternoon. Maybe not comfortably, and not every day, but often enough to remind myself how far I've come.

I didn't know when I first ordered the combination at Guy's that potatoes and roast beef drippings filled the original po-boy sandwiches, which most written accounts and people old enough to remember agree were constructed at a sandwich shop called Martin's. During a streetcar strike in the 1920s, the brothers Bennie and Clovis Martin began feeding strikers potato and gravy sandwiches on French bread for free (some sources say that they charged a few cents), calling them "poor boys" in a double-entendre: the protesters were losing wages and the sandwiches were made with the cheapest possible ingredients.

That's the story, anyway, and nobody challenges it anymore. Just thirty-odd years ago, when Richard Collin published *The New Orleans Underground Gourmet*, a debate over who created the sandwich still raged. "The battle can be seen in several signs throughout the city, each claiming the invention," he wrote in a chapter devoted solely to po-boy vendors. Martin's Poor Boy Restaurant, still functioning at the time, served as Collin's pick for best po-boy.

Careful readers have noticed that while the Martin brothers called their invention a poor boy, I call it a po-boy. A minor dispute smolders over the spelling. The restaurant writer and food-media personality Tom Fitzmorris has lived in New Orleans longer than I have by nearly five decades. During a discussion of the topic on the Web message board he moderated, he made the following almost convincing argument for "poor boy":

> I have in my collection the final menu from Martin's, of which I was a regular customer. It says, "Martin's Poor Boy Restaurant. No Branches. We Serve Margarine." Its sandwiches were called poor boys. Not po-boys. It's

their baby—they get to name it, and spell the name however they want. And I use their spelling.

Tom is among about a dozen people whom I've ever heard properly enunciate the *poor* in *poor boy*. It's possible that I don't hang out with enough natives; maybe, like the fried potato po-boy itself, the correct pronunciation is an endangered species. What I know is that it took me too long to perfect saying *po-boy* without cringing (for a long time I felt like a bad white rapper) to change tracks now. And besides, it's Guy's Po-Boys.

Martin's is gone, the fried potato po-boy is a relative obscurity, the sandwich's pronunciation has gone to pot—is anything sacred? More than not: overall, the po-boy hasn't shifted much from its original foundation. If the Martins fattened their first po-boys with odds, ends, dregs, and drippings from the roast beef pan, they must have done a respectable trade in roast beef. Roast beef remained New Orleans' favorite po-boy filler up to the 1970s, according to *The New Orleans Underground Gourmet*, and it still lights the fuse of po-boy passions more quickly than any other filler today.

Roast beef po-boys generally follow one of three basic styles: tissue-paper-thin wisps of beef wetted with beef jus; thick, leathery slices of beef, often cut from a processed loaf, dampened with gravies of various consistencies; or CrockPot-tender beef that has become one with its gravy during the process of stewing. Garlic may or may not flavor any of the three styles. New Orleanians of a certain roast beef persuasion take seriously only those po-boy joints that follow a rule of inverse proportion: the messier the sandwich, the flimsier its napkins. My own standby, Parasol's in the Irish Channel neighborhood, is dead on in that regard, and also regarding a po-boy shop's preferred ambiance, which is spartan. You may eat in Parasol's bar, which extends to encompass its entire residential block on St. Patrick's Day, a hard-partying holiday in New Orleans no matter your heritage. Or you may rest your elbows on one of the utilitarian tables back near Parasol's short-order kitchen. Either way you'll passively consume enough cigarette smoke with your beef to make a persuasive substitute for barbecue. (A law banning smoking in Louisiana restaurants that took effect in 2007 has not improved the air quality, nor ruined the ambiance, in bar-restaurants like Parasol's, which remain at least partially exempt from it.)

Literature on the menu at Mother's Restaurant brags that the kitchen there produces more than 100,000 pounds of roast beef per year. A sort of neighborhood cafeteria opened in 1938 and sustained (mainly owing to its downtown location) by tourists, Mother's is the kind of old-school haunt you expect to maintain a straightforward po-boy selection. While the restaurant does specialize in basic baked ham sandwiches, the Famous Ferdi Special po-boy overshadows them with a whopping combination of roast beef, baked ham, gravy, and debris, dressed as all Mother's po-boys are with shredded cabbage. Debris, explains a glossary on the back of Mother's menu, is "the roast beef which falls into the gravy while baking in the oven." If you add cheese to your Ferdi, it's called a Ralph.

Debris was an enchanted word in New Orleans up until the storm, but for months afterward residents used it in nearly every uttered sentence to sum up the miserable detritus plaguing the city. The painful word association did not prevent New Orleanians from sating their roast beef po-boy cravings. Mother's and Parasol's were two of the first po-boy shops to reopen, and they filled with reuniting friends. I shared my first post-Katrina Parasol's roast beef feast with Judy Walker, the food editor at the *Times-Picayune*, who at the time was trying to repair her flooded home so that she could cook for herself again.

Though Mother's po-boys enjoyed a heyday prior to my own in New Orleans—a time when, locals say, the gravy was more robust—the Ferdi still sets the bar for messy beef-and-ham copycats, and it probably provided the template for some of the more absurd po-boys sold around town. Absurd such as Verti Marte's All That Jazz po-boy, described on the store's takeout menu as "a medley" of grilled ham, shrimp, turkey, tomatoes, mushrooms, Swiss and American cheeses, and a mystery "Wow Sauce." Before Katrina, Verti Marte was a twenty-four-hour deli with bicycle couriers who delivered directly to barstools in the neighborhood. (At the time of this writing, it closes at midnight.) French Quarter partiers who develop a late-night famishment on their walk home are still liable to find themselves dining on an All That Jazz atop a trash receptacle on the street corner outside the store and then regretting the sandwich, among other possible misdeeds, the next day.

If extended observation serves as proof, the second most popular po-boys in New Orleans are those stuffed with fried oysters. Long before the Martin brothers uttered "poor boy," this design was archived under the name *la médiatrice*, which translates as "peacemaker." Picked up after a night of carousing, fried oyster sandwiches reportedly keep husbands out of the doghouse. "It is a foolish husband who does not rely on it in case of need," wrote Mary Moore Bremer, who apparently hadn't a taste for jewelry, in her 1932 cookbook *New Orleans Recipes*. Bremer's peacemaker calls for a loaf of French bread, its top crust cut away and its insides hollowed out. She instructs toasting the whole long, boatlike affair in the oven and filling it with about two dozen fried oysters before buttering the toasted top crust and replacing it like a lid. A nearly identical recipe appears in the *The Picayune's Creole Cook Book*.

Both books, and others that followed, offer a third name for the peacemaker/fried oyster po-boy: oyster loaf. A handful of New Orleans restaurateurs still call their fried oyster sandwiches loaves, thereby denoting (at least in theory) a larger-than-average oyster sandwich. The most advertised oyster loaves are at Ye Olde College Inn, on the exterior of which a period mural devoted to the sandwich distracts drivers motoring down Carrollton Avenue. The most revered are at Casamento's, the Uptown oyster house of wall-to-wall tiles where the chef-owner, C. J. Gerdes, fries his oysters in lard and piles them between slices of toasted and buttered pan bread (essentially Texas toast without the garlic). Uglesich's Restaurant first opened in 1924 with one menu item, fried oysters on toasted and buttered bread; oyster loaves remained on the menu when, in 2005, its second-generation owners, Anthony and Gail Uglesich, closed their comfortably worn-in lunch spot.

I've never encountered Bremer's hollowing-out technique in a restaurant. I have, however, noticed this subtle differentiation between those oyster sandwiches called po-boys and those called loaves: order-takers always ask whether you want your po-boy dressed; they ask less frequently when you order a loaf, perhaps assuming that inherent in the order is a desire for an oyster sandwich prepared as simply as Bremer prepared her *médiatrice,* with butter and then maybe a dash or two of hot sauce. My inner traditionalist (or is it my inner Californian?) recognizes the brilliance of the undressed version, of the oysters' hot brackishness surging against naked fried batter and toasted bread like sea spray over stone—a timeless, complementary, necessary relationship. At the same time, I cop to a learned weakness for mayonnaise, an appreciation for the clear white crunch of iceberg, and a lust for pickles with everything. It was an oyster po-boy, fully dressed, at Jazz Fest that convinced me I had heard Ti Martin correctly.

Ti (pronounced "Tee") Martin is the daughter of Ella Brennan, the reigning matriarch of haute Creole cuisine, who with her siblings purchased Commander's Palace in 1969. With other family members of her generation, Ti manages the day-to-day operations at Commander's, a responsibility that by New Orleans standards is the culinary equivalent to owning the Hollywood Walk of Fame. Every day of the year (except the year following Katrina, when extensive water damage meant that the restaurant was closed for an overhaul and the family became contractors), she oversees the production of classics—turtle soup au sherry, pecan-crusted Gulf fish, bread pudding soufflé—and the release of flashy new blockbusters such as sugarcane-lacquered foie gras and oysters with Cajun bowfin caviar. Ti is the kind of woman on whose every word an aspiring New Orleanian hangs. At least, that's the position in which I once found myself, during a telephone interview regarding the opening of a short-lived gourmet-to-go market the Commander's group ran in Metairie. I was not yet an oyster po-boy zealot, and so it struck me as curious when Ti, in describing Foodies' sandwich menu, revealed this weakness: "I'm queer for oyster po-boys."

The word *queer*, as my editor pointed out when I wanted to call this book *Queer for Oyster Po-Boys*, is inflexible for our lifetime; the primary definition in contemporary American language is the one that refers, not always kindly, to sexual orientation. Historically, however, New Orleanians concern themselves with the contemporary only to the degree that smart marketing requires. An upstanding New Orleanian, Ti chose style over convention in relaying her affection for the sandwich. Instead of saying she was obsessed with or crazy about, or even, to use Merriam-Webster's synonym, *mildly insane* for oyster po-boys, she used a common word in a charming, arcane way, thereby ensuring that I would never forget it. I became engrossed with the notion that one could be queer for a po-boy. I needed to know that feeling.

And I do now, thanks to one illuminating sandwich. The day was toe-burning hot, dustier than the fan at Guy's, sticky with sunscreen and spilled beer, and otherwise not the kind of afternoon that encourages appetites anywhere but at Jazz Fest, where the regionally relevant food is subject to quality control of robotic standards. I ordered a fried oyster po-boy. The bread's fluff, the tomatoes' summer sweetness, the cool lettuce, the still crackling oysters, the tart pickles, and the ungodly slathering of mayonnaise all combined in the queerest, most breathtaking way, and I understood exactly what Ti had meant.

That same day, the songstress Charmaine Neville caught her breath between numbers by musing, "Love is an oyster po-boy," which is another fine way of saying it.

The most popular po-boys are also the most traditional, but that doesn't preclude allowances for innovations, aberrations, and peculiarities. Guy's owner and solo cook, Marvin Matherne, accepts customer creativity—"a sushi bar attitude; you don't see it, ask for it"—which inspired members of the local jam band Galactic to create Da Bomb: catfish and shrimp seasoned to kill, seared on the flattop griddle, and covered with a melt of Swiss and cheddar cheeses;

mayo if you dare. Matt created his own favorite at Guy's: fried catfish and potato salad, fully dressed. Jack Leonardi, a chef who batters and deep-fries mini roast beef and cheese po-boys as appetizers at his raucous dinner restaurant, Jacques-Imo's, purchased a seafood market with a sandwich counter in 2001. He called it Crabby Jack's, staffed it with cute girls, and set about experimenting with the genre. Roasted duck sopping in its own thin juices and panéed rabbit became quick classics. The chef name-checks Mother's by calling his baked ham, roast beef, gravy, and debris po-boy the Not Famous Fergi.

The most out-there po-boy I've encountered, and also genuinely liked, was the pepper wiener with beef chili, yellow mustard, and mayonnaise at Domilise's. An extinct product according to the Uptown po-boy maven Dot Domilise, who no longer is able to source it, the pepper wiener was essentially a dense hot dog speckled with a meteor shower of cayenne pepper and preserved in shiny red casing, most of which Domilise's cooks found time to pare off. Guessing that my hesitation to order one for the first time had something to do with its name, Miss Dot assured me, "It doesn't have that wiener flavor."

Two steps inside Domilise's and your clothing has absorbed the friendly reek of fried seafood. The first exchange you overhear inevitably goes something like this: "I've been eating here all my life." "Oh yeah? I've been *working* here all my life." In keeping with everything else in the restaurant, so outdated it's glamorous, are the toothpicks pushed into empty Tabasco bottles, a faded beer can collection, a hand sink against one wall, an aluminum can crusher mounted near the bar, and Miss Dot herself, whose home is attached to the restaurant.

Miss Dot was just a toddler living on a plantation in rural Louisiana (where her father worked as a mechanic) when her future father-in-law opened up shop at the corner of Annunciation and Bellecastle Streets. She fell for Samuel Domilise as a teenager while spending summers with relatives in New Orleans, and she ate a small pepper wiener po-boy every day during their courtship. After having children, Miss Dot took over her in-laws' business. Years later, her own daughter-in-law, Patti Domilise, joined the fold. The young blood promised that if the pepper wiener disappeared, at least there still would be a Domilise's.

Hurricanes notwithstanding.

I thought about Miss Dot often during my storm-mandated vacation from the city. I'd heard that other Uptown food icons of her generation, Mary Hansen and Joseph Casamento among them, did not survive their evacuations. Miss Dot's spirit and drive had been hardy before the storm—her hands rocked steady and her hair was always set—but she was in her eighties. There were so many things that the city couldn't afford to lose, and Domilise's was one of them. Three months after Katrina, having heard no news, I drove to Domilise's corner and peered inside the dark, wind-battered shop. Hoping against hope. There, on the other side of the glass side door, stood Miss Dot, her hair set as neatly as always, wearing a pastel yellow sweatsuit. As she opened the door to greet me, a carload of fans wheeled through the stone-silent neighborhood, shouting hellos in our direction. "I'm reopening!" Miss Dot shouted back. "Just waiting for the new refrigeration!"

Domilise's pepper wiener po-boy wasn't as artistic as the deep-fried boudin po-boy at Johnny & Josie's (a cylinder of French bread hollowed out, stuffed with seafood jambalaya, and dunked in hot oil to puff and stiffen like a beignet), and it wasn't as challenging as the brilliant but punishing Hots Delight at Guillory's Grocery & Meat Market (hot sausage patties, beef chili, orange cheese sauce, fried onions, and pickled jalapeños), but it did manage to pull off tasting like a classic while looking a little freakish, which is an accomplishment for food of any kind.

There may be po-boy vendors that excel with every sandwich, but I've never met one. For me, shopping for po-boys is like shopping for ice cream: coffee and dulce de leche from Häagen Dazs, cookie dough and New York Super Fudge Chunk from Ben & Jerry's, mint chocolate chip from Breyer's, French vanilla from Edy's, hot sausage patties at Gene's, fried shrimp at St. Roch Seafood Market (which has been closed since the storm), soft-shell crawfish at Jazz Fest, cochon de lait at Walker's Southern Style BBQ, meatball at R&O's, Italian sausage with olive salad at Radosta's, fried pickle at Fiorella's.

Our Statue of Liberty, where we drag guests whether they've brought their cameras or not, is Liuzza's by the Track, a corner bar near the Fair Grounds horseracing track (the site of Jazz Fest), where the frosted beer schooners could house a nuclear family of goldfish and the BBQ shrimp po-boys break all the rules. They contain no barbecue sauce, they require one butt end of the French loaf (in most restaurants the ends are thrown away or tossed aside to stale for bread pudding), and they must not be dressed. Craning from a barstool to observe the kitchen, I've watched cooks jab the end of a wooden spoon into the bread to mat its fleecy innards, creating a deep hollow within the loaf and shoring up a crusty barrier to contain the sandwich's sauce. They toss the bread bullet into the oven to toast and finally fill it to overflowing with pint-sized shrimp in an aggressive buttery slurry sharpened with garlic, lemon, and black pepper (when teamed with shrimp, these ingredients somehow provoke the idea of barbecue in New Orleans). The toasted bread holds its bounty like a chalice; Liuzza's cooks prop the po-boy on a plate by positioning little buttered toasts beneath it to prevent spillage. I cannot manage to eat it without knife and fork.

It's a sandwich that changes your life, just as a friend promised it would moments before I locked down on my first one. Its shrimp seem infinite, and its tart, peppery gravy thickens over time as it soaks into the bread. At a minimum, this po-boy alters your priorities. One afternoon a pickup truck and a Corvette with corresponding dents blocked the intersection at Liuzza's corner. There were no drivers in sight. I found the vehicles' owners inside the bar, borrowing the phone and ordering a snack.

My second father-in-law, Kurt Brown (Matt's stepfather), is immoderately moderate. He never eats red meat more than once a week, he allows himself exactly three disks of dark chocolate every afternoon and two spoonfuls of frozen yogurt every night, and if he ever drinks coffee with caffeine, it's because someone has tricked him into it. But since his maiden BBQ shrimp po-boy at Liuzza's by the Track, he insists on heading there directly from the airport. What greater compliment for a kitchen than a hypochondriac willing to compromise his health for lunch? On the other hand, Anthony Bourdain, the badass New York chef, television personality, and author, declined even a bite of a po-boy one afternoon at Liuzza's, where I kept him company between press engagements. He did empty two schooners of Abita Amber, and that after we had shared a Sazerac and a Ramos gin fizz at the Fairmont Hotel (where the Ramos gin fizz is said to have been invented), so he cannot be accused of missing the point entirely.

The problem with introducing guests to the po-boy by taking them to Liuzza's by the Track first, as we did with Kurt, is that you rob them of perspective. You cannot expect a po-boy neophyte deflowered by the BBQ shrimp spectacle to appreciate the plain but perfect fried catfish at Guy's, or the hamburgers grilled à la George Forman at the out-of-commission Rendon Supermarket, or the griddle-curled ham with melted white cheese at Parkway Bakery & Tavern.

Parkway's proprietor, Jay Nix, is a contractor by trade, a curator at heart. When history filters through his vision and his hands, it emerges in the present distilled, as sharp and clean as a perfect memory. The Timothy family, Parkway's original owners, who opened shop in 1922, baked their own po-boy bread until a flood damaged the kitchen's brick ovens in the 1970s. By the time the Timothys gave up the business entirely, in the 1990s, the building had gone to seed. In one of numerous nostalgic gestures while restoring the restaurant, Jay constructed a permanent foot rest at the bar out of the old oven bricks. When he first reopened Parkway, after eight dark years, citizens arrived en masse just to peruse the antique wall memorabilia that he had hung, from a Woolworth's luncheonette billboard to a menu from the old Roosevelt Hotel. Before Katrina made everyone famished for information, news of a renovation like Parkway's was the main reason that some New Orleanians still read the morning paper.

In addition to its preserved architecture and cultural showpieces, Parkway is a museum of the region's ongoing edible history, a place where brand names like Barq's (root beer), Blue Plate (mayonnaise), Zapp's (potato chips), and Hubig's (fried pies) are hallowed. And the po-boys themselves are of the straightforward sort that cause old-timers to say things like "Now *that's* a po-boy."

Which raises the question, What defines a po-boy? Is there an ingredient besides geography and mayonnaise that makes a po-boy a po-boy instead of, say, a submarine sandwich or a grinder or a hoagie? Easy answer: the bread.

New Orleans' bread culture may not be as strong as it once was. Before World War II and industrialization, the city's population supported a couple hundred small, family-run bakeries specializing in French bread. Old-timers tell me that up until a few decades ago, New Orleans French bread bulged at the center and tapered at the ends; it was longer than a supermarket bread loaf but shorter than a French baguette. The mass production of po-boys eventually birthed a longer, uniformly cylindrical loaf called po-boy bread, which can be cut into three standard sandwiches. Today the old style of French bread with tapered ends is uncommon in New Orleans; for newcomers like me, as well as younger New Orleans natives, "po-boy bread" and "French bread" are essentially one and the same, in size, shape, and taste characteristics.

The moniker "French bread" is a stretch, first off because the majority of French bread bakers in New Orleans—a century ago and now—are of Italian or German heritage; also, because other than a shared yardstick-length silhouette, the difference between a typical French baguette and a loaf of New Orleans French or po-boy bread is as pronounced as the vocal gulf between Etta James and Madonna. Mature and rich versus thin and flyaway.

Each style has its place, so I've learned. In reviewing Liuzza's by the Track in 2001, I wrote that the bar's BBQ shrimp po-boy (which requires sturdy bread) and bread pudding "might be the only reasons for continued production of the brittle, mostly hollow bread that plagues so many New Orleans sandwiches." I'm still shocked that no readers called for my resignation. I'm blushing as I write about it now.

New Orleanians are zealous about their French bread traditions, and while the look and mouthfeel vary some from bakery to bakery, the idea is the same: airy inside, brittle out. In his cookbook *Homegrown Louisiana Cookin'*, the late Cajun humorist and cook Justin Wilson raved about the irreplaceable quality of New Orleans French bread as if referring to a baking genre as poorly imitated as the New York bagel or the Parisian croissant. "This bread is very light, with uniform air spaces, tender, even porous in character—it seems to melt on the tongue," he wrote. This precisely is why I study cookbooks. Had I not run across such a poetic analysis, recorded by a man deep in the know, it never would have occurred to me that New Orleans bakeries produced bread that melts on the tongue *on purpose*.

I've made serious progress. New Orleans' unique bread now tastes angelic to me when it's served warm, with butter, before a meal; pressing my elbows into the liberal shatterings of its brittle crust scattered across a white tablecloth is a comfort. And I'm convinced that this is the perfect style of bread for a po-boy. Whether filled with ingredients as bold in flavor and heft as roast beef with gravy and mayonnaise or as properly delicate as fried oysters with butter, a more aggressive bread would throw the sandwich out of whack. I do, however, maintain that untoasted New Orleans French bread passes its prime within a few hours. The next day, it's good only for the stale bin. (Many New Orleanians insist that the bread must be toasted before it's made into po-boys. I make an exception at Domilise's, where the bread is not toasted but is ultra-fresh; Leidenheimer's bakery delivers there twice a day.)

There are a few exceptions to all of the above. Certain Italian-oriented neighborhood restaurants build their po-boys with seeded Italian bread. That works, as New Orleans Italian bread is similarly well ventilated and could also, if I was forced to do it, be compared to Styrofoam.

Alois J. Binder and Leidenheimer's bakeries are the city's primary sources of po-boy bread at the time of this writing, the first being also a pastry shop with exceptional doughnut holes in the Faubourg Marigny neighborhood, and the second being the most conspicuous because of its near-monopoly of the local bread market and also the colorful design of its trucks. Shaped like bread boxes on wheels, Leidenheimer trucks at first appear to be victims of graffiti; a closer look reveals an intentional design by the cartoonist Bunny Matthews, who created Vic and Nat'ly Broussard. Owners of a pretend po-boy shop in "da Nint' Ward," Vic and Nat'ly speak in colloquialisms, some of which are translated in a glossary on Leidenheimer's Web site. "Sink ya teeth into a piece of New Orleans cultcha," the couple exclaims on the flanks of the trucks. (In July 2006, Matthews opened a real-life Vic and Nat'ly's restaurant, in Covington, on the Northshore.) Locals like to spread the word when they spot a bread truck double-parked outside a po-boy shop for more than five minutes, as it means the driver is taking lunch inside—an indisputable endorsement. Binder's is a smaller operation; truck sightings are rare but exciting. Above the grill, a Binder's truck reads "Po-Boy Express."

The siblings Robert J. ("Sandy") and Katherine Whann descend from George Leidenheimer, a German immigrant who opened his first bakery in New Orleans in 1896. They now run the business together, with Sandy at the helm, and in so doing defend a vital piece of New Orleans cultcha. At a certain point, supplying demand for their breads didn't seem proactive enough, and so in 2004 they founded the New Orleans Po-Boy Preservation Society, an organization with the mission statement "to elevate the status of the po-boy sandwich in and around New Orleans as a delicious and nutritious cultural treasure and thereby increase the exposure of the city's po-boy shops and neighborhood restaurants."

Their initial effort was to call a series of meetings that convened around the metro area, inviting more than one hundred po-boy shop owner-operators to attend, regardless of their bread suppliers. I observed the final meeting of the series, at Mike Serio's Po-Boys and Deli downtown. Including the Whanns and Mike Serio, who supplied a muffuletta loaf as refreshment, only five po-boy preservationists made an appearance. Previous meetings had suffered similarly low attendance, no doubt for the very reason that a po-boy preservation society seemed necessary: hardworking small-business owners all, po-boy purveyors possess neither the time nor the money to compete effectively with national sandwich chains operating on multimillion-dollar advertising budgets. No one in the room dared to name the obvious competitor, though Mike Serio referred to it with a wink as "the underground train."

The group spent most of the meeting brainstorming marketing concepts, focusing on children as their target audience. ("Parents are more drivers than decision-makers" when it comes to choosing where to eat, Sandy, a father of two, said.) A po-boy exhibit at the New Orleans Children's Museum, po-boy Mardi Gras beads, outfield advertising, maybe a po-boy festival in the fall. But executing any idea would require money, culled from membership dues, which would require members, which they didn't have. Discouraged but not defeated, the group launched into personal po-boy testimonials. Jay Nix admitted that cooking had terrified him before he opened Parkway—he developed his now-famous roast beef recipe by asking "old ladies" for tips. Mike Serio remembered a time when parents would give their teething babies the hard ends cut from French bread loaves . . . "And fill them with sweetened condensed milk," Katherine Whann added.

I left the meeting feeling exhilarated despite its low attendance. *These are my people*, I thought, *real food-cultcha geeks*. Outside, someone had leaned a brown bag of day-old po-boy loaves against a parking meter at the curb. In the quiet twilight of the business district, the streetcar's antique trundle echoing as a backdrop, the po-boy—and New Orleans itself—seemed as worthy of preservation as Chilean sea bass, osetra caviar, the Great Pyramid at Giza.

And that was before Katrina. Before every last po-boy shop was forced to close indefinitely, some forever. Before the ovens at Leidenheimer's and Binder's went cold, and before the ovens at the adored United Bakery, which has not reopened, sat underwater for weeks. Before hundreds of thousands of New Orleanians spent long hours wondering whether they'd ever get to sleep in their own beds again, wave hello to their neighbors, walk on a levee, or eat a roast beef dressed. A hundred-year storm can do the work of a thousand po-boy preservation societies in highlighting what a culture takes for granted. If any New Orleanian in the diaspora did not fear the permanent evaporation of New Orleans' indigenous foods, then let her eat at the underground train.

The Whanns resumed baking after five weeks, having first cleaned up 10,000 pounds of melted yeast in their production facility. The New Orleans po-boy rose from the dead. If there was a silver lining during the mandatory shut-down, they say it was the way the community rallied in their favor. Strangers e-mailed to offer their garages as temporary bake houses. In an expression of allegiance, the Washington, D.C., chef Ann Cashion hung a note on the door of her restaurant, Johnny's Half Shell, explaining that she wouldn't be serving fried seafood po-boys until Leidenheimer's could ship her their bread again.

During an interview, Sandy described how the storm had fitted him with "a mantle of responsibility." He worried less about po-boys themselves in the early postdiluvian days than about the thousands of New Orleanians who couldn't work and thus eat without them: bakers, truck drivers, po-boy shop owners and their employees, shrimpers, meat purveyors, and so forth.

For the time being, the mantle of responsibility at Leidenheimer's does not include the Po-Boy Preservation Society, which is on hiatus. It was difficult to ask owner-operators for time and dues before the storm; now more than ever, a day's success is measured by just managing to keep up.

While I'm sorry that the society has suffered a setback, perhaps it will give the think tank time to reconsider that part in the mission statement about nutrition: "to elevate the status of the po-boy sandwich . . . as a delicious and nutritious cultural treasure." The idea of marketing po-boys as a healthy meal alternative doesn't seem dishonest, exactly. You can hold the mayo and get your catfish broiled, *if you want*. But let's say it caught on—let's say New Orleans found its Jared. Wouldn't that further imperil the fried potato po-boy? Wouldn't it tarnish the fried oyster loaf's sterling reputation? Wouldn't the Famous Ferdi's ancestral line face the danger of dying out? Wouldn't we be edging a little too close to California?

Our most recent California visitor was also the most difficult. Raised in Palo Alto, a homeowner in San Francisco's Noe Valley, and always tanned a shade darker than is probably healthy for a blonde, Julia is Northern California to the bone. She's a food elitist without the least bit of bon vivant: freshness trumps luxuriousness, familiarity trumps originality. Julia was my chef during the year I worked in San Francisco and the closest thing I've ever had to a food guru. I wanted badly for her to taste what I loved about New Orleans.

Fried chicken was the first disaster. Julia bit into what may have been the only medium-rare drumstick ever to escape the fingers of the genius fry cook Austin Leslie. Hungry, she poked through a basket of warm white French bread. "Do you think they have sourdough?" she asked. It was only the first night. The week stretched long before us, but not nearly so long as it would become. Pampy's, Mosca's, Lilette, Jazz Fest—Julia remained hungry. She was especially horrified at watching me finish a small fried potato po-boy, dressed, at Guy's. "What happened to you?" she asked.

Julia's last supper in New Orleans, a big happy salad at my sister Stephanie's house, was her favorite. She still talks about it. That night a palmetto bug—the polite term around here for a flying, sparrow-sized cockroach—crawled into bed with her. She hasn't recovered.

TURDUCKEN

Tales of a Poultry Chimera

A turducken makes no apology. A deboned and stuffed chicken enfolded in a deboned and stuffed duck sewn into a deboned and stuffed turkey, all roasted together for half a day and wetted with duck-fat gravy—what could it possibly say in its own defense?

Given the lengths to which I've admitted going in an effort to think, live, and eat like a New Orleanian, I fear I risk sounding like the ultimate poseur by divulging that I find turduckens, the envelope pushers of local cookery, not just freakishly beguiling, what with their slouchy postures and terrinelike innards, but also good to eat.

I didn't set out to like turduckens. Early indications predicted just the opposite. In preparation for an article I wrote for *Gambit Weekly*, I phoned up a cadre of good-eating advocates whose numbers were in my slim Rolodex at the time; the results of my informal poll did not favor the avian aberration.

David Olivier, who is tied to this city and its food traditions by a long line of Creoles on his paternal side, had never considered the turducken. "Isn't that a fairly new thing?" he asked.

"I had one once, but it isn't something that I'm dying to learn to make myself or buy for the family," said Lolis Elie, the *Times-Picayune* columnist and author of a poetic book on barbecue.

Mary and Greg Sonnier, who ran Gabrielle Restaurant, met while working for Paul Prudhomme at K-Paul's Louisiana Kitchen in the 1980s, the era when the turducken debuted there and when Chef Paul's celebrity exploded nationally. Mary shuddered audibly at mention of the *t*-word. "When I worked for [Prudhomme], I made thousands of them, probably. The turducken sounds better than it actually is. Things kind of get lost," she said.

Poppy Tooker, the efficacious leader of New Orleans' Slow Food convivium, agreed: "As far as I'm concerned, a turducken is a medieval pile of poo. I've never seen one that, when carved, didn't look like that and didn't taste like a big pile of mish-mash-mush. Anyone who knows anything about food thinks the same."

She had a point.

Thanksgiving Eve is the only day of the year that turducken is served at K-Paul's. As I spend Thanksgiving with my family in Wisconsin, where the holiday spread is traditional American mish-mash-mush, I ate my first K-Paul's turducken from a foam takeout box at Louis Armstrong International Airport, where I had sped after waiting in line outside the French Quarter restaurant until its doors opened for dinner. Hearing about my exploratory mission and tight timing, the generous gaggle of locals and tourists also in the queue let me cut to the front. I remember one of them cheering when I crossed the threshold, though it could have been an auditory mirage—racing planes for turducken gives a good adrenaline rush.

Matt, Stephanie, and Stephanie's now-husband Nathan joined me on the floor in Concourse B, where we located some sort of footstool for a tasting table. The turducken was still hot when we lifted the box's hinged lid. "What part is what?" Nathan asked rhetorically. The individual portion (I can't say it resembled a slice) had splayed out like . . . well, like part of an overweight spineless bird, in various shades of a single color, and it was impossible to identify the pieces and parts. Its appearance offered one theory why more restaurants don't serve the dish.

Having devoured it, the four of us agreed that in spite of our still not knowing what was what, the turducken mostly tasted like Thanksgiving. "I liked that brown dressing best," Nathan said, entirely without irony.

. . .

To make a turducken at the last minute, you must begin three days in advance. Especially if you're making it from one of Chef Paul's recipes. The one I've used spans more than fourteen pages in *The Prudhomme Family Cookbook*. It involves a small hammer, a carpet needle, and thirty-nine different ingredients, including your entire spice cabinet, except the Indian section; it produces two gallons of stock and thirty-five cups of dressing; and it calls for twelve hours of roasting, at a minimum.

To begin, instructs the recipe, be sure your oven temperature control is accurate. After making it from one end of a turducken to the other for the first time in my kitchen, I knew why the Prudhommes had stressed this step above all: liability. If, after three days of building a forty-pound tri-bird, I had had to serve my guests Popeye's takeout owing to faulty calibration, I would have stuck my own head in the oven.

My oven worked fine, and I still lost my wits.

The first challenge was finding a butcher to debone the birds, a concession that Chef Paul himself allowed during a phone interview. An accidental hole in the turkey's skin will cause stuffing to ooze, and duck breast is particularly delicate. You really can screw it up if you don't know what you're doing, he said. Such a relief. Except that butchers willing to debone are a disappearing breed in New Orleans; when I finally found one, he neglected to remove the leg bones, an oversight I didn't notice until I was ready to begin the turducken's climactic assembly. As all three birds' legs are essential stuffing receptacles, and as you cannot properly carve a turducken that hides a scattershot boneyard, I had to extract the forgotten bones myself.

Extract is a gentle verb often used to describe a violent procedure. I was conscious when a dentist extracted my impacted wisdom teeth. I still can feel the thump of his wrench hitting my sternum when the force of his yank exceeded his grip on it. My deboning technique was about that graceful.

Besides a general lack of skill, exhaustion and a foreboding urgency debilitated my dexterity. On day one, it took visits to three grocery stores to locate everything on my shopping list. On day two, I prepared industrial amounts of dressing—smoky and spice-pummeled andouille dressing for the turkey, cornbread dressing enriched with gizzards for the duck, and an aromatic oyster dressing for the chicken—and finished washing the dishes way past midnight. On day three, I overslept. My guests would arrive in fourteen hours, and I hadn't even begun the hard part.

A few days before, I had spent the morning with Glenn and Leah Mistich at their Gourmet Butcher Block shop in Gretna. Thanksgiving had just passed, Christmas was looming, and it was peak turducken season. Between their two stores, they would sell roughly six thousand before the New Year. Production was in high gear.

The star players at Gourmet Butcher Block that year could debone a turkey in just over a minute, a chicken in forty-three seconds. Distributed around stainless steel tables in a cool production room, the Mistichs' crew sprinkled raw poultry wetsuits with dried seasonings, paved them with stuffings, folded them into one another as if closing a book, sewed up the turkeys' seams with the ease of zipping a hoodie, propped the assembled turduckens on their rear ends for two final slipknots at the neck, slid them into plastic bags, and tossed them into trash cans for storage. (These were hygienic trash cans. I threw my dried-out ballpoint pen into one of them before learning its function and caused a sanitation emergency.)

It had looked so easy.

At home, the sprinkling and paving and folding went all right, but the next step was like zipping Santa Claus into a toddler's snowsuit. And the sewing . . . I had passed a sewing course in junior high school only because, as my diplomatic teacher said, I had picked a challenging pattern. Now it was twelve hours until my guests would arrive. I had been wrestling with raw poultry for so long I thought surely the birds had grown continents of salmonella. The Prudhomme family's cookbook claims that to "do" a turducken doesn't take magical cooking ability, just care. Oh, I cared. I cared so deeply that my pending failure caused me to melt into a heap of crusty dressing and poultry goo on the kitchen floor.

Then—*ding!*—I remembered that I had married a medical student.

Suturing skills and a hand trained to keep steady under pressure are useful when assembling a turducken. So is an extra-large turkey. No matter what poundage proportion Chef Paul's recipe specifies (a twenty- to twenty-five-pound turkey, a four- to five-pound duck, a three- to three-and-a-half-pound chicken), no one has yet bioengineered turducken-specific birds to fit together as precisely as you want them to—like Russian nesting dolls would be nice. You're a slave to what the butcher has, or to what he thinks you need. My New Orleans butcher went too small on the turkey for a novice like me. I should have known he was trouble when he advised replacing the duck in my tur*duck*en with country ham.

The good news: once your winged Frankenstein is in the oven, you can catch a twelve-hour catnap. Remember, though, that the turducken is a self-baster, weeping pints of duck fat from within. In order to prevent it from deep-frying in its own drippings, you must remove them from the roasting pan every few hours. Interrupted sleep is a price all parents pay, and you've just created your own little monster.

The next Christmas, having heard about our turducken-making adventure in New Orleans, Matt's family requested a repeat. They thought it sounded like three days of good fun—me in the kitchen, them doing Christmas in New York. Matt took their side. Having grown up in Belgium, where the natives eat well but tend not to cook so excessively, he never tires of American holiday leftovers—the more, the better. With a turducken, there's more *and* better: a cross-section of roasted-and-rested turducken resembles a terrine; cooled and congealed, it makes the best next-day sandwiches.

After several calls, I eventually found a New York butcher willing to debone, at Citarella, a grocery store so posh it makes Whole Foods look like Circle K. Citarella's organic, free-range birds bumped up what was already guaranteed to be a daunting grocery bill, but I took comfort in knowing that Chef Paul would approve. His parents were sharecroppers who produced everything the family ate barring sugar, rice, and flour, and the chef is vehement about integrity of ingredients.

I ordered discreetly at Citarella, never uttering the *t*-word and asking for a thirty-pound turkey, but the butcher caught on. When I picked the birds up on day two, they came bundled together in one plastic bag affixed with a computerized price sticker reading "turducken."

I was aware that turduckens had migrated. When I spoke with Chef Paul he marveled at how Americans had embraced the creation. "It's going crazy around the country. It's just mind-boggling, it just don't make sense," he said. Jonathan Gold, *LA Weekly*'s restaurant columnist and my go-to guy for advice literary and culinary, confirmed that his local gourmet store in Pasadena sells them frozen. John Madden is largely responsible for the turducken's rising star; the NFL announcer tried one for the first time while on the clock at the Superdome, and he has torn into one on camera on Thanksgivings since. One year, even PETA (People for the Ethical Treatment of Animals) noticed. Still, Citarella's sanctioning the recipe with space in the computer system was beyond mind-boggling. *I* couldn't find a fashion foothold in Manhattan. How had the turducken managed it?

Making groceries had taken patience in New Orleans, but no one had scrutinized the loot in my shopping cart in that town. Nothing on the ingredient list would cause a Louisianian alarm, turducken fan or not. It went down differently in New York. Matt's stepfather, Kurt, the turducken's greatest proponent at first, insisted on accompanying me through each step of the process. That changed when he saw the four sticks each of butter and margarine, the pound of turkey giblets, the two and a half pounds of sausage, and the dozen eggs in my cart. I tried to reassure him that I would use only eight of the eggs. The final straw was his asking me about the quart container of wet, steely stuff I had been trying to shield beneath nine green bell peppers. Shucked oysters, I answered truthfully when he asked about them, for the chicken's stuffing.

Somehow despite the mashed-together quality of its name, the inevitable mish-mash-mushiness of a turducken itself had escaped Kurt prior to our grocery run. Over the next two days of production, he entered the kitchen only to check on the oysters' status. It's unclear what disturbed him more, watching them slosh around raw in a plastic tub or imagining them stuffed into the hollows of some boneless bird.

Again that year the turkey was too petite for my abilities. Again Matt peeled me off the kitchen floor, this time with help from his mother, Laure-Anne, who's a whiz with knitting needles.

I cannot say that the idea of a turducken never turns my stomach. After more than six solid years of eating in New Orleans, my stomach sometimes feels permanently turned. I arrived here with all the bragging rights of a beaten-down but still standing line cook: callused feet, screaming upper back, wood-grill-singed eyelashes, fingertips charred numb, face permanently glossy, forearms scarred with horizontal brands from having brushed against the oven door, stomach of steel. Julia, my California chef, taught me that a good cook eats all day long because she tastes all day long—a slice from each beet to make sure none is bitter, a spoonful of each vinaigrette, as much soup as it takes to hone the seasonings, a few leaves from each dressed salad, a forkful of each pasta prepared à la minute. Every night of the year I worked for her, it fell to me to make and taste the gorgonzola mashed potatoes; it's a mystery how I still can tolerate blue cheeses at all. If line cooking nearly broke my spirit, it bolstered me to know that I could wash it all down with bourbon after a twelve-hour shift and wake up hungry the next day.

More mornings than not in New Orleans, I wake up vaguely nauseated. I can't pinpoint the exact moment my gut met its threshold, but sometime during my second year of reviewing restaurants I woke in the dark of night and instinctively grabbed the antacids Matt keeps near him like a security blanket. He stores a bottle in his work locker, a roll in his glove box, and a Ziploc of loose tablets in his skateboarding bag, which gets so knocked around I imagine him snorting the pastel dust between swigs of Gatorade. Until my nocturnal acid attacks became a regular occurrence, I secretly believed that Matt had a weak will—I would sooner amend my diet, I thought, than snack on chalk. But that's not so easy, and it's definitely not fun. Not here.

A few measures lessen my chances of stomach distress: no after-dinner coffee, choose bourbon over wine, beware raw garlic and butter. Even so, years of self-study have proven that it's generally not about individual components; it's the combinations, the all-inclusiveness, the nondiscriminatory quality of a perfect New Orleans restaurant meal that kills me. Consider this amalgam, my ideal supper at Galatoire's: a Sazerac; hot New Orleans–style French bread with butter; horseradish-fueled shrimp rémoulade; fried eggplant spears dusted in powdered sugar; twice-fried pommes de terre soufflées dipped in béarnaise sauce; fried trout meunière amandine (that's awash in brown butter and lemon); creamy Rockefeller spinach; bites of someone else's broiled pompano; a glass of Chardonnay; cup custard; and café brûlot (flaming liqueurs and spices doused with coffee whose tar-colored stream emits no light). If it's possible for anyone to sleep well with such an assortment communing in her belly, I'm certain that she's not me.

A superlative New Orleans meal doesn't have to be so elaborate to be debilitating. It could be—but, mysteriously, isn't always—a bottle of Barq's, an oyster po-boy, and a Hubig's coconut pie; or a bowl of red beans with hot sausage and sweet tea. I'm no more likely to give up these pleasures than I am to wear a costume next Halloween. Which is why Matt and I now have one more thing in common, solidarity in Tums—and why when I'm not eating New Orleans I'm steaming white rice.

It's possible that I'm fond of the turducken for the utter rebelliousness of it, for the ability of one lopsided bird to contain a blow-out meal's worth of dissonant, stomach-churning combinations and still come out tasting harmonious. At its best it does taste harmonious, though something I heard once—that you're always sure of your gallbladder following a meal at K-Paul's—holds true post-turducken too. This peculiar creation is additionally appealing for its associations with Chef Paul Prudhomme's daring culinary sensibilities, which most of the world has accepted as Cajun.

It must be noted that Chef Paul may not have been the first Louisianian to make a turducken. Sammy Hebert, Leah Mistich's brother, claims that it all started at the meat market he runs in the Cajun town of Maurice with his brother Widley. One day in 1984, a customer walked in with fresh kill and asked for his wild turkey and duck to be deboned and stuffed. Then, said Sammy, the old man asked for his wild duck to be stuffed inside the turkey and for one of Hebert's already famous deboned and stuffed chickens to be pushed inside the duck.

The Heberts hadn't heard of Chef Paul's turducken in 1984. Sammy believes that his is a spin-off of theirs. "He's trying to claim he's the first one to make [a turducken], but he doesn't have any proof, just like we don't have any proof we made it first," he told me over the phone. "He gives us a lot of credit, though. I think he knows who was the first one."

To understand how difficult it can be to pin down the true origins of foods, imagine that this old man had been making turduckens in his cottage on the bayou for half a century, and that the only reason he enlisted the Heberts' help in 1984 was that he had misplaced his carpet needle and the local five-and-dime was out of stock. Would that make *him* the turducken's legitimate originator?

Marcelle Bienvenu, the part-Cajun author of several cookbooks who worked at Commander's Palace in the 1970s, when Chef Paul was a relative unknown there, told me her version of the story. Chef Paul, she remembered, "found a historical note on [multiple stuffed birds] and introduced it to the modern world." The historical note could have been in any number of books, as the practice of roasting animals within other animals is ancient. Alexander Dumas' *Le Grand Dictionnaire de Cuisine* includes a recipe for an anchovy in an olive in a turkey in a pig.

Chef Paul concurred with Marcelle. "I don't think there was an exact moment of invention. It was more of an evolution . . . The evolution took ten, maybe twelve years, starting in the 1960s," he said, adding that "if memory serves me correctly, Frank Davis participated in naming turducken" during a radio show broadcast from K-Paul's.

Whoever made the first turducken, the Hebert brothers' boneless chicken with spicy pork stuffing is worth the two-and-a-half-hour drive from New Orleans to Maurice, with an ice chest; and whatever its origins, in spirit the turducken is 100 percent Chef Paul.

There's a common misconception on the outside that all New Orleans food is fired up to three-alarm levels with Tabasco, cayenne, and fresh hot peppers. It's true that a bottle of hot sauce is always within reach, that hot sausages add zing to traditional New Orleans dishes, and that Creole cooks lean heavily on salt and dried seasonings. But for the most part, New Orleans food, Creole-based dishes in particular, is not characterized by intimidating heat. Some of the confusion may arise from the use of the adjective *spicy* among Creoles and older New Orleanians, not as a synonym for chile-pepper hot but to mean something like "made with many spices" or "exhibiting a complex spice profile."

The food of Acadiana is another story (not always, but in general Cajun cooking carries more heat than city cooking does). Chef Paul, born on Cajun soil, brought the heat of his people with him when he came to New Orleans. He also brought his imagination, and together they resulted in an individualized cuisine that, before turduckens, was most famous for a technique called blackening. According to *The Prudhomme Family Cookbook*, to blacken a fillet of redfish, you wet it with melted butter and season it beyond reason with paprika, salt, thyme, oregano, onion and garlic powders, and red, white, and black peppers. Then you cook the fish in a cast-iron skillet that has been heated just below the white ash stage, basting it with butter, until your nose burns and the seasonings form a nice crust. Chef Paul writes in the cookbook that properly blackened fish and meats are sweet, not spicy. Having been raised in a culture where a packet of dried onion soup was the ultimate in seasoning, I guarantee that he underestimates. While the three peppers involved do not overpower the dish, they do taunt the inexperienced tongue.

Also in the family cookbook, which includes recipes from his twelve older siblings, Chef Paul outlines the keys to successful blackening, beginning with trying it either in a commercial kitchen or outdoors. Without a restaurant's powerful ventilation system, the process creates enough smoke to trigger the neighbor's fire alarm. "Don't push your luck," he writes. Matt owned one of Chef Paul's cookbooks before I met him, which perhaps explains his current favorite, ultra-safe dish to "cook" at home: barbecue sauce poured over pasta. The one time he experimented with blackening orange roughy, in an apartment in Oakland, California, he neglected to heed Chef Paul's warning. His neighbors had to evacuate the building, and representatives from the fire department gave him a dressing-down.

The popularity of Chef Paul's blackened redfish reached fever pitch in the 1980s, and the species' natural existence dwindled in inverse proportion. Today, though farmed redfish is plentiful, K-Paul's kitchen blackens tuna and drum fish instead. Pork chops, chicken, hamburgers, lamb, and steaks also respond well to the technique.

I once heard Ruth Reichl, the editor in chief of *Gourmet* magazine and an early Chez Panisse contemporary, say in a radio interview that Chef Paul's unintentional blackening revolution touched off America's still burgeoning interest in regional cooking. But blackened redfish, though an innovative riff on the standard high-temperature searing of protein, was no more a traditional Cajun dish thirty years ago than turducken was. When I asked the chef how he characterizes the ethnicity of the tri-bird invention, he answered, "It's a Paul Prudhomme thing, and I'm from Louisiana, and I'm a Cajun, so you can draw your conclusion from that."

Fried turkey, he said, is more of a traditional Louisiana thing. The frying of turkeys, a widespread practice I encountered in a catering kitchen less than a month after moving to New Orleans, is extreme—you dunk the whole bird into a tub of hot bubbling oil—until you compare it to a turducken. Or until you taste one for the first time. Injected beforehand with a seasoned brining solution, a culinary first-aid procedure that tenderizes and flavors the meat, the ultimate fried turkey has crackly bronzed skin and luscious moist meat untouched by the oil. Carved, a fried turkey looks just like a roasted turkey. Which is another reason that I prefer turduckens. Multiple stuffings dilute a turkey's turkeyness.

My dad's oldest brother, Dan Crabill Roahen II, is a retired elementary-school teacher and a lifelong gourmet in the most down-to-earth sense of the word. His Christmas bread, bejeweled with candied fruit and almonds, which he serves hot for Christmas brunch, shames doorstop fruitcakes right out of their cans. He digs the meat from fresh pumpkins for his Thanksgiving pies and decorates winter fruit salads with pomegranate seeds. Whether a sign of the times or of his inner farmer, Danny's culinary interests in the 1970s skewed more earthy than they do today. I remember jugs of dandelion wine fermenting in the basement and a duck in the backyard, and for a few years his garage was a poultry coop. My cousins told stories of watching the chickens and turkeys run around the yard headless and crazed. The closest I ever came to participating in the butchery was the Thanksgiving when Danny roasted one of his turkeys for the extended family. The adults tried to keep its origins hush-hush (surely this wasn't the first time), but I overheard them whispering about its broken leg, an injury sustained during its final sprint.

While it's my firm belief that omnivorous humans ought not to ignore the fact that our sustenance comes at another's sacrifice, I greedily wish I had never seen that mangled drumstick. Would it have seemed more natural if Danny hadn't lived near the center of town? The question is moot, as the resulting hangup has kept me from eating more than a few bites of our holiday centerpiece since childhood. And now my family knows the truth behind the year I forced them to eat beef tenderloin for Christmas dinner instead.

. . .

However many thousands of New Orleans–area families roast turduckens each year, results of my ongoing informal polling suggest that locals haven't taken to the six-winged creature with the same "mind-boggling" vigor as Chef Paul reported springing up in other parts of the country. While tweaking this chapter at Rue de la Course coffeehouse, I asked a couple of strangers at the table beside me whether they ever had eaten from a turducken. Both were New Orleans natives. "Isn't that a turkey in a duck?" one asked. The word *turducken* was so foreign to his companion that he couldn't pronounce it.

The guests who gathered around our table on the random weeknight of my first turducken party in New Orleans all stuffed themselves, but there remained skeptics. One of them still insists on describing it as a poultry malt. Another, put off by the thick layer of duck skin within, suggested that duck ought to be the exterior bird. This, he rightly posited, would produce an outer shell of duck cracklin', and who wouldn't die for that? We'll have to wait on heirloom baby microturkeys, or body-building ducks, before attempting the modification.

I don't know why my New York turducken audience was more wholly enthusiastic. Kurt even rejoiced upon excavating a whole oyster from the mess on his plate. New Orleanians more or less have accepted other Prudhomme inventions as their own; his blackening technique, exuberance with debris, and Asian-influenced duck preparations have gained traction at K-Paul's and in the restaurants now run by his early protégés.

Easy access to premade, overpriced, frozen turduckens can't help its cause down here. Whimsy and shortcuts are worse disasters. Most local turducken producers allow customers to choose their own stuffing combinations, and some of them use duck and chicken breasts instead of whole birds. If it's possible to be a purist about something as impure as turducken, then I'm one of them. The wrong stuffing combination (say, boudin plus alligator sausage plus Mexican) can taste as haphazard as a turducken sounds, and too much or too little of any component throws off the proportions.

Because the chicken is so much smaller than the turkey, a turducken proportioned à la Prudhomme already contains fewer than a dozen complete slices, all of them at the turducken's center, where every layer is evenly present; using too much of one stuffing or using breasts instead of whole birds can slash the perfect slices in half.

In his solo cookbook, *Chef Paul Prudhomme's Louisiana Kitchen*, Chef Paul writes that he seasons his cooking to taste "round," in order to touch every one of the taste buds (using ground black, white, and red peppers in one dish, for example). His turducken is a stellar example that this rounded idea doesn't just look good on paper. Despite its overabundance of ingredients and seasonings, a centermost slice of Chef Paul's turducken does manage to taste circular, even. While each bite changes shape as you chew, there are no jagged edges or jumps and starts. The taste experience is full and smooth.

Chef Paul has never purchased a turducken for comparison's sake. "I'm not that curious. That would be like an automobile dealer buying a car from another automobile dealer just to see what would happen," he said.

After two consecutively stressful holidays in the kitchen, I did order a premade turducken last year, one made with whole birds and the proper proportion of stuffings. Never again. It was a lemon. The Prudhomme turducken, meanwhile, has Rolls-Royce potential, providing you buy whole birds, use Louisiana smoked andouille, set margarine prejudices aside for one day, and follow the chef's Sweet Potato Eggplant Gravy recipe, scary as it may sound and look. When my culinary-school-trained sister-in-law Maëlle found me stirring sweet potato chunks into a simmering grayish purple liquid and reaching for the Grand Marnier, she mentioned that it might be interesting to taste it against a more, you know, traditional gravy. In the end, while some eaters at our table did prefer the more familiar, and less "spicy," recipe that Laure-Anne whipped up, everyone appreciated the way Chef Paul's oddball concoction added a silken, highly seasoned, elusively elegant dimension to the dish. It seems that a repressed turducken is not the best turducken. Skimping on the extravagances throws it off-kilter, like wearing a turtleneck with hot pants.

The one way in which I do suggest altering Chef Paul's instructions actually compounds the dish's extravagance by adding an extra hour to its resting time (that makes two hours for resting, total). While our house didn't flood after the levees broke, it did shift and settle a few weeks later, compacting door frames and causing the living room ceiling to bow. It's the same concept with a well-rested turducken, only the results are more appetizing: the extra hour compresses and sets the layers completely without significantly cooling the interior.

I wouldn't have come upon this revelation if a melodrama hadn't erupted in the kitchen just as my turducken reached the ideal 165°F. Barry, my common-law brother-in-law, insists every Christmas on making his English mother's potatoes crisped in duck fat, parsnips roasted with carrots, and Yorkshire pudding, and every year the learning curve is reset to zero. That year he got a late start. So two hours after I pulled the turducken from the oven and several brandy Alexanders and a narrowly avoided house fire later, we were finally ready to sit.

I have a photo of the New York turducken open on my monitor as I type. Though some poor sport named the file "Turmonster," it shows a cross-section at the turducken's center: compressed, terrine-like, stunning in its landscape of browns. Each meat is a different shade, each stuffing distinct. In the next photo, taken just moments later, the camera captured us all at table, candlelit, in ties and pearls, Christmas crackers sent from England in shiny red wrapping at each place setting, our glasses filled with Penfolds 1990 Grange Hermitage. On our plates: mish-mash-mush. You can take the turducken out of Louisiana . . .

Martha Rhodes, a poet and publisher by profession and a member of my New York turducken audience, generously agreed to share some lines inspired by the prospect of her first turducken feast.

FEATHER ALERT!

turducken
pluckin
feathers and down
all over everything
all over town
turducken
pluckin
in the house of brown
take your allergy pills
cover your sills
turducken feathers
stuck on the walls
turducken feathers
floating in the halls
turducken pluckin
in the house of brown
turducken a cookin
in the house of brown
o turducken
turducken
it's coming your way
i hope it's dead or it will
break a gallé
cuz turduckens can fly
turduckens can swoop
turduckens can swim
turduckens can poop
turducken pluckin
on christmas day
turduckens turduckens
oy vey oy vey

CRAWFISH

A Crawfish Is a Darned Beast!

Whereas a turducken levels the playing field, being equally alien to born New Orleanians and to me, other indigenous foods bare the discrepancies between native bloodlines and the rest of us. The ability to peel boiled crawfish is not inborn for someone who grew up shelling nothing more challenging than peanuts, and that only as a between-meal diversion. Every crawfish season in Louisiana, the heart of which runs roughly from January through May, I teeter through relearning the technique. And every season I undergo the crustacean eater's equivalent of a fashion crisis, feeling about as dexterous with the peel-and-eat routine as I do on the nude beaches of Europe with my naturally bronzed Belgian in-laws—a bowlegged ghost loping around in a one-piece.

But given that a Louisiana spring without boiled crawfish is as unthinkable as a Louisiana summer shrouded in wool, practice makes me a little more agile, and the crisis gets a little less dramatic, by the year. Indeed, the most recent retraining session went down peacefully at Hawk's, a corrugated tin, end-of-a-gravel-road, hardly-ever-open boiling point in Cajun country.

As usual, the tutorial amounted to looking around. At the table to my left sat a woman well into middle age, her spine finishing-school straight, her hair set in a permanent wave, and her elbows hovering at the table's edge without ever touching it. Looking more like the cottage-cheese-and-oat-bran type, she worked with pinkies raised through five pounds of antennae, pincers, and insectile leglings as if each flame-orange shell were a Tiffany's box looped in ribbon. One after the other, she twisted the crawfish in two, placing the tail ends temporarily aside in order to free the manicured trigger finger of her right hand; this she used to excavate savory mustard-colored fat from inside each head. After licking the fat from her finger, she turned to the crawfish's other half, pinching the curled tail meat from its segmented armor with the ease of extracting tissues from a box. She did not pause, or even speak, until the tidy beheadings were complete. As a final act, she wiped her hands with her clean, dry napkin.

A more realistic role model sat at the table to my right, wearing low-rise corduroys, her hair knotted back in a rubber band. With one foot tucked beneath her rear end, the other bobbing with excess energy, and her elbows planted on the table, she attacked her mound of crawfish as if she feared the boiling pot hadn't completely snuffed the life from their claws. After wrenching each of them in two as aggressively as you might go after a pickle jar with a stuck lid, she sucked the fat from their heads with a backward whistle and tore their little legs asunder to get at the tail meat. Some of the crawfish were big enough to have good meat in their claws; these she cracked open with her front teeth. If the prim woman to my left ironed underwear and alphabetized spices by day, this one crashed funerals and terrorized kittens. She finished eating suddenly and bolted to the restroom, presumably to wash her hands. When I did the same some time later, the doorknob was sticky and rough: boil juice and seasonings.

Matt and I tried to appear in control at Hawk's. We ordered our crawfish spicy (but not drizzled with jalapeño juice, which we figured would be touristy) and our beer domestic. We casually traded peeling tips as we ate, as if engaged in real conversation. But we could not resist posing our largest crawfish over a piece of boiled corn so that it resembled a sci-fi mutant hauling itself up from the deep, antennae splayed, beady bubble eyes fixed on the middle distance. Our waitress caught us taking its portrait. "It's all right, lots of tourists do that," she said. "You want me to take one with you and the crawfish together?"

To say that Hawk's is a three-hour drive from New Orleans is to misrepresent how distant it really is. Because New Orleans is still such an adventure, I'm always surprised by how doubly exotic it feels out in Cajun country, where many elders still speak a singsongy French dialect, teenagers play the accordion in bars on school nights, and the most accessible fast foods are artisan products like cracklin's, boudin, and stage planks (molasses-sweetened gingerbread cakes). Cajun country is also where the rest of Louisiana finds most of its crawfish, both the wild variety that trappers catch in the unearthly green Atchafalaya River Basin and the more abundant farm-raised kind that feed on rice shoots and other plant life in flooded fields.

When the crawfish are "running," which is how Louisianians describe their harvestability, you could go snow-blind cruising through the countryside from the blur of seafood stores, sheds, temporary tents, and roadside-cooler entrepreneurs, each one advertising hot boiled crawfish to go (some places sell crawfish cold, but they don't brag about it). On the backest of back roads you happen upon secreted boiling points like Hawk's, where the seasonal drill is so specific and tied to place that you recover hope for America's culinary destiny: it's not sealed in prefab burger patties or warehouses retailing pretzels by the five-pound barrel just yet.

A few years ago Matt, his father, Louk, his stepmother, Christine, and I passed a whirlwind evening in a country cider house (*sideria*) outside San Sebastian, Spain, where from January to May the diners gather around communal wooden tables in brightly lit rooms partaking of traditional *sideria* feasts: salt cod, slabs of beef roasted to rare over an open flame, Idiazabal cheese with quince paste, and crack-your-own walnuts. There was no menu and no instruction manual; we learned from watching the locals that you're expected to smoke an unfiltered cigarette with each course. Spaniards in the area tend to be loyal to one or two *siderias*, something like Cajuns and their boiling points. At this one, everyone seemed to know each other. We followed them when they staggered in groups to a row of wooden cider vats against a far wall. One person opened the tap while the others stood back eight feet to receive the hard cider in their glasses as it gunned toward them in a powerful arch. Spanish cider begins to oxidize immediately, which alters its flavor, so it behooves connoisseurs to chug. We got so into the ritual, which is to say so tipsy, that eventually a crowd gathered around our table to cheer us on. Similarly, seeing that we were enjoying his crawfish, Hawk Arceneaux stopped by our table to chat this year. He asked where we were from. "Everyone else is family. Y'all are the only ones I didn't know in here tonight," he explained, and invited us to come back next year.

I first learned to eat boiled crawfish in the city, but perhaps not as quickly as I should have. The crawfish were running strong the day the editorial staff of *Gambit Weekly* took me to lunch to celebrate the publication of my first few restaurant reviews. Someone had chosen Sid-Mar's for its lovely, and rare, view of Lake Pontchartrain. Many of my colleagues ordered boiled crawfish and returned to their keyboards with hands smelling like fishing bait. I ordered a shrimp po-boy and hoped they wouldn't notice. My first staff outing didn't seem like the appropriate time for divulging that the paper's new critic hadn't ever experienced skin-on-shell contact with a crawfish. Fortunately, the peeling ritual is a public one; I became a voyeur at once.

For urban families, Mardi Gras revelry often involves dumping sweet corn, potatoes, whole onions, lemons, garlic, celery, sinus-clearing seasonings (sold in liquid concentrate), and crawfish by the dozens of pounds into barrels of water brought to a boil over portable propane burners—all of this curbside, within scalding distance of marching bands, debutantes rolling by on floats, and children on the loose. If you hang with the right crowd, someone will have parked her pickup truck nearby so the bed can be lined with newspaper and scattered with the steaming finished product. A card table or the lid of a cooler will do. My best voyeuristic memory of Mardi Gras 2006 is of a group of teenagers standing around a cascade of crawfish that one of their fathers had just tipped from the pot. The kids were in the same position when I passed by again an hour later, still chatting and twisting and sucking, carcasses beginning to bury their feet. I wondered how much better socialized we would be today if my teenage friends and I had rallied around mounds of boiled crawfish in plain view rather than cases of warm Blatz beer beneath the bleachers.

Mardi Gras crawfish boils were particular triumphs in 2006. Storm surges from Hurricanes Katrina and Rita had scoured south Louisiana's fields with saltwater, killing the greenery and thus hampering the crawfish life cycle; droughts before and after the storms had stymied the Atchafalaya Basin's wild production. In February, live crawfish were going for three times the usual price, if you could find them at all. While the harvest improved over time, the early-season prices caused more local outrage than three-dollar-per-gallon gasoline, which hit here two months later.

Crawfish have a long history in Louisiana as a poor man's food—in reputation, in stigma, and in reality. In *Stir the Pot: The History of Cajun Cuisine*, Marcelle Bienvenu and Carl and Ryan Brasseaux record that even as recently as the 1930s, Cajuns limited their crawfish harvests to times of flood, when they were too plentiful to ignore, and Lenten periods of fasting. The authors found newspaper articles from the 1870s that referred to crawfishing parties, "but these ventures frequently sought only bait for fishing expeditions."

The United Houma Nation, after whom the Cajun town of Houma was named, was ahead of its time in choosing the *saktce-ho'ma*, or red crawfish, as its tribal war emblem. But it wasn't until the city council of Breaux Bridge marked that town's centennial in 1959 by naming it the Crawfish Capital of the World ("La Capitale Mondiale des Ecrevisses") and instituted an annual crawfish festival that boiled crawfish entered the Cajun mainstream and began its climb toward unofficial Louisiana mascot.

It took longer for boiled crawfish to find traction in the urban diet, even though crawfish bisque, a time-consuming delicacy of the elite, has been served in New Orleans restaurants for more than a century. I found one rare early reference to boiled crawfish in the city; it appears on a New Orleans Press Club dinner menu reprinted in Celestine Eustis's 1903 book, *Cooking in Old Creole Days*, with this still-true caveat: "A crawfish is a darned beast!"

By the 1980s crawfish boils had finally stuck fast in New Orleans; by the time I arrived, the practice was as integrated into the city's seasonal culinary fetishes as Hubig's sweet potato pies, strawberries from Ponchatoula, and Creole tomatoes. During cooler months, when the seasons of crawfishing and Sunday second lines collide, boiled crawfish take prominence along the street routes, joining grilled sausages on white Bunny bread and the spaghetti and bouillon soup called ya-ka-mein. I once paid just three dollars for a hot brown-bag feast from a woman on Orleans Avenue who had thrown turkey necks and smoked sausage into her crawfish boil.

Both of these are common additions, and I'm always grateful for them. Hard-core crawfish lovers probably consider the turkey necks, the sausages, the potatoes, and the sweet corn to be lagniappe, little extras to nibble at between pounds of tails. For most of my crawfish seasons, however, these trimmings were my only hope of getting enough to eat. In fluid environments, like parades and backyards, crawfish grazing can last all day; intake is limited only by stamina and the will to peel. It took me years to develop such a will. My technique was so clumsy and my fingers were so torn up after tackling the first dozen that I burned more calories peeling crawfish than eating them. When we knew that crawfish were on the agenda, Stephanie and I always ordered extra fries.

Peeling inefficiencies don't just make you look like an outsider; limited crawfish eating keeps you from fully appreciating your prey. In trying to describe the taste of crawfish a few years ago, I always focused on the most obvious flavor: the boiling seasonings, a contentious subject. Wet or dry (meaning dissolved in the boiling water or sprinkled on the crawfish after boiling)? Cloves? Mustard seed? How many lemons? How much bay? Celery? One chef told me that her secret is throwing a pound of butter into the pot. Louisianians are as particular about what seasons their crawfish as they are about what thickens their gumbo. Some aren't happy unless their tongues vibrate from the aftershocks of pepper, while others don't like them peppery at all. At Guiding Star, another Cajun country boiling point, the boilmasters use Tabasco pepper mash (what's left over from Tabasco peppers after their juices have been extracted for the hot sauce), which imparts a husky flavor. Straight Tabasco is lighter, brighter. It's possible to be so taken with the seasonings that you miss the point, the point being the crawfish.

Crawfish tails have a mellow flavor that's independent of, and easily disguised by, overpowerful flavorings. Unseasoned, they taste earthier than shrimp and subtler than lobster but similar to both. And like both, their tender pink flesh is easily overcooked. Crawfish are sweet when fresh, often mildly muddy (a flavor many Louisianians like), and they have an elevated potential for fishiness when peeled and frozen. I found crawfish immediately interesting but not obviously tasty. Some people develop allergies from overexposure to shellfish; I developed awe. The better I got at peeling crawfish, the more I wanted to eat and to taste. At Hawk's this year, I didn't even finish my potato.

One spring morning my friend Brett Anderson, who lives in the Faubourg Marigny, a neighborhood directly downriver from the French Quarter, called to tell me that he had just stopped his car to let a crawfish cross the road. Must've escaped from King Roger's, a nearby takeout joint and seafood purveyor that has been known to advertise coon and live turtle. Midwesterners both, we had a good laugh—oh, this wacky, wacky town!

Rural Louisianians are accustomed to living cheek-by-claw with crawfish. The miniature lobsterlike crustaceans have earned the nickname "mudbugs" for their propensity to burrow into the earth where the terrain is damp, meaning nearly everywhere. Though freshwater animals, crawfish live for months in the ground; you can tell where they've entered by the tall mud volcanoes, or "chimneys," they kick up on their descent. Chimneys are the bane of a rural lawnmower's existence. Pest control message boards buzz with tricks for eradicating them.

Gary Duhon, a pediatric intensive-care doctor at Children's Hospital in New Orleans who grew up down the road from Hawk's, talks about playing with the crawfish that lived in his backyard like I might talk about . . . honestly, I have no childhood comparison. We had squirrels and sparrows in Wisconsin, and we shone flashlights on earthworms at night. But we had limited context for understanding crustaceans. Once I had a pet hermit crab, but I left his cage in the sun and he crawled out of his shell and died. I also remember capturing a "crayfish" from the pond near my grandparents' house, but my cousins and I poked at it for a while and then got bored. Gary, meanwhile, used to tie pieces of ham to string, which he would then lower into the mud chimneys to trick crawfish out of their holes. From there, the days held endless possibilities.

Crawfish shape the New Orleans metro area's landscape in more static, even decorative ways. The twenty-plus crawfish preparations on parade at Jazz Fest—crawfish pasta, crawfish étouffée, crawfish sausage, crawfish bread, crawfish beignets, and so on—cast doubt that the annual intersection between the music festival and crawfish season is coincidence. While festival grounds crews excel at controlling what could be a garbage catastrophe, by the end of the second weekend trampled crawfish exoskeletons texturize the Fair Ground's topography like white quartz in a Florida mobile home park.

It's the same at the Fly, an open space directly behind the Audubon Zoo (signs call this area Riverview, though locals still use the nickname Fly, inspired by a butterfly-shaped building that stood in the area before my time). I've taken countless sunset walks along the Fly, but no matter how colorful the sky, it's always eclipsed by the strange silvery beauty of barges pushing around the Mississippi River's narrow bend at eye level, almost close enough to touch. A picnic on this ledge of the river is a straight shot down Carrollton Avenue from K-Jean's, a superb takeout seafood stand and boiling point in Mid-City. Or it *was* a straight shot. Working on this chapter gave me a hankering for K-Jean's evenly spiced boiled crawfish, and for the routine my brother-in-law Nathan had developed of stopping by a frozen daiquiri shop on his drive back uptown with dinner from K-Jean's in the passenger's seat. I knew that floodwaters had battered K-Jean's turquoise building nine months earlier, but I drove to it anyway, looking for signs of life and quietly hoping for lunch. Instead of crawfish, I found a demolition company's sign stuck in a field of groomed dirt (K-Jean's has since been rebuilt).

You don't want to be overheard romanticizing litter in post-Katrina New Orleans. It was always a problem here. Before the storm, you'd see McDonald's bags tossed out of car windows at busy intersections; your blood pressure would soar, but it would be just another day. Now, though, when slow debris pickup, rat armies, and toxic mold are such a broken-record problem, a beer can in the yard can cause a migraine. Earlier this week, from my car, I saw a man walk past a water-stained sofa that someone had hauled to the curb weeks ago. He got a few feet beyond it and then doubled back to arrange two of the sofa's cushions that had gone askew. My throat tensed at this small gesture toward fixing our overwhelming mess. I choked up again the following day, this time while stepping over boiled crawfish leftovers scattered on a sidewalk at the Fly. Shards of orange, vacant eyeballs, trampled heads. Maybe the crawfish hadn't come from K-Jean's, but the detritus was still a lighthearted sign of our culture's survival, of hope.

Food idolatry is not a post-Katrina phenomenon. It blankets New Orleans, from the novelty T-shirts festooned with crawfish pinching ass, to the shrimp playing the accordion on the menu at Pascal's Manale, to the $3,500 Keishi pearl "gumbo necklace" ornamented with 14-carat gold shrimp, crabs, and okra at Mignon Faget, a jewelry store that is to Magazine Street what Harry Winston is to Rodeo Drive. One Father's Day early in our New Orleans tenure, Stephanie proposed buying our dad a golf shirt from Perlis that featured a distinguished-looking crawfish where Ralph Lauren would put his polo-player logo. I agreed, as long as Dad didn't embarrass us by wearing it in New Orleans. What I didn't realize at the time is that Perlis is a by-locals-for-locals kind of store; every season brings new additions to its popular crawfish line. This spring, for instance, they stuck the crawfish logo on a pair of gingham boxers. Making Dad feel ashamed to wear his crawfish polo in New Orleans would have been like telling a Packers fan that his foam cheesehead is an embarrassment to Green Bay. Sometimes it makes perfect sense to represent at home.

I would clear several hurdles before I understood this. For one, I would learn how to order boiled crawfish properly, at Sal's Seafood in the West Bank suburb of Marrero, where the first item to hit the table is always the newspaper. I considered it a good omen on my initial visit that Dick Cheney's face bore the brunt of my crawfish waste. "How many pounds? Ten? Fifteen? Three to five per person usually does it," a waitress educated my group without asking first whether we'd come for one of the noncrawfish dishes scribbled on sheets of white paper and taped to the wall. She taught us by omission that during crawfish season you don't eat shrimp. On the flip side, crawfish ought to be off-limits when they're out of season in Louisiana, even if they remain as accessible as apples. Frozen crawfish imported cheaply from places like China have a compromised flavor, and they hurt local crawfishermen by oversupplying demand and driving down prices.

By the time I discovered Perino's Boiling Pot, another crawfish hot spot on the West Bank that quickly became my standby, I had begun to grasp that the more serious you are about eating shellfish, the more natural it feels to goof off in its presence. When you enter Perino's, which backs up against a Days Inn motel, you pass between two folk-art murals: one of an alligator grinning as he's fixing to boil a crab, and one of a colossal crawfish hauling itself up onto dry land. Inside, you can buy Perino's T-shirts embellished with the outline of an oyster and the caption "Cajun Viagra." After several visits there, I relaxed enough to understand that such silly regional contrivances are profound in a place where table centerpieces are rolls of paper towels and where card-holding natives peel and crack shellfish until their fingers wrinkle into insensate flaps of flesh. It's like when genuine western wranglers straddle the saddle barstools at the Million Dollar Cowboy Bar in Jackson Hole, Wyoming. They don't just get the joke, they own it.

. . .

Not quite owning the joke yet myself, I invited no one to my first crawfish miniboil. I had cooked sketchier foods—sweetbreads, pig's feet, hormone-plumped chicken breasts—but either as part of my restaurant training or in the privacy of my own kitchen. A crawfish boil is a public event, a backyard demonstration that in the man-versus-nature campaign, we occasionally come out on top. I didn't know whether my first attempt at boiling crawfish would be such an occasion, and I didn't want anyone else to know either.

I am *so* smart.

Matt didn't eat shellfish with legs when we first moved to Louisiana. "Bottom feeders," he would say. "Insects of the sea." Emboldened by the gustatory cowardice of a man whose calves are as big as my head, I ate enough for both of us, in front of him. It helped me save face that Matt was out of town the day I bought my first live, farm-raised crawfish from Big Fisherman, at the time Uptown's most reliably stocked local seafood purveyor. A saleswoman set the crawfish, packed in a cardboard box, on the counter, which put me in earshot of a familiar sound, something like soft but persistent rain falling on a tin roof. A reader could approximate the sound by barely touching her fingernails to any page of this book and then wiggling her fingers back and forth as rapidly as possible. Hear it, that delicate little patter? Like a beetle rustling around in the trash. Also like ten pounds of live crawfish taped inside a cardboard box. I kept my cool as the saleswoman ran my credit card, if opening the box and taking several photos counts as keeping my cool.

A standard unit of live crawfish is a burlap onion sack. One sack holds between thirty-five and forty-two pounds. It's hardly worth firing up the boiling pot for less than that; once you commit to more, you might as well make a party of it. A spontaneous get-together with friends: two to three sacks. A family reunion: twelve to twenty. As I wasn't having a party, the folks at Big Fisherman did me a favor by splitting up a sack and selling me ten pounds: just enough for a bisque; more than enough to challenge my abilities.

The first step to my bisque recipe, for which I had cobbled together pieces and parts from a variety of cookbooks, was to purge the crawfish by bathing them in saltwater, rinsing them, and repeating. You do this enough times to cleanse the crawfish of the matte-gray sheaths that betray their natural habitat, and also to wash out their intestinal tracts. I've overheard locals pooh-poohing purging as unnecessary. I found a crawfish production manual put out by the Louisiana State University Ag Center that corroborates those rumblings by reporting, "Local consumers in Louisiana are not overly concerned about the presence of a full intestinal tract." I will never be a local in this regard.

If you're someone like Hawk Arceneaux, with artisan springs at your doorstep, you purge your homegrown crawfish for twenty-four hours in a live well of fresh aerated water to achieve the unmuddiest mudbugs with the pinkest tails and brightest yellow fat ever to be served on a plastic Bud Lite tray. If you're a home purger like me, you need a large tub, a hose, and a broomstick handle. None of these cooking implements will be found on your Williams-Sonoma gift registry. It caused me some anxiety that our hose is located in our very public front yard; needlessly so. Judging from my neighbors' unfazed responses, the sight of a woman swirling a broomstick around inside a bright red tub in her front yard in the middle of the day is no reason for alarm. Not even when she screams.

During my ten-block drive home from Big Fisherman, I had talked myself down from the idea that I was about to kill a box of insects for sustenance by convincing myself that crawfish clearly aren't as evolved as the average cockroach. The proof: if I had been transporting cockroaches, every last one of them would have found its way out of the box. I don't know why this thought comforted me, but I know now that I was wrong.

The moment I dumped my box of crawfish into the tub of salted water, their fight-or-flight reflexes kicked in with such zeal that one of them managed to attach itself to my hand in two places without my seeing it happen. Feeling it instead, I screamed and jerked my arm back. The predator slammed to the ground behind me; claw marks darkened the knuckle of my pinkie and the side of my thumb. *Good aim,* I thought. How humiliating and impressive. Cockroaches just run in circles.

Initially I considered letting the escapee go free—to burrow beneath the house, wander into the street, or become a cat toy like all the house bugs do. But somehow that seemed less humane than granting it a quick, scalding death. And besides, my thumb throbbed. So I made for the nape of its neck (or where its neck would have been if crawfish weren't built like defensive linemen), the only spot on its body that a crawfish's claws can't reach. But my foe had already assumed an offensive stance, reared up onto its haunches, tail flattened, waving its claws like a gladiator. Prior to this battle, I'd figured that the other Indian tribes had claimed all the fierce animals first. My bad, Houmas. I took a breath, reminding myself that *I* was the human, and poked a stick at the crawfish's chest. While its claws were busy defending against that insult, I pinched the fanlike shell at the end of its tail and lobbed it into the tub. The broomstick facilitated all future contact.

Crawfish are similar to lobsters in many respects, beginning with biology. Both are crustaceans of the invertebrate phylum Arthropoda, the class Malacostraca, and the order Decapoda. Cajuns spin a yarn that crawfish actually originated as lobsters, in Nova Scotia, where the Acadians lived until the English ousted them in 1755. They imagine that the Nova Scotian lobsters followed them south and that their current minuscule form is a result of muscle mass lost during the arduous journey.

Also like lobsters, crawfish aren't good unless boiled alive. Some people say that you can detect a rotten crawfish once it's cooked by a straightened tail (healthy crawfish tails curl). You definitely detect it when you bite into its decaying flesh. I did my best to locate the deceased before boiling them. About a dozen hadn't survived their trip to our front yard; these I flung into the monkey grass, remembering having read someplace that fish make healthy fertilizer. For the next few days, breezes through the kitchen window carried with them a lesson that dead crawfish, like live ones, would do well *underground*. While I don't find the smell of decomposing crawfish waste pleasant, I do appreciate how universal and accepted it is in New Orleans. By contrast, if my parents had a bag of shellfish remains and if the next garbage truck weren't scheduled to pass by for three sun-baked days, they would have no choice but to find a trash receptacle in some park or empty lot, to avoid the wrath of their neighbors. In New Orleans, you simply wait for the night-blooming jasmine to take over.

After completing the purge, I carried my still-living crawfish through the house and into the kitchen, where I had set seasoned water to boil. I learned something while executing this step that's not included in recipe books: when transporting live crawfish, it's best to use a vessel deep enough for their double antennae not to have easy access to your forearms; the tickle is creepy.

I never regretted making my crawfish bisque from scratch, meaning with live crawfish rather than prepeeled and packaged tails, and yet I was eager to regain solid footing at the top of the food chain by the time I got them into the kitchen. Which is why, when two of my captives demonstrated the origin of the underused verb *to crawfish* (Merriam-Webster: "to retreat from a position : back out") by back-diving to freedom, I in turn demonstrated hyperventilation. It's one thing for a water insect to assume the warrior stance in your front yard; quite another when it does so centimeters from safety beneath the stove.

In these tense and sweaty moments, I decided that a more accurate and respectful term for *crawfish boil* is *crawfish kill*. As in, *We're having a crawfish kill on Mardi Gras—bring the kids*. I may not have trapped these crawfish from my own pirogue, but that didn't keep me from experiencing the thrill of the hunt, the pride of the hunter. If I'd previously thought that fishermen exaggerated the size of their catch because of their own weak egos, I now know that they do so out of respect for the dead. All my crawfish were the size of alligators.

I also instantaneously understood the genius of outdoor crawfish kills. Even in abbreviated amounts, live crawfish do not belong in a domestic kitchen. Unlike lobsters, they come in swarming armies, their claws unfettered by rubber bands. They defend themselves valiantly right up to submersion, at which point they stiffen in silence, their lackluster shells brightening to lush shades of red and orange.

The transformation is immediate and humbling. The least we can do, I now believe, is grant them a fitting funeral setting—grass and open air rather than dirty linoleum and a clanging ceiling fan.

Bisque is a superb and reverential resting place.

New Orleans' veneration of crawfish bisque predates its first recipe collections. Lafcadio Hearn, an emigrant writer who, like me, fell in love with the city through its food, included a recipe for "crayfish bisque" in his 1885 *La Cuisine Créole*. Elizabeth Bégué, who gained renown for the midday "second breakfasts" she and her husbands (Louis Dutrey, followed by Hypolite Bégué) served early-rising French Market vendors, recorded fifty of her best dishes in 1900. To make Madame Bégué's "bisque of crayfish," you first "choose about forty nice crayfish and let them have a good boiling." She sounds like the evil caretaker at an orphanage for naughty children, which, come to think of it, is an apt metaphor.

If I learned one thing while conducting my private crawfish boil, it's that no Louisianians—not the early cookbook writers, and not my contemporary friends—are aware of how completely *not normal* the practice is. When I mention the weirdness to natives like my friend Brooks Hamaker, known on the eGullet.com forum he used to moderate as Mayhaw Man, they always require explanation. "Haven't you ever boiled a lobster?" Brooks asked me. As if the one or two special occasions a year on which I might send a live lobster to its screaming death begins to approach the hundreds of pounds of wriggling antennae and swimmerets (the technical term for all those little legs) that the average Louisianian scalds over a lifetime. Oh yeah, and then eats.

I pointed out that no one would ever mistakenly call her exterminator if she suddenly saw a lobster scurry across the living room floor. Other Louisiana crustaceans are insectlike in the wild, but crabs do not look larval when peeled, and shrimp are DOA.

"Yeah, I guess you're right," Brooks, a boilmaster himself, finally conceded. "If someone could just find a way to incorporate explosives and car racing into a crawfish boil, men would do it every weekend."

At an earlier time I might have passed off this talk as typical guy-takes-the-kitchen machismo, but I was still feeling the rush of my own crawfish kill. The thought of a crawfish tattoo had crossed my mind. At the very least a shirt was in order. Imagining a crawfish stretched across my chest—a warrior image, not an ass-pinching cartoon—made me feel strong and connected, maybe the way Uncle Danny had felt about his Thanksgiving turkeys years ago. I ventured down Magazine Street, where since the storm two design-your-own-T-shirt shops had made a cottage industry out of fleur-de-lis emblems and boosterish sayings like "Make Levees Not War." I asked a saleswoman if she had any crawfish graphics. "No, the only New Orleans animal we have right now is a cockroach."

The old-school method of making crawfish bisque extends to the crustacean kingdom the southern value of using everything from the pig but the squeal. As soon as the boiled crawfish are cool enough to handle, you tear off their claws, mash the claws with a hammer (a meat tenderizer works, but why get civilized now?), and toss them back into the boiling liquid to reduce into a more robust stock. Then you peel your kill. It took me two hours, eighteen minutes, and twenty-nine seconds to peel ten pounds of boiled crawfish. A real Yankee time. In my defense, it was the end of crawfish season, so the shells had grown long and tough. The tails, however, were fat and meaty. Tightly packed, they filled a quart yogurt container.

The more fat in your bisque, the deeper the flavor. Some recipes suggest tapping the heads in order to empty them of excess fat. Others instruct you to run a finger around the inside of the heads, like I saw the spice alphabetizer doing at Hawk's. In the cookbook Paul Prudhomme wrote with his siblings, he says to discard any "gray or dark matter" that might emerge with the fat. Which raises the question, Fat? Crawfish *fat*? Certainly this is code for something just short of the squeal (a crawfish's head matter is in fact equivalent to a liver).

At this point you dispose of the exterior tail parts and the face—

the part of the head where the eyeball stalks attach and where the forehead dips into a needle-sharp snout. But you clean and keep the remaining cylindrical thorax, to fill later with crawfish stuffing. Lined up on my kitchen tabletop, the hollow orange receptacles looked so much like beetle shells that my mind turned to Styrofoam and stickpins. I had bombed my eighth-grade-science insect collection project. If only Mr. Wanie could see me now.

Moving forward, you use a portion of the tails to make crawfish stuffing, which you then force into the hollowed-out thorax carcasses, which you then flour, fry, and refrigerate. It's been a long day. The next step is to take a bath. It will do nothing to mediate the deeply fishy aroma embedded in your hands, but it will steady your breath and clear space in your head for meditating on your newfound (or reinforced) machismo, whatever your gender. Tomorrow you will wake up and make a roux gumbo using standard seasoning vegetables, the remaining crawfish tails, and the rich stock that has been simmering on your stove. You will garnish your brown, velveteen soup with the stuffed and fried thoraxes, little crawfish meatballs floating in shell boats.

The authors of *Stir the Pot* call crawfish bisque "that quintessential example of Louisiana haute cuisine." In the early twentieth century, they write, only cooks in upper-middle-class and upper-class homes had two days to devote to the process. I would add procrastinating writers to the updated list.

Unlike the other bisques plentiful in New Orleans (oyster and artichoke, corn and crab, eggplant and shrimp), and as opposed to the conventional definition of *bisque*, traditional Louisiana crawfish bisque contains no cream. Whatever a particular crawfish bisque's peculiarities—made with tomatoes, beef stock, or veal, or without the stuffed thoraxes—it's thickened with a roux, filled out with fat, and left largely to the concentrated essence of crawfish. That essence is as complex as it is pure, beguiling and chaste, of the earth and of the swamp.

In general, you're apt to find thicker, lighter-colored bisques in New Orleans and thinner, darker-roux versions in Cajun country. I followed the instructions of one Creole recipe and added sherry and thyme at the end of cooking. A country chef would be more likely to leave it at red pepper and green onions. In both country and city, crawfish bisque is customarily eaten as a stand-alone main course with rice rather than as an appetizer. It's worthy of center stage—because its flavors are sincere and eternal, and because of all that transpired between cook and beast to make it so. When I served mine, I politely insisted that my friends eat their salads second.

POISSON MEUNIÈRE AMANDINE

The Creole Conundrum, and the Alibi

If this were a guidebook, somewhere between crawfish and Mardi Gras I would be obligated to include a clever line about how there's a flesh to sate every hunger on Bourbon Street. And it would be true, particularly if you number poisson meunière amandine among the street's temptations.

Speckled sea trout, a specialty of the Gulf of Mexico, is a silver-scaled, black-spotted, white-fleshed finfish that conceivably was given life to fulfill orders for poisson meunière amandine, a specialty of the house at Galatoire's. Served unapologetically à la carte, the trout steams within its crinkly balloon of fried batter, which sort of hovers around the fillet, a loose second skin doused in nutty brown butter and shingled with sliced almonds. The fish itself remains sweet, pristine, untouched by—but more interesting for the company of—its rich companions. A squeeze of lemon brightens and completes the composition like the opalescence of pearls against a dark dress. The first bite is light, ethereal; the last is saturated with regret. No one who finds love on Bourbon Street wants the night to end.

The French Quarter is a misunderstood neighborhood, mostly because of the overexposure of a seven-block stretch of Bourbon Street, the stretch that's famous for frozen daiquiri shops, strip clubs, and the century-old, jacket-required, white-tablecloth restaurant Galatoire's. While Bourbon Street's gone-wild reputation is no exaggeration, I get defensive when visitors judge the city, or even the rest of the French Quarter, by the compressed bacchanal. For instance, the time during a Jet Blue flight when I sat beside an electrician from Connecticut who had been working in New Orleans since Katrina, aiding and capitalizing on the city's recovery. He told me that he had stayed at a hotel on Bourbon Street during his first few work trips but had later moved his base an hour east of the city because the hotel had been too rowdy for him, crowded with "disgusting" and "obnoxious" people. Those weren't New Orleanians, I wanted him to know. Locals don't need Bourbon Street to be obnoxious.

Oh yeah, well what about the two girls working the door at Oz, who had lured him in with their cleavage and then set him loose without mentioning that it was a gay club? "What about them? They work there, they must be New Orleanians," he challenged.

Yes, but that was *funny*. I wanted to giggle. As he clearly was reliving a low point in his manhood, I kept quiet and adjusted my headphones.

A few weeks later, as I walked through the mellow residential end of Bourbon Street, down toward Esplanade Avenue, a car slowed to a stop beside me. The driver rolled down his window—for directions, I assumed. "You need a job?" he asked me. "I have a café in Metairie and I need to fill three night shifts." I didn't need a job, but I knew friends who did. With land lines still kaput in much of the city and displaced people shacking up in strange neighborhoods, networking was the post-Katrina way. I pulled out a pen and notebook to take down his number.

"You sure you don't need a job?" he asked again. "What do you do—cocktail waitress? Dance?"

Only then did I register his faded black polyester pants, the Band-Aid on his cheekbone, the smell of deodorizer wafting from his car. I'm often embarrassed to claim that I'm a writer, because it's so often a dishonest way to describe the sitting-before-the-computer I do every day, but this was the first time I'd felt shame for my profession because it sounded unsexy. Our exchange also verified that the French Quarter has a PR problem, even close to home. How else to explain that a man from the suburbs had mistaken a thirty-five-year-old woman wearing Gap jeans, Chuck Taylor knockoffs, and a padded 36A petite bra for a stripper?

Fact: stereotypes always contain some element of truth. I *was* walking Bourbon Street for a subversive reason that day. A friend and I had met for lunch at a culinary speakeasy, a takeout restaurant that a musician and his wife had been running from their living room since the storm. We had enjoyed Thursday's fried pork chops and smothered cabbage on a shaded knoll in Louis Armstrong Memorial Park. This "restaurant" may have been less legal than much of what transpires on Bourbon Street, but our participation in it was for a good cause: the propagation of local cooking and of a local musician's liquidity during the city's postdiluvian slump.

Culinary speakeasies have long proved a viable way for sometimes-entrepreneurs to make a buck in New Orleans. A chef whom I will refer to with the pseudonym Miss Patricia raised her five children as a single parent by holding three-day-long "suppers" every few months. She would clear the furniture out of her "straight-through" (what she called her shotgun house) and arrange tables in the configuration of a restaurant. Some of her customers hung around, played cards, and got their drink on until she swept them out at the end of three days, but most of them picked up their food and took it home to their families. The New Orleans Police Department busted the operation more than once. Miss Patricia never said so, but I like to imagine that the officers ate well on those nights.

Later in life, after retiring from legitimate restaurant work, Miss Patricia resumed doing suppers, this time following a more conventional single-day program. For a typical one, which she ran from her home in the Gentilly neighborhood, she fixed more than two hundred packaged dinners, each one consisting of a choice of fried catfish, fried chicken, or seafood-stuffed bell peppers, plus baked macaroni, potato salad, a slice of cake, and a cold drink. Some customers came to the house to pick up their orders; with the help of family members, Miss Patricia delivered to others. One of her daughters took orders from city hall employees, another from coworkers at the New Orleans Credit Union. Having distributed fliers, Miss Patricia received orders from the post office, the fire department, and NASA's Michoud Assembly Facility. Her pastor stopped by. Charging six dollars a plate, she netted enough profit to take eight of her grandchildren to Disney World.

Suppers were a big business on Fridays at University Hospital when Matt occasionally worked emergency room shifts there during his pediatric residency, and the hospital's nurses were speed-dialed into the subculture. Over the years I've met and heard about people who work the suppers angle in lieu of a formal job, or between formal jobs, or as once-in-a-while personal fundraisers. Once I came across a flier for a supper on Marais Street in Treme (fried fish, fried chicken, stuffed peppers, baked macaroni, potato salad, peas, bread, dessert, soda; six dollars; free delivery for five or more orders). I asked a friend who lived in the neighborhood and knew the woman running it whether she did suppers regularly. "No, it's probably for her outfit for the Sidewalk Steppers," he guessed, referring to the social aid and pleasure club to which the cook belonged. "People have suppers to raise extra money for rent, choir robes," he said. I've also heard of suppers benefiting Mardi Gras Indian costumes, band uniforms, vacations, medical bills, and wedding dresses.

It could go without saying that New Orleans is a town of make-you-holler-good homegrown cooks, including spot-on Friday fish fryers—perhaps a fortunate relic of faded Catholic values. I wouldn't hesitate to follow the directions on a random flier to any stranger's supper. With any luck, it would return me to Miss Patricia, whom I haven't been able to locate since the storm. I did, thankfully, get to observe her running a supper before all that mess, and her catfish, which was as thick and thickly seasoned as a Popeye's fried chicken breast, did not outlast my drive home.

Being one of the least expensive and most abundant edible aquatics of the South, wild and farmed catfish is ubiquitous every day of the week. It turns up in po-boys, on fried seafood platters, in court bouillon, and in catfish-centric restaurants such as Middendorf's in

Manchac and the late, great, *great* Barrow's Shady Inn, where the only dinner option was cayenne-pricked catfish pan-fried the golden color of dried corn, so hot when it hit the table that you had to eat your buttered toast first. (Barrow's flooded and as of this writing hasn't shown signs of reopening.) One of my most memorable catfish experiences was unsolicited. Upon taking my order for speckled trout amandine, a waiter at Mandina's (where the dish approaches Galatoire's in its fineness) informed me that the kitchen had run out of trout but I could have the preparation with catfish instead. He delivered this as good news and advised me: "If you find a bone in the catfish, consider yourself lucky. We employees eat the amandine with catfish, and we eat it with a spoon so we can scoop up the sauce with each bite. That's what *we* do." Imagine having a job in which your duties include encouraging diners to feed themselves as much butter and nuts in one bite as possible. In some cities, that's borderline illegal.

All of which is to explain, again, how New Orleans is a unique and complex place. In the French Quarter, that complexity is concentrated into a throbbing intensity. Contrary to media snapshots and Web cams, however, the best observation point is not a balcony on Bourbon Street, where the vices on display are fairly straightforward, but in the dining room at Galatoire's.

The restaurant's regulars know this. Two of them, Kenneth Holditch and Marda Burton, wrote *Galatoire's: Biography of a Bistro*, a sort of society gossip memoir masking as a history lesson. When the book was released, I attended a society gossip session masking as a book signing, during which Burton and other Galatoire's regulars cut up, remembering all the ways in which they'd misbehaved while wearing their finest and eating poisson meunière amandine over the decades.

I first glimpsed the restaurant's naughty/nice personality a couple of years before I ever heeled across its cool pharmacy-tile floor. Out-of-town visitors provide locals with an excuse to experience the bawdy Bourbon Street scene now and then, kicking and screaming and secretly titillated all the way; Matt and I humored my dad's desire to check it out on his first visit (and his second, and his sixth). At the time I knew about Galatoire's in the same way I knew about Carnival balls and mint juleps on wraparound porches—as scenes from a southern fairy tale so foreign to my Yankee aesthetic that I couldn't imagine myself as a character in it, not even as the disenfranchised stepsister. I did know enough to be curious about the restaurant, though, and so as we passed with our frozen daiquiris, I pressed my face against the front window, peeking through the sheer curtains for an after-hours look. The view: the back of a tuxedoed waiter as he pushed through a swinging door into the kitchen, and behind him a mouse racing across the tiles from one French-bread crumb to the next.

It could happen anywhere, and yet that first glimpse was emblematic. Two tails, one ravishing, one rodent. There exists a precarious balance within Galatoire's, and extending out into the city at large, between decorum and debauchery, decency and seediness. Sometimes it tips one way (little boys in sports coats eating steaks with knife and fork), sometimes the other (an unfamiliar hand on my behind as I move toward the restroom). I'm still exploring how it is that I feel so at ease in there, and out here.

When my girlfriend Corrie called to say that she would breeze through New Orleans for six hours on a Saturday afternoon, I knew instantly where we needed to spend them. In an earlier life Corrie had managed a restaurant in Wisconsin where I had cooked. At the time we were both pseudovegetarians; our friendship gelled one seditious evening at Madison's L'Etoile Restaurant, where we shared a hulking filet mignon cut from a grass-fed cow that no doubt had blinked with the eyelashes of our dreams. That meal was a springboard for a solid alliance that we continue to feed in restaurants whenever we find ourselves in the same area code.

I planned an afternoon with Corrie that would mimic my own first Galatoire's meal, because there was no way I could improve upon the long Saturday lunch I had taken there with the writer

Jonathan Gold, who isn't a New Orleanian but who knew how to order just like one. Lustrous oyster-artichoke soup; fried eggplant sticks powdered with confectioners' sugar; fat oysters wound in bacon and deep-fried; a cold crabmeat salad jeweled with capers; a bottle of Sancerre; and, thank goodness, the poisson meunière amandine, which Jonathan later honored in *Gourmet* magazine with the spare but admiring description "fried fish with slivered nuts on it."

Galatoire's has forever after been my French Quarter Creole antique restaurant of choice. Other biggies in the genre are Antoine's, one of the country's oldest restaurants, and Arnaud's, opened in 1918 by Count Arnaud Cazenave (a count in name only). Tujague's, Broussard's, Brennan's, and the Court of Two Sisters also deserve mention for upholding antiquated culinary traditions in the face of trends, tourists, and tempests. But I have little to report about these others, because a person of moderate means can afford to know just one old-line French Quarter Creole restaurant with any kind of intimacy. Galatoire's is my one and only.

If ever there were a good time to address the tricky word *Creole*, this must be it. (It remains questionable whether there is a good time. After writing that sentence, I avoided this chapter for a week; it took another month to type anything succinct, and I use *succinct* with my fingers crossed. I previously thought that reading *Crime and Punishment* while backpacking alone in Northern Europe during the rainy season in my early twenties was the pinnacle of angst.)

To begin, an important clarification: by Creole, I do not mean Cajun. Acadiana, or Cajun country, encompasses most of southwestern Louisiana. Native Americans occupied the region when the French-speaking people of Acadie, Canada, for which the area is now named, began to arrive in 1755. Originally of French descent, the Canadian Acadians refused to take an oath to the British crown, which would have pitted them against their ancestral homeland. Their disobedience begat a sort of ethnic cleansing; taking the opportunity to leave winter forever, some of the ousted Acadians resettled nearly as far south of Canada as possible without crossing an ocean.

Over time, Cajun cooking has asserted itself on New Orleans' eating habits, but the city is not Cajun in tradition any more than it is in geography. In fact, common Cajun ingredients and food preparations—andouille, boudin, tasso, boiled crawfish, and brown (tomato-free) jambalaya—didn't enter the city limits in significant amounts until the latter part of the twentieth century. A New-Orleans-as-a-Cajun-place myth transpired during the 1980s because of Paul Prudhomme's worldwide omnipresence at the time. With a man raised in Cajun country running New Orleans' best-known restaurant, confusion was guaranteed. Additionally and continually confusing is that much of Chef Paul's cooking isn't even emblematic of his people; rather, his culinary style is a little bit Cajun, a little bit Creole, and a whole lot of his own ballsy genius.

But detailing the finer points of Cajun is for another book. For this moment, it helps to know simply that from the beginning, the Creoles and the Cajuns have shared one important influence: France, which colonized Louisiana once it was finished with Canada. French names decorate Cajun and Creole family trees; the French language, however maligned, peppers their respective dialects; and French technique informs both Cajun and Creole cooking.

Creole is used as both a noun and an adjective. The noun denotes a language or a race (as in "Her mama's people are Creoles, but her daddy's from Hawaii"); the adjective describes a thing (as in "Creole cuisine is the aristocrat of all cuisines"). The word derives from the Spanish *criollo* and the Portuguese *crioulo*. The most general and noncontroversial meaning I've come across, in texts and in an etymological dictionary, is "person native to a locality." It immediately gets more complicated.

Louisianians dispute exactly which natives belong in the Creole club. Sometimes it seems that the only sources in agreement are those that quote one another. In Natchitoches, a town in central Louisiana known for its fried meat pies, a plantation guide explained to my tour group that only those people whose ancestors owned land before the Louisiana Purchase can claim the Creole title. It sounded so clear-cut, so easily determined, that I wanted it to be true. But the theory doesn't fly in New Orleans, where land is hardly a solid foundation, whether you're building a fence, a levee, or a premise.

Fundamentally, New Orleanians concur that, beginning three centuries ago, the first Creoles were the offspring of foreign-born parents—in other words, first-generation natives of this locality. The stickler is, *which* foreign-born parents? Five main ethnicities populated New Orleans in the decades immediately following its 1718 founding: French, French Canadians, Africans, Indians, and a few Germans. It was a feral place to live at the time (not so difficult to imagine)—hot, wet, overgrown. In 1746 the population hovered around 4,000, including African slaves (mostly male), Indian slaves (mostly female), and a handful of ne'er-do-wells from France banished to labor in the New World. Interdependence in all regards was the law of the land; the French crown favored assimilation and was friendly to interbreeding. Franco-Indian battles and well-organized slave revolts transpired, but so did interethnic alliances and marriages. DNA mingling began at once, and the pool continued to expand. The colony fell under Spanish rule in the 1760s; over the next forty years, Anglo-Americans involved in the river trade and refugees from the Caribbean-French colony Saint-Domingue joined the melting pot.

Handpicking which of the earliest combinations and bloodlines produced Creoles and which didn't seems impossible but has proven to be irresistible. In the end, the multitudinous theories break down into two basic camps: those who contend that the truest Creoles are of unsullied white European blood, and those who believe that the truest Creoles are black—either of straight African blood or the mixed-race result of unions between white Europeans and Africans.

To prove the point, consider George Washington Cable's 1884 book *The Creoles of Louisiana*, in which the author grants Creole status to the white descendants of the French and Spanish colonists for their "excellence of origin." He adds that "later, the term [Creole] was adopted by—not conceded to—the natives of mixed blood, and is still so used among themselves."

Then consider the work of Gwendolyn Midlo Hall, a more modern historian who cites Cable in her works. She contends the opposite in an essay titled "The Formation of Afro-Creole Culture": "In Spanish and French colonies, including eighteenth-century Louisiana, the term *creole* was used to distinguish . . . American-born from African-born slaves; all first-generation slaves born in America and their descendents were designated creoles." The word *creole* was redefined *later on* (my italics), writes Hall, to mean people of exclusively European descent born in the Americas.

Cable and Midlo Hall represent the dozens (hundreds? thousands?) of historians who disagree about the origins of the first Louisiana Creoles. It's not so different on the streets of New Orleans. I consulted one white friend of German Creole heritage who conceded the validity of dark-skinned Creoles (commonly called *gens de couleur*, or Creoles of color) but noted that *his* people were Creoles *first*. Conversely, a black friend said he'd never encountered the notion of a white Creole until he left home, and the Seventh Ward, to go to college. A third friend, a white Creole of French ancestry who also grew up in the Seventh Ward, said that she knew black Creole families who shared her last name and always assumed that they were her distant relatives.

When I asked Leah Chase which Creoles she refers to when she relates what the Creoles do and don't do (Creoles never set their purses on the floor, for instance, and it's bad luck to store your shoes above your head), she laughed. "The ones that look like me," she said.

Mrs. Chase's skin is the creamy caramel color of café au lait. Along with being a genealogical Creole, she's a prime visual example of a contemporary folk understanding of what makes a Creole, such as this one found on the Louisiana Creole Heritage Center Web site: "Creoles are generally known as a people of mixed French, African, Spanish, and Native American ancestry, most of who [*sic*] reside in or have familial ties to Louisiana. Research has shown many other ethnicities have contributed to this culture including, but not limited to, Chinese, Russian, German, and Italian."

In support of this relatively nonspecific, mixed-race, street understanding of *Creole* is the story of my redheaded, Minnesota-bred friend Katy Reckdahl. When she pushes around town with her gorgeous milk-chocolate-skinned son, Hector, whom she produced with a black New Orleanian, people of all races comment on her pretty Creole baby. They do this without asking to see his family tree first.

Fortunately, there seem to be two points of consensus among all New Orleanians who call themselves Creole: a) that they belong to an elite set based on biological eminence, not economics, and b) that while they may be proud New Orleanians, their American identities are secondary to their ancestral identities. Whatever your favored strain, New Orleans Creoles descend from colonials and immigrants who forged a blended culture, and an immeasurably important place, all their own. America may have claimed them by way of the Louisiana Purchase in 1803, but while the Creoles conceded their former nationalities, they never fully abandoned the cultures of their various homelands. To me, this begins to explain why New Orleans, identified as Creole itself, can still feel so foreign, and why Creole cooking has such a distinctive taste.

Understanding the evolution of New Orleans' Creole cooking is both simpler and more confounding than charting the evolution of the city's Creole people. Like the people, Creole food is a consequence of immigration and integration, and it's absolutely indigenous to this place. It's a by-product of how all the above-mentioned ethnic influences, and more that arrived in subsequent centuries, interact on the stove, in the pot, and on the plate.

The Creole cooking rule-cum-cliché that *first you make a roux* is true to a remarkable degree. Even some versions of red beans and rice begin that way. It's also true that the holy trinity (onion, celery, and green bell pepper) permeates the Creole kitchen; that French influences are palpable (such as in the preponderance of first-course soups); that Africa continues to assert itself; that Creole gumbos are generally thicker and lighter in color than Cajun gumbos; that rice trumps potatoes; that pork and veal trump beef; and that, for New Orleans Creoles anyway, fresh seafood is the ultimate object of exaltation.

But truisms are just the beginning.

"If I have to explain it to you, it's hopeless," Gene Bourg told me, paraphrasing Louis Armstrong's famous quip about jazz, when I asked him to define Creole cooking. Gene is a Cajun-Creole hybrid, descended from a French man and an Acadian woman who fell in love on the boat to America. (Upon being ousted from Canada, some Acadians took a detour to France, which felt no more like home than Indonesia would have. Good thing boats left regularly for the wilds of Louisiana.) Gene grew up on the West Bank of New Orleans, in the 1940s and '50s, a time when ice, milk, coffee, and dry cleaning were delivered to each family's doorstep. A journalist, he covered local food and restaurants for the *Times-Picayune* from 1985 to 1994.

I realized while laboring over this section and talking to Gene that although I've studied the subject extensively, my best knowledge of Creole cooking still exists in the part of my brain that stores sensory impressions and taste memories, not the part that deals in words. Words aren't what enables a diner to identify the smoked soft-shell crab loaded with butter and crabmeat at Clancy's Restaurant, and the fried soft-shell crab over crawfish linguine at Irene's Cuisine, as belonging within the realm of Creole cooking—as opposed to the sautéed softshells sauced with mint vinaigrette at Uglesich's (no longer open), which despite tending toward heaven didn't taste Creole at all.

Gene, who as a young military man lived for two years in France, divided traditional Creole cooking into three subgroups for me: French Creole (as at the old-line, sauce-specific French Quarter restaurants), home-style Creole (long-cooked pot dishes), and black

Creole (often identified as soul food). "What most Creole food has in common with French food is that if you put it in the refrigerator, it's better the next day," he said, citing the gumbo at Praline Connection, the smothered pork with onion gravy at Brigtsen's, and the sweet turtle soup at Restaurant Mandich as three of his favorite examples.

To Gene's taste, Mandich was New Orleans' archetypal Creole restaurant. A pink-painted dinosaur of a place in the Ninth Ward opened by the Croatian immigrant John Mandich in 1922 and expected (by me, anyway) never to go extinct, Mandich remains a depressing Katrina casualty. To sit at the bar while the owner, Lloyd English, mixed you an old-fashioned and his scotch-drinking pals talked up the veal Parmesan was the friendliest of initiations. Every one of Mandich's dining room windows was curtain-sealed, I assumed to protect appetites from the concrete panorama outside, but perhaps also to keep the kitchen's secrets within. Lloyd's wife and Mandich's chef, Joel, used butter like she meant it, sugar in salt amounts, and lump crabmeat as if it were parsley. These were the most appetizing or stupefying of culinary decisions, depending on your sensibility. It tasted like home to Gene, like some tripped-out Creole bedtime story to me.

Just when I thought Gene had provided a definition of Creole cooking I could follow by creating three workable categories, he took a drag on his predinner scotch and added, "What makes New Orleans food an authentic cuisine is that there's this matrix of Creole and Acadian . . . and then we have lots of subcuisines, like in France." Provençal, Parisian, Breton, *marseillais*; French-Creole, Cajun-Creole, Creole-Italian, contemporary Creole. We may be edging toward a Vietnamese-Creole category, and a population boom of Latin American immigrants occasioned by the poststorm labor shortage has already spawned a number of taco trucks and Latin American cafés, not to mention provided New Orleans restaurants with dishwashers and cooks.

Perhaps it's the persistence of the we're-all-in-it-together attitude of the earliest French settlers that's responsible for the city's continuing policy of acceptance. Immigrants, whether from another country or another American state, can't help but be absorbed into the culture and contribute what they know. Like the apothecary and bitters-maker Antoine Amédée Peychaud did with his tonic. Like Paul Prudhomme does with his Cajun-influenced cooking. Like the Vietnamese do by calling their traditional sandwiches po-boys. Like I'm trying to do. Given the city's assimilationist culinary history, it's hardly a stretch to imagine a Creole *cocina* in the future: "I'll have three fried catfish tacos, please, dressed."

The pool of immigrants from which Creoles originate was set around the time of the Louisiana Purchase—there are no new strains of Creole people. Creole cooking is more dynamic, of the here and now. New Creole dishes—fried green tomatoes with shrimp rémoulade at Upperline, shrimp with tasso cream sauce over grits at Herbsaint, alligator sausage cheesecake at Jacques-Imo's, pecan-crusted Gulf fish at Commander's Palace, sautéed sweetbreads with sherry mustard at Bayona, farmer Jim Core's kale and sausage jambalaya—are constantly generated, often in the hands of cooks who aren't Creole themselves. It's not necessary to pulse with Creole blood in order to be a good Creole cook or to identify a Creole dish (though certainly it helps); you need only a developed sense for that inexplicable Creole flavor, which Creoles concur is all in the seasoning. This flavor is best defined by the tongue, not the typewriter. You know it when you taste it, as you would know a New Orleans brass band from five blocks away even if you were in Anchorage. It wouldn't be the tuba exactly, or the trombone, or the bass drum. It would be all of them, but something else too—something rooted so deeply, so early, in this place that it precedes a common language. It is itself a common language.

For me, Galatoire's is the beginning and the end of Creole cooking in New Orleans, not because it's always the best and not because it incorporates all possibilities of the Creole kitchen, but because it leads to and from all possibilities. Often when I've been unsure about the historical or regional legitimacy of a dish, because it's something I've never encountered before—stuffed eggplant, court bouillon, cup custard, chicken Clemenceau—its presence on Galatoire's menu has acted as my rubber stamp, giving me license to entertain it as a valid contender. At Galatoire's you see the big picture, the goal at which all the minor, less focused stabs at Creole cooking are aiming. Diners familiar with the other French Quarter restaurants of Galatoire's genre may opine similarly about them, and diners who knew Galatoire's fifty years ago, back when waiters chipped ice by hand and none of the bentwood chair seats ever had been denigrated by denim, may accuse me of having arrived too late. But that wouldn't change the fact that Galatoire's shapes the first principles for my experiential understanding of New Orleans Creole cooking.

I'd eaten in the city extensively before ever trying Galatoire's, and so my first lunch there was a climax. I sometimes wonder whether it would have been more instructive to have dined at Galatoire's first and had my subsequent meals around town serve as little acts of deconstruction. That's the precedent I was eager to set for Corrie. I visualized unveiling the restaurant to her as if it were the Smithsonian or the Louvre, a cultural cornerstone. She would always have it, an immovable edible entity, a consistent point of safe return. Looking back, I understand why she hasn't. Returned, that is.

When Corrie and I passed from the hot, sour street into Galatoire's dining room with its neat tiles, lazy ceiling fans, and gilded fleur-de-lis wallpaper, a hostess asked whether we had a waiter preference (Galatoire's has employed waitresses, a bone of contention—like the forsaken ice chipping—with some regulars, though none were working that day). I now carry the name of a Galatoire's waiter around in my purse notebook, not because I like him any better than the others but because it's in a diner's favor to appear as though she has a favorite waiter at a place like Galatoire's. Still agreeable Wisconsin girls, Corrie and I left our waiter assignment up to the fates, who must have been having a bad day.

Our assigned waiter played it perfectly at first. He congratulated me on my Sazerac order and complimented my engagement ring. Should the alarm have sounded when he noted aloud that Corrie wasn't wearing one? All part of the game, I thought. One of Galatoire's most highly requested waiters had recently been fired for sexually harassing a female coworker. Knowing almost no details about the incident itself, the town stood divided: half the populace paying attention looked favorably on this sign of gender enlightenment in Old World New Orleans; the other half was convinced the victim either had been asking for it or had overreacted. I hadn't chosen a side, but in the interest of showing my friend a good time, I allowed our waiter his weak moment with her and then, like the high-class subservient you're meant to be as a diner at Galatoire's, I asked him to forgo bringing menus and order for us.

Galatoire's is a restaurant where the servers know more than the customers do, which ought to go without saying at every restaurant but rarely does. Even in his worst-behaving moments, a Galatoire's waiter would sooner cinch his throat closed with his bow tie than utter zingers that are common in other dining rooms: "I don't know what the chicken tastes like—I'm a vegetarian"; "The crawfish are fresh from China tonight"; and "All of our desserts are homemade from Sysco." On the contrary, a Galatoire's waiter keeps notes on his regular customers, and he knows at a glance whether you're a soup or fried-eggplant table, whether you'd take better to the cold seafood salads or the leafy ones, what fish is freshest, what sauce is weak, and whether it isn't really more of a lamb chop or omelet day. While I have an unshakable attachment to the trout amandine, Galatoire's crème de la crème of fish preparations is pompano from the Gulf of Mexico, so fresh that it flinches when it feels the broiler heat, served simply with butter and lemon. It's rarely available. Our waiter scored an order for Corrie.

The introduction to *Galatoire's Cookbook*, published in 2005 and written with the cooperation of the Galatoire family, reads, "Galatoire's cuisine is not the handiwork of a single superstar chef, but rather of a family that has carefully safeguarded its traditions of quality in the tangible culinary product and the restaurant's intangible image and ambiance." During my six years in New Orleans before Katrina, the food at Galatoire's changed so little that this statement seemed plausible; you could imagine some French-speaking ghost from Galatoire's past running the kitchen from his grave. The waiters and managers were character actors in the restaurant's old-fashioned theater, but the kitchen was faceless. Not a single white toque emerged from its swinging doors during my meals there; looking through them from the dining room, I was privy only to flashes of stainless steel and steam.

But carefully safeguarded traditions don't run kitchens. Tireless men and women run kitchens, and on the days of my lunches there with Jonathan and Corrie, the chef running the kitchen at Galatoire's was Milton Prudence. He had begun his tenure as a dishwasher in 1968, when he was twenty-one years old and just out of the Marine Corps. It was meant to be a transitional job; he wanted to be a schoolteacher. But Mr. Prudence's mother and several other family members also worked behind the scenes at Galatoire's, and he quickly took to cooking. By the time he did move on, in 2003, ultimately taking a job at Tommy's Cuisine, Mr. Prudence had held the top post in Galatoire's kitchen for fifteen years. He was the first—and as of this writing, the only—black man to do so. (Speaking of tradition, the food at Tommy's is half New Orleans Italian and half Galatoirian Creole specials from Mr. Prudence's background. The last time I dined at Tommy's, seafood-eggplant stuffing, oysters Rockefeller, shrimp linguine, and veal Marsala shared one table.)

I didn't know anything about Mr. Prudence beyond his name until one afternoon during the writing of this book, when he sat down with me for an interview. Our conversation confirmed that even in a restaurant as seemingly static and shrinelike as Galatoire's, the melting-pot quality of Creole cooking compounds with every hand that stirs a pot, peels a shrimp, or measures tarragon into a batch of béarnaise sauce. In unison with its Old World ambiance, the restaurant's mythology prescribes that no recipe, ingredient, or cooking technique has changed over the past one hundred years, when in fact Mr. Prudence learned sauce-making techniques from Paul Prudhomme during a free cooking lesson at Mr. B's Bistro in the 1970s, and he gleaned tips for making what would become Galatoire's standing crawfish étouffée recipe from a Cajun waiter who worked there.

Mr. Prudence learned soups from one coworker, stocks from another. While he primarily cooked from the Galatoires' written recipes, there was always room for personal touches and improvement, as long as they passed the family's taste test. Naturally, this is the key to the survival and evolution of Creole cooking, more than workable categories and sensible definitions: careful, caring Creole cooks, and eaters who wouldn't want to live here without them.

Lunch with Corrie was progressing just as I had hoped it would. The Sazeracs, the seafood, the time of day. I'd purposely planned our meal to take place between the lunch and dinner rushes. These quiet, breathing hours in a restaurant tend to be the most interesting for people who love restaurants themselves, not just eating. You get to hear a restaurant for what it is then, not for who it contains—its intimate sounds of working, clocks ticking, fans clinking, ice machines dumping their loads. And you get to observe the staff as people, which can be so refreshing, even inspirational, if you've ever been in their shoes. For instance, having cashed out all his clients for the day, one waiter sat alone at a corner table with a glass of red wine, a newspaper, and a muffuletta from Central Grocery. He kept his vest on but loosened his bow tie. This was his restaurant too.

Galatoire's is a lingerer's place. Servers generally follow the precept not to drop a check until it's called for, and even then not until they've at least offered a final round. It's a Friday afternoon ritual at Galatoire's to come for lunch and keep your table through dinner. I'm not sure who has more fun when this happens, the participants in the all-day-long lunches or the observers who catch up with them at dinnertime, after the long-lunchers' eyelids have grown two inches, their blouses and teeth have been stained with wine, and their movements have begun to resemble those of small children just learning the Frankenstein toddle. Having arrived for a late afternoon/early evening meal, my family and I once looked on as a woman readying to leave slouched over to pick up a twenty-dollar bill she had dropped on the floor. Her knees had lost their ability to bend, and her fingers couldn't reach the money because her heels were too high. Apparently she had also lost control of her abdominal muscles, because she just hung there, arms flopping around, long hair sweeping against the French-bread crumbs on the floor, until a friend noticed and helped her straighten out. Afterward, we felt terrible that we hadn't helped, that we'd just sat there entertained, but the early dinner hours (or late lunch hours, take your pick) at Galatoire's have a television-like quality to them—we didn't feel as though we were in the same time zone as the people who had arrived at noon.

The dressed-up debauchery at Galatoire's is why many New Orleanians love being there—that and the poisson meunière amandine, the pungent red shrimp rémoulade, the anise-perfumed Rockefeller spinach, the possibility of fine fried chicken (sometimes made by special request) with fine wine, the airy double-fried potatoes dipped into béarnaise sauce. It's consistent with the liberal atmospheres at other white-tablecloth restaurants favored by locals (Clancy's in Uptown, for example), where "white-tablecloth" is code for a place where you wear your best jewels, where smoking is (was) allowed, and where the night is a dud if the waiters haven't led at least one communal round of "Happy Birthday."

I hadn't planned how long lunch with Corrie would last. I thought we'd chat awhile, have some of the thick house coffee, and then split an order of crêpes maison. This specialty is an appropriate way to end a meal with a visitor, as its particular style of tacky sweetness reflects those characteristics of the city. If you ask an experienced server for a description of crêpes maison, he'll tell you that the crêpes are filled with currant jelly and sprinkled with Grand Marnier or Cointreau. A busboy gave me an unedited rundown: "Grape jelly rolled up and dunked in orange liquor." Creole? You decide.

Corrie and I never got to the crêpes. Even before I could order coffee, our waiter asked permission to settle our tab and take us out for a drink. His shift would be over when our lunch was, and he was ready when we were, he said. My only explanation for allowing what transpired next—our meal to fall apart prematurely and our waiter, annihilating the third wall, to usher us out the front door with a scandalously large tip from me in his pocket—is that Galatoire's, like the street that fronts it, is a ball of surprises. Not all of them pretty.

He led us around the corner and up Iberville Street, stripping down to a T-shirt as we walked. Halfway up the block, he stopped before a bar called the Alibi and stepped aside to let us enter first. "You girls like beer?" he asked. My dad makes a point of passing the Alibi when he's in the French Quarter. Sometimes he snaps a picture. Once he bought a T-shirt for a buddy. He always snickers to himself to see it again. As its name suggests, the Alibi is the kind of bar that when your dad snickers over it, you don't ask why. Our waiter, whom I never saw again—not in Galatoire's or otherwise—and who in my experience is not representative of the other gentlemen who wait tables there, bought Corrie and me each a beer. Then he pulled a roll of cash from his pocket, said good-bye, and left us for a video poker machine.

PHO

If at First You Don't Belong . . .

To get to Vietnam from Galatoire's, you scoot through the French Quarter and wind around to I-10, then follow it in the direction of Florida. You scale a bridge that traffic reporters aptly call the high-rise, crossing the Industrial Canal, and you merge onto Chef Menteur Highway, the first exit into New Orleans East. You've gone six and a half miles; you're more than halfway there.

Even before the flood broke its windows and soaked its mattresses, Chef Highway was a visually bleak place: a hot, whitewashed runway of auto mechanics and detailers, taverns with tinted windows, apartments without gardens, and low-rent motels that would look right at home in a David Lynch film. Friendly cul-de-sacs and neighborhoods with groomed yards broke off from the thoroughfare, but they didn't affect your impression of the long, straight road itself. This used to be swampland, but it feels like the desert. I've always dug it out here.

And not in the least because six miles to the east of the exit you reach perhaps the most dramatic juxtaposition in the whole city. To your right, NASA's Michoud Facility, a sinister collection of gray smokestacks, white emissions, and complicated scaffolding as viewed from afar. To your left, Alcée Fortier Boulevard, a doorway into the business district, moist farmland, and lawn iconography of a tight-knit Vietnamese community that often prepares its café sua da (thick coffee and sweetened condensed milk) with coffee and chicory from Café Du Monde.

The turn onto Alcée Fortier (named for a nineteenth-century educator and historian) takes you down a short corridor of storefronts—groceries, karaoke restaurants, male-dominated cafés, video and jewelry stores, pharmacies, travel and insurance agencies, tax preparation offices—displaying Vietnamese signage, only some of it translated into English. While it seems to non-Vietnamese interlopers like a whole other world, this strip encompasses only one block; soon enough you're on a short bridge, crossing a bayou that's like so many other bayous in the area, except that it's entirely different.

Out one window, you see the roof of a car projecting just above the water's surface (it's not always the same car, and it's not always on the same side of the bridge, but there's always a car). A dark swamp bird—crane? cormorant?—suns itself on a tangle of branches, wings outstretched like a clothesline, and then disappears underwater to hunt. An elderly Vietnamese man rolls past on a bicycle, edible greenery strapped into a wide basket behind his seat.

When your gaze turns out the driver's side window, it lands on a panorama that may explain the bicyclist's loot. While the hieroglyphs on the Vietnamese businesses appear alien, this is where it begins to feel as though the earth has missed a rotation, or spun out of orbit, or turned inside-out, or undergone some other physical transmutation that resulted in your vehicle having transported you to Southeast Asia. Garden plots crowd the bayou's far shoreline, dipping into the channel itself, so that no barrier separates water from leafy green. The emerald carpet climbs up and around tilted wooden fencing and skeleton trelliswork; it looks lush enough in some places to live beneath, completely protected from the elements. So fertile are these gardens, slanting uphill toward the outer edge of a residential neighborhood, so verdant and economical in their use of space, that even up close it's impossible for the untrained eye to distinguish one plant from another. In certain seasons a profusion of water lilies obscures even the bayou's water. Reflected in the sunlight, the green geography is blinding, the only visual interruption being the occasional conical hat bobbing among the plant life—Vietnamese gardeners tending their plots.

Three blocks onward, Alcée Fortier dead-ends at a larger garden that you might pass off as untended jungle if you didn't stop to take a closer look. Legions of mating monarchs flutter at ground level while dragonflies the size of bats buzz overhead. A conical hat and beneath it a man at work materialize from behind a fence of banana trees, whose leaves flap in the wind like elephant ears.

Around and between the commercial strip and the garden greenery and extending for acres are the mostly single-story, ranch-style homes of Vietnamese families, the older generations of which began to immigrate to this area in the 1970s, fleeing communism in their homeland. (A few newer subdivisions contain larger, multistory homes constructed of cream-colored brick and high archways.) Front yards bound by chain-link fences and semishaded with fruit trees display religious yard art: stone sculptures of the Blessed Mother; life-sized statues of Mary and Joseph kneeling to pray, watched over by an angel; a stone dolphin poised in midjump, watched over by the Blessed Mother.

The normally tranquil pulse of this neighborhood quickens to a drum roll on Saturday mornings between five and eight o'clock, when the parking lot of a tired strip mall situated between the bayou and the larger garden becomes an open-air marketplace. You know you're getting close when you see shoppers in their church clothes (having come from an early mass at Mary Queen of Vietnam Catholic church) meandering back to double-parked cars carrying red mesh sacks wriggling with live chickens, purple mesh ones wriggling with white rabbits, and clear plastic bags stuffed like feather pillows with long bean sprouts. Beside a cart of squawking fowl parked at the curb, a man sells eggs.

A narrow passageway, dark and cool at this time of day, cuts between Ly's Supermarket and a butcher shop; it's crowded with vendors selling traditional silk outfits for toddlers alongside bundles of green herbs: cilantro, sharp-smelling mints and basils, and *ngo gai*, a jagged, acerbic herb with a metallic aftertaste. The dim, busy estuary spills into an inner courtyard where mostly old Vietnamese women push past each other and where other mostly old Vietnamese women sit or squat behind their wares, which change with the growing season: more herbs, sprouts, shallots, spring onions with pink bulbs, lettuces, black-skinned potatoes big as garden rocks, bitter melons, roots knotted and curled like arthritic fingers, green squashes shaped like Little League bats, brilliant maroon banana buds. Star fruit, longan, and Dr. Seuss–looking fruits without apparent English names have been trucked in from Florida and elsewhere. In the courtyard's shady corners, customers use their bare hands to pick through different coolers of silvery fish, frozen squid, and spiny shrimp of every size.

Then there are prepared foods. Warm, gummy noodles folded on themselves and crammed with caramelly onions, with cups of sweet/salty/sour/hot fish sauce on the side. Steaming banana leaves wrapped into triangles and bound with twine, hiding odd mixtures of sticky rice, mealy yellow bean paste, red beans, and a brick-orange something or other that tastes like Mexican chicharrones. Sometimes the matriarch at Ly's Supermarket fries glutinous sesame balls filled with lotus root and mung bean pastes.

The butcher shop is transformed into a buzzing minimarket on Saturdays. One woman stands behind a display of pastel-colored sticky rice wrapped in cellophane. Alongside a butcher who does more knife work before 8 A.M. than seems safe, an assembly line of supersonically quick women and girls stuff yellow-mayonnaise-slathered pistolettes with garlicky meatballs, cold cuts, carrot sticks, green chiles, and cilantro. These sandwiches are called *banh mi;* in New Orleans–speak, Vietnamese po-boys.

For foreigners, which is to say non-Vietnamese New Orleanians, spending a morning out here is like visiting Vietnam without a guidebook or the option of hiring a cabdriver interpreter. Probably a few more people speak English than at your typical market in Vietnam, but only when pressed. Whether out of respect, humility, or sleep deprivation, members of the younger generation of Vietnamese Americans who accompany their elders to take money or help restock only reluctantly step in to translate. Every time I make it out here for the market I just kind of wander around, buy a couple bunches of purple basil and maybe a root or two (which shrivel and rot in my produce bowl at home while I fret over how to use them), and wait for something suddenly to make sense.

Food is a common language and all, but that doesn't preclude valid questions. How long do you let those rabbits live before . . . ? How many people does it take to eat an eight-pound squash? Are there fetuses in those eggs or just yolks and whites? Do you grow plants *in* the bayou water? But this Vietnam is not a place for getting questions answered. This is a place for wondering. It's the one place in New Orleans where I feel on a level with the rest of the city (barring, of course, the Vietnamese)—just as lost, just as confused, just as newly hatched. It's awesome.

I write in the present tense even though the last time I visited the Vietnamese market, in August 2006, only about half of my description of it held true. Katrina's winds and storm surge, and a few weeks later Rita's, nearly exterminated New Orleans East, an area boxed in by the disappearing wetlands to the east, the Industrial Canal to the west, Lake Pontchartrain to the north, and the Mississippi River Gulf Outlet to the south. The bayou gardens of what some people call Little Saigon, others Versailles, became one with the bayou. Homes flooded. Portions of the roof peeled off Mary Queen of Vietnam. About one hundred parishioners holed up in an adjacent school for days, while hundreds of others slept out on Chef Highway awaiting rescue. Their pastor shuttled between his followers, often in a boat. The butcher shop wasn't open on my last visit. Neither had enough market vendors returned to put the inner courtyard to use; all the action was concentrated in the parking lot and the shadowy alleyway. While the bayou gardens were in full green again, the larger garden at the end of the boulevard appeared more overgrown and jungly than ever.

Nevertheless, it seems so certain that the Vietnamese market's post-Katrina shortcomings are temporary that I've decided to describe its past glories as if they exist. It's coming back, and at relative warp speed—not just the market but also this area's businesses, its homes, and the ravaged shrimping industry (Vietnamese Americans and Vietnamese nationals awaiting citizenship form the backbone of the Gulf Coast shrimp trade). The Vietnamese community in New Orleans East has rallied faster than perhaps any other sector contained in the 80 percent of the city that flooded. In newspaper articles and on the evening news, members of that community and journalists observing them have explained why: the Vietnamese people lost homes and livelihoods once before, in 1975, in Vietnam. They'd had practice, had set a precedent for gathering resources and starting completely over. I heard one journalist opine that it's easier for the Vietnamese to rebuild because they have no nostalgia holding them back from the future, no template for living in New Orleans that was drawn by their ancestors here; he theorized that this enables them to think more freely, and with innovation, about how to begin again. Whereas other New Orleanians, myself included, look around the city and see a war zone, Vietnamese New Orleanians, who remember a literal war zone, see the consequences of a strong hurricane and a terrible flood.

On the one hand, I embrace these explanations and observations, because they make a happy ending possible, one in which the Vietnamese section of New Orleans East makes a full recovery—and also because on the surface they make sense. But upon deeper reflection, it strikes me as appalling to suggest that rebuilding a life is any less arduous the second time around. That losing your home again is less spirit-breaking because you're already familiar with hardship. That governmental betrayal is easier to swallow in the country of your refuge.

During a Southern Foodways Alliance symposium held in Oxford, Mississippi, roughly two months after the storm and a year before he passed away, R. W. Apple of the *New York Times* told an audience that the Vietnamese people of this country are "incredibly sinewy, resourceful, unbeatable people." Which is the lens through which I prefer to view their post-Katrina triumphs. Not that rebuilding is easier for the Vietnamese of New Orleans East, but that they're sinewy, resourceful, and unbeatable enough to take it on.

. . .

Katrina may have put the Vietnamese market through the shrink cycle, but that didn't make it any easier for me to determine what to do with myself there. I paid a woman wearing a pretty embroidered blouse one dollar for one of her mottled green baseball-bat squashes. While the language barrier prevented her from understanding my request for cooking tips, another customer stepped up when she overheard me ask. "Soup," she said, and then pointed out into the parking lot to indicate where to find another ingredient I needed to buy for it. I couldn't see where she was pointing, and when she spoke the name of the mystery ingredient again, all I could hear was a jumble of letters. She pointed and called the ingredient by name a third time. I stood there, mute and sweating.

In hindsight, I understand that my panic reflex triggered by unfamiliar accents—any accent: Vietnamese, Russian, Yat—had kicked into overdrive and prevented me from understanding her. Eventually she dragged me into the parking lot and over to a Coleman cooler. "Shrimp," she said in perfectly audible English.

As I had on a market trip before the storm, I kept orbiting back to a vendor of live rabbits and the only non-Asian vendor I've ever seen out here. Gringo, he calls himself. Some shoppers pay twenty dollars for his soft white pink-eyed bunnies to take home as pets; others as dinner. A female vendor who set up beside him also sold his rabbits, but she had killed, skinned, deboned, frozen, and bagged them first. While I stood chatting with the rabbit sellers, a man with a gray crew cut pulled a black, double-cab pickup truck alongside the woman's stand and handed her money through the window for a dozen of her prepared rabbits. I was dying to know where this man had a restaurant, but the vendors told me he was only stocking up for home use.

I've been exploring New Orleans' Vietnamese restaurant culture ever since the first friend I made in the city, John Ales, introduced me to his favorite, Tan Dinh, where we feasted for the first of many times on roasted quail with sticky rice cakes, a squidgy rehydrated jellyfish and herb salad wetted with fish sauce, and springy shrimp paste molded around sugarcane skewers and grilled. Over the years,

I've also celebrated with the seven-course beef dinner at Kim Son on the West Bank, across the river from New Orleans, where another Vietnamese community thrives. I've enjoyed vinegary seafood fondue at 9 Roses. I've learned to crave the *banh mi* of livery Vietnamese pâté, spongy "ham," and hot peppers (and an iced jasmine milk tea with tapioca pearls to go) at Frosty's Café. And I've hung around long enough at the now-closed Pho Quang on Alcée Fortier for a table of fishermen to offer my friends and me a bowl of their off-menu, soft-shell turtle and ginger stew as well as some sashimi, cartilage and all, that they had cut from a bluefin tuna caught that day. ("See why we're so skinny?" one of the men said to me. "Vietnamese eat only fresh food.")

A personal triumph was finally getting to eat from the handwritten, untranslated Vietnamese menu at Pho Son, a short-lived restaurant in Gretna. The first time I tried to order from it, the server refused: "No, that's food for drinking beer." As I already had ordered a café sua da to drink, I settled for a vermicelli bowl.

I adapted with a more proactive strategy on my next visit, taking John with me (he speaks fluent menu Vietnamese) and ordering a round of Heinekens before broaching the beer-food menu. "No, no, no!" the server said, laughing, when I asked for the first item, *tiet canh*. "You can't eat that."

"But I'm drinking beer."

"That's duck blood." She grimaced, pointing to the veins in her arm in case her words hadn't been sufficiently disturbing.

"No problem," I pleaded. "I eat duck blood *all the time*."

But she stood her ground, shaking her head like a mother hiding the candy. And she had an out: every dish on the beer-drinking menu served six people and had to be ordered ahead of time. John and I settled for soup.

On my third visit, the protective staff at Pho Son had no choice but to comply. John had stopped by the restaurant days ahead of time to preorder and then again a few hours before our scheduled dinner. I brought four other friends with me, and we ordered a battalion of Heinekens to start. It took the staff twenty minutes and a dozen round trips from the kitchen to fill our table with wide bowls of sticky rice and opaque vermicelli; platters of fresh basil; minced ginger and red chiles steeping in fish sauce; premixed salt-and-pepper seasoning; lime wedges; and variously sized bowls for dipping sauces and individual portioning.

The most stunning of the forbidden beer-drinking dishes we tried was a room-temperature sort of salad involving thin, ragged slices of rare veal, ginger shards, and herbs, all stuck with a mosaic of sesame seeds. John had ordered us a heap of quail split in half and shellacked with a sweet/salty glaze—Vietnamese Buffalo wings.

And the duck blood, naturally, which was beautiful and paralyzing, like standing on the edge of the Grand Canyon on tiptoes: chewy nubbins of duck, minced ginger, and forest-green herbs held together on a shallow platter in a viscous, cranberry-hued semifluid. If the radiant color appeared unnatural, the blood revealed itself as real by depositing a thick varnish and a metallic aftertaste on the tongue. A server instructed us to stir basil, lime juice, and gingery fish sauce into the blood salad before eating it. "It will make you strong," he said, which we all agreed was duck blood's best selling point.

Duck blood is uncommon in New Orleans–area Vietnamese restaurants, as far as I know, but it beats rabbit, which I've never seen listed on a Vietnamese menu in English; nor have I knowingly eaten rabbit in a Vietnamese restaurant preparation. I want to, especially after witnessing what a commodity rabbits are at the market in New Orleans East. But rabbit seems to be a housebound delicacy in the Vietnamese culture here, something like squirrel gumbo, cowan (turtle) stew, and turducken are to south Lousianians. These dishes rarely, if ever, appear on restaurant menus.

I've been inside a Vietnamese home in New Orleans East—once—but the kitchen was quiet at the time, and I didn't see any rabbits. I was too mesmerized by the gilded, life-sized Sacred Heart of Jesus portrait hanging on a wall in the living room to notice much of anything else.

When I asked the live rabbit seller for Vietnamese rabbit recipes, he mentioned that one of his customers makes an amazing rabbit and herb salad. He phoned the man up and told him that I was willing to pay bank for a portion, but the man declined. I'm used to close calls like this one. Once a young Vietnamese American who responded to a classified ad and bought our old washer and drier told me he knew a woman who sold the city's best *banh mi* out of her house. He gave me a phone number, but it had been disconnected by the time I tried it the following week. And for years I heard about the boiled duck fetuses sold at the Vietnamese market, but I could never locate them. Not until our vacation in Cambodia, anyway.

One afternoon in Siem Reap, after a mystical morning touring the ruins of Angkor Wat, I left Matt in our hotel room to sleep off the "extra happy" pizza that had zombified him the previous evening. (Marijuana is used in some traditional Khmer cooking; tourists from naughtier cultures spend their vacations eating revolting pot pizzas and watching Ping-Pong tournaments on their hotel's three-channel televisions.) I found the town market, where, just as in New Orleans East, mostly women squatted behind their wares: herbs, vegetables, fruits, roots. The market operated in a warm, dank building with a low ceiling and little evidence of an electrical current; I had to bend down to get a full look at the produce in the faint light, and the butchers had no refrigeration in their stalls. I had been sweating fish sauce for two weeks, since we had begun our culinary excursion in Bangkok, and I felt like a soup or a salad ingredient myself as I perspired my way through the offerings.

Near an opening along the exterior of the long, crowded structure, I came upon a counter at which customers were dunking spoons into eggshells cracked open at one end. The vendor confirmed that they were duck eggs. "Make you strong," he said. I guessed from the grayish masses emerging from the shells that the eggs had been fertilized and allowed to develop. Here I was, a gazillion miles from home and finally in a position to crack one of the New Orleans Vietnamese market's secrets. One problem: the Cambodian vendor wouldn't sell me one. He shook his head and pointed to my blond hair. I pulled out five thousand riels, but he couldn't be bought.

The next morning I asked our bilingual cabdriver, Thuong, for help. Thuong had brought me a lotus pod from his home one day so that I could try its green, peanutlike seeds, and he had driven us to an off-the-strip restaurant that specialized in dried fish salads. He understood the culinary tourism thing and even offered to help me eat the duck fetus if it wasn't to my liking.

The egg vendor remained stoic as Thuong explained that I understood what I was ordering. Then he chose an egg from a small pot of simmering water, placed it in a red plastic bowl, and handed it over with a saucer of premixed salt and pepper and some wedges of lime. Thuong cracked open the top of the eggshell and told me to dip my spoon inside. I complied, but instead of scooping up the wet gray goo I had seen others enjoying, my spoon jabbed against an impassable hardness. I took another stab, then another. Confused, Thuong broke the egg all the way open; out spilled a fully formed baby duck, feathers, limbs, bill, and all. The yolk sack that was supposed to form the bulk of the egg's insides was just a pale yellow lozenge at this stage. Thuong pushed back from the counter and withdrew his offer to help me eat it. "That one's too old for me," he said.

I benefited, as I so often have—while eating in New Orleans and traveling elsewhere—from not having had any expectations for my boiled duck fetus. I'd had no idea how big or small, young or old it should be. And so it was no more or less pleasant to learn upon taking a bite that a downy duck fetus tastes mostly like warm, salty protein. It gave some resistance when I chewed, but not enough to sound a crunch. The yolk sac was like organ meat in its richness. In a country where so many children are starving, there's no question about finishing your food. This snack packed additional satisfaction: I'd finally tasted a hidden delicacy of the Vietnamese population in New Orleans East.

. . .

Before Katrina, citizens of Vietnamese heritage formed the largest Asian population in both Orleans and Jefferson Parishes (New Orleans East is in Orleans Parish; most of the West Bank and all of Metairie are in Jefferson Parish). If duck fetuses, duck blood salads, and rabbit salads remained fairly secret, other Vietnamese food traditions had crept into the city's common eating habits, largely because Pho Tau Bay, a restaurant that had been operating in Gretna since the 1970s, had sprouted three additional locations in high-profile spots around the metro area during the few years immediately preceding the storm. While all three satellites have so far remained closed since Katrina, they represented an integration of Vietnamese flavors into New Orleans' popular dining culture that's here to stay.

Pho, often referred to as Vietnam's national dish, is second only to spring rolls as the major food of Vietnamese integration in New Orleans. Pronounced something like "fuh," it's a quick-serve, aromatic beef broth soup presented in deep, wide bowls and consisting of delicate rice noodles and an anatomical survey of beef parts. At less Americanized pho houses, you can find combination-offal pho bowls that testify to the Vietnamese affection for challenging textures. Omosa, or tripe, which looks like the fringe on a cowboy's white chaps, has just a bit of musty stomach flavor and falls apart in the mouth like brittle crepe paper. Navel is milky white and tubular, with a little crunch and a lot of give, like cartilage. Hunks of tendon look like opaque gelatin cubes, taste like nothing really, and feel like pearls of tapioca between your teeth. For straight-up beef eaters, there's pho made with rare flank steak, fatty brisket, eye of round, and meatballs.

The first slurp of pho's clear broth and delicate seasonings may not rock the world of someone whose tastebuds developed while lapping at dark-roux gumbos. But the soup's refreshing shades of star anise, ginger, and cinnamon, overlaid with a float of fresh cilantro, green onion tops, slivered white onion, and fried shallot, tend to haunt novices into returning for more. Accompanying baskets of fresh herbs and bean sprouts, as well as table condiments like hoisin, chile, and fish sauces, are meant to be used in the rigorous sport of at-the-table seasoning. I can think of few more seductive fragrances than the steam that swells when torn basil hits hot beef broth and then discharges its damp, sweet anise essence. When visitors reach the inevitable tipping point and beg for a break from typical New Orleans eating ("Can't we just get a salad and be happy?"), pho is our best recourse.

Once every diner has tweaked her own, no two bowls of pho taste alike. It's often said and written that Vietnamese immigrants feel more at home in south Louisiana than they might in, say, Nevada, because of similarities in climate, topography, and fishing opportunities between this area and their homeland. I would add that New Orleanians have slowly but honestly begun to appreciate Vietnam's food culture, in part because of its familiar precept of seasoning for yourself. Tabasco on red beans, filé in gumbo, ketchup and soy sauce in ya-ka-mein, Tony Chachere's on everything—naturally pho would catch on.

A shared appreciation for mayonnaise-moistened French-bread sandwiches likely also helps. Dong Phuong, a bakery on Chef Highway, is the Vietnamese Leidenheimer's, supplying the pistolettes for *banh mi* sandwiches throughout the area. While the Vietnamese market's early hours prevent all but the most masochistic among us from experiencing it regularly, the Chinese/Vietnamese bakery is a popular destination for culinary adventurers who also enjoy sleep. Here you find eggy coconut-scented breads; squishy ginger-banana candies coated with sesame seeds; coconut-covered gummy worms made from steamed yucca; "newton" bars filled not with fig but with mealy mung beans or stinky lotus paste; cream puffs; savory steamed buns; clear plastic cups filled with sweet soups and custards; and rack upon shelf of other sweets and pastries that contribute to making the world a better place.

All of this since the 1970s. Another sixty years and Vietnamese cooking far beyond pho and *banh mi* could well be as entwined in the local cuisine as Sicilian flavors have become over the past century.

. . .

My duck fetus encounter in enchanting Siem Reap emboldened me to order the delicacy at two Tet celebrations marking the start of the lunar new year in 2006, one held on the grounds of Mary Queen of Vietnam, in New Orleans East on Super Bowl Sunday, and another at a church on the West Bank. Whether responding to my glow of confidence or to the cross-cultural joy we all felt at being able to celebrate anything in our city again, vendors at both festivals complied with my order with smiles and advice on how to eat the eggs. This time all the fetuses were young: no feathers, no beak, no bulging eyes; just fleshy blobs clinging to light, custardy yolks mapped with geographies of brown veins. On the West Bank, the vendor provided a little cup of premixed salt and pepper and more of the biting herb *rau ram* than I could find use for in a year. In New Orleans East, a Vietnamese woman with whom I shared a communal table found the eggs repulsive; she couldn't bear to watch me eat them.

At both festivals, kids raced around mummifying each other in spray foam. Blaring Vietnamese pop music threatened to rupture any unprotected eardrums. Signs advertised "duck pizza," aka duck blood salad, abandoned plates of which sat to coagulate on cluttered tables among emptied Heineken bottles and half-drunk bubble teas. I passed on the duck blood at both parties but enjoyed fresh-pressed sugarcane and tangerine juice, homemade blood sausage, and shrimp-stock soup with cellophane noodles on the West Bank, and a sweet, meaty goat curry, battered and fried bananas, spring rolls, grilled sweet corn, and okra gumbo in New Orleans East.

That last dish, which a middle-aged Vietnamese woman was selling, is not the sort of thing I typically seek out in the Little Saigon of New Orleans East. But while the crowded pho tent across the lot was emitting clouds of star-anise steam and good cheer, her gumbo didn't have a single taker when I passed by. So I stopped. We tried to conduct a conversation as she ladled out my quart, but it didn't go anywhere, what with the loud music, her apparent shyness, and my inability to speak two words in Vietnamese (I can make myself understood with "fuh").

From what I could gather, she had made the gumbo in anticipation of more non-Vietnamese visitors to the Tet celebration than attend most years. The festivities had been talked up more, and in broader forums, than usual—the newspaper, AM radio programs, and everyday English-language conversation. Six months after Katrina, the prospect of such an event in New Orleans East was a rare sign of life and hope. Electricity was only a recent luxury there. The bayou gardens hadn't yet begun to be revived. The market was months from reopening. Nothing on the scale of this celebration had been attempted in similarly flooded areas like Broadmoor, the Ninth Ward, and Mid-City.

Katrina had connected New Orleanians in a way that caused most of us fortunate enough to be here to look at one another's traditions more squarely. The general populace acknowledged that reviving the Tet festival—the biggest holiday of the year in the Vietnamese community—was just as essential as preserving St. Joseph's Day altars, po-boy sandwiches, and Mardi Gras Indian traditions.

I didn't need the woman's gumbo, but I ate it anyway, and it was so nice: a milk-chocolate-brown, okra-slimed broth in which smoked sausage, dark turkey meat, turkey skin, and hard sections of crab were bobbing. It was nice of her to make it, nice of me to buy it, and nice that we could share the moment: a Wisconsin native buying gumbo from a Vietnamese immigrant on the recently dewatered Louisiana floodplain we both called home.

COCONUTS, KING CAKE, AND YA-KA-MEIN

Taking It to the Street

It took me five years to get a Zulu coconut, arguably the most iconic (though uneaten) food of the street on Fat Tuesday in New Orleans. Five years and a connected mailman, though that could go without saying, mail carriers being the obvious arbiters of all things street. It was our two mailmen—the main carrier, Huey, and the Wednesday guy, Powell—who properly initiated Matt and me into Carnival season in the first place. On a Friday afternoon in 2000, the off-duty duo staked out a spot at the end of our block and called us over to share a six-pack as the first uptown parade of the year rolled into place.

At the time we had no context for understanding what was beginning—that roughly thirty more parades, some lasting hours, would clang past our corner over the upcoming weeks. When we moved into the eastern side of a double shotgun near the corner of Constance Street and Napoleon Avenue, our landlord handed us two keys, an operator's manual for the dishwasher, and a handwritten letter extolling the virtues of the house, including its proximity to Ms. Mae's—a twenty-four-hour dive so raw that the aluminum cans of Diet Coke sold there taste of old cigarette ash—and to the start of the uptown parades.

As there's no imagining the adrenaline rush of Carnival until you're in the thick of it, we'd filed the letter with the dishwasher manual. That first parade proved our landlord a sage: with its gaudy colors, creepy masked riders, and deluge of flying beads, all measured by the bass drum's hollow boom, it was a mind-bending, only-in-New-Orleans experience of the limitless sort that continues to hold me so riveted to this city's peculiar movements. In the days following our first Mardi Gras, we could barely absorb the mania and move on with our usual routines. I've no doubt that our lives would be less rich now if we hadn't accidentally moved onto the parade route.

To clarify, Carnival begins with Twelfth Night, the Feast of the Epiphany, on January 6, and concludes at midnight as Mardi Gras (Fat Tuesday) turns into Ash Wednesday, the first dark day of Lent. The length of Carnival season is determined by the same calendar that sets the date for Easter, which means that it lasts between four and nine weeks. An early Mardi Gras is hard on New Orleans' tourism-driven economy, as most Americans are still pretending to keep their New Year's resolutions in early February, but locals don't complain about the compressed partying or the extra elbow room. Mardi Gras may be a Christian holiday, and New Orleans may be a God-fearing town, but Carnival's priorities are purely pagan. At least by Rome's standards.

Mardi Gras merriment in the neighborhoods is not the same Bourbon Street debauchery that the otherwise puritanical networks are so eager to broadcast once a year. On Bourbon Street, women (mostly out-of-towners) score chintzy strings of beads in exchange for baring their breasts. In the rest of New Orleans, and reaching out to the suburbs, the celebration is more of a block party. As long as you don't mind your kids seeing the neighbor staggering or high school baton girls gyrating in sequined bodysuits to the hump and groove of a marching band, it's family-friendly fun. Scoring beads from parade riders takes nothing more than solid eye contact and a strategic smile—at the most, some shameless begging. Often the beads bonk you on the head when you're not even looking.

In 2005—the year of the coconut, to me—Mardi Gras fell on February 9. More than a month before that, around New Year's, Powell and I exchanged tips: he got twenty dollars for delivering our magazines and bills on time, and I got the breathtaking news that he would be riding in the Krewe of Zulu parade. "Float number one, second car, first level, river side, in the middle," he said, rattling off his future position with a choppy formula that New Orleans kids learn before their multiplication tables. "Write that down," he said, but I didn't need to. Anticipation had seared the coordinates into my memory, for hidden in Powell's revelation was a long-awaited promise: a Zulu coconut.

Along with common parade throws—metallic and pearlescent beads, plastic cups etched with a krewe's, or Carnival club's, slogan, and doubloons (aluminum coins printed with a krewe's insignia)—parade riders toss limited specialty throws, like the Krewe of Proteus's red beads with the white seahorse pendant, and the doubloon imprinted with Frodo's portrait that flew from Elijah Wood's pale hand to mine the year he rode in the Krewe of Bacchus parade. It's dog-eat-dog along the avenues, everyone rabid for the rarest throws, even if the best of them will be tossed in the corner to gather dust bunnies come morning. During the all-female procession of the Krewe of Muses, the most treasured throws are high-heeled shoes: glittery red soaps shaped like pumps, furry pumps, plastic pumps, actual pumps painted and glittered. I once ran for cover as a man tackled my willowy girlfriend for a string of white beads punctuated every few inches with battery-powered, blinking, hot-pink pumps. My friend caught the pass even while he sprawled on top of her, and the two shared a shrug as she wiggled her fingers and toes. But even a Muses shoe has nothing on the Zulu coconut.

The Zulus, predominantly a black krewe, began parading on Fat Tuesday between 1901 and 1909, through black neighborhoods, the only neighborhoods in which they were allowed. The krewe's own historians have written that the Zulu Social Aid Club was officially founded in 1916. (Historically, social aid clubs, also called benevolent societies, provided members with financial help with medical bills and burials during segregation, when blacks couldn't get insurance. Italian immigrants formed similar societies.) In 1968, with segregation laws lifted, the Zulus integrated themselves into the city's white Mardi Gras rituals by diverting their parade route down part of St. Charles Avenue, through the Lower Garden District, past Gallier Hall (formerly City Hall), and up Canal Street downtown. The Zulu parade is still the only major parade that travels through the projects and other neighborhoods of the sort that guidebooks are obligated to advise against.

No one is sure when the Zulus began distributing coconuts, but legend places them as far back as 1910 (before that they tossed walnuts). In *Gumbo Ya-Ya: A Collection of Louisiana Folk Tales*, written as part of the Works Progress Administration's Louisiana Writers' Project in 1945, documentarians recorded the following about the 1940 Zulu parade: "The King [Zulu] heaved a slow curve at the proprietor of the saloon and the coconut fell right smack on his head . . . It was an indication His Majesty was drunk."

Back then the coconuts literally were throws. These days, because of a successful damage lawsuit and high insurance premiums that annually threaten to banish the coconuts altogether, Zulu riders usually hand them off delicately, as if passing a relay baton, sometimes with two hands. Tyrannical insurance regulations notwithstanding, the coconuts deserve to be treated with care. Most (though not all) have been skinned of their brown hair, drained of their milk, painted, festooned with feathers, googly eyes, glitter—anything from the arts and crafts department—and slipped into protective plastic bags. Each Zulu purchases his or her own coconuts, and anything else he or she wants to throw (the same policy generally holds for riders in other parades). The Zulu vice president in 2006, Namaan Stewart, told me that he gave away six hundred coconuts the previous year.

While Zulu coconuts are not meant to be eaten, they are emblematic of New Orleans' gastronomic heritage. Cakes, candies, and puddings prepared with freshly grated coconut, as well as ambrosia, a sweet dish of fruit and coconut, are old Creole specialties, included in the area's earliest cookbooks. The distribution on Mardi Gras of food as fun, rather than as sustenance, is in harmony with the spirit of the grand street party.

In the Zulu Proclamation, a droll document that establishes rules of fair play and revelry, His Royal Highness King Zulu, "Beloved Defender of the Gods of Fun and Toleration," decrees the essence of the holiday:

> That in proper consideration for the glory of his regal state and the desires of royal subjects, daily laborers shall be suspended and all impediments that may interfere with public enjoyment shall be removed.

And that's exactly how I've experienced the day, as one of pure and public enjoyment. Whether you're in the street begging for beads, shaking your hips at the curb, searching the back streets for Mardi Gras Indians, or peeling boiled crawfish in a friend's yard, it's impossible to imagine that it's just another Tuesday elsewhere. I write this knowing that plenty of New Orleanians must work on this locally sacred holiday, to keep the rest of us safe and to keep the party going. Matt has never had Mardi Gras entirely free. For him as much as for me, I needed to bring home that coconut.

The fog was thick, the air pale and wet, as it always seems to be on Mardi Gras morning. My usual Zulu viewing post is the corner of Jackson Avenue and Carondelet Street, just a block shy of the parade's crowded, climactic turn onto St. Charles Avenue. Mayor Ray Nagin, whose shiny brown skin and smoothly shaved pate made him a touch foxier that day than is typical among political figures, led the procession on horseback. Next appeared the formidable Zulu Walking Warriors swishing along in grass skirts; mobile platforms ferrying past and present Zulu royalty dressed for a storybook; bass-pumping radio station vans swarming with partiers swigging from Crown Royal bottles; loose-limbed high school marching bands high-stepping and playing tight as a symphony orchestra; teenage girls twirling batons and parasols and busting out of sequined body-suits; cowboys from the West Bank, across the Mississippi; old-timers in Cadillacs. Ninety minutes passed. The sun burned pinholes through the clouds, a boy suffering from diabetes passed out beside his mother, who was selling pralines the size of dinner plates, and a sweating parade-goer beside me begged three coconuts off Zulu float riders—all before float number one, towed by a farm tractor, finally rolled into view.

The coconut glutton to my left represented what had always vexed me about the Zulu parade. Why did he feel so entitled? Before Powell divulged that he would be riding in Zulu, I'd considered a coconut beyond the reach of a Johnny-come-lately like me. Displaying one on the mantelpiece over a nonfunctioning fireplace, the designated coconut resting place in homes all over town, is an honor that ought to be earned not by luck or begging but by bowing to the profundity of the Zulu tradition. Through my years of friendly relations with Powell, a New Orleans native, I had *earned* the right to a coconut. Or at least that's what the priggish aspiring New Orleanian in me believed.

I was wrong. The fourth guideline in the Zulu Proclamation states that "all spectators on the route of King Zulu's Parade are hereby declared Loyal Subjects." The proclamation's generous spirit puts everyone on equal footing, including greedy perspiring men as well as the parade-goer to my right, who screeched that it was her birthday at the approach of every float. Some of the Zulus responded by asking to inspect her ID; her birthdate sufficiently corroborated, they showered her with coconuts too.

At the sight of Powell's float, I pushed past both of them, cleared the police barricades that are meant to keep the crowds at bay but never do, and made up-close eye contact with every Zulu on the first level of the river side of the second car. And then my hopes plummeted to the pavement. Powell wasn't there.

The Zulus mask in blackface, smearing their skin with tar-black paint and outlining their eyes and mouths with zinc-oxide white, a tongue-in-cheek tradition that historically has caused controversy among blacks and self-consciousness among whites (Louis Armstrong donned blackface the year he was King of Zulu; Spike Lee did not). The paint, along with the Zulus' wild Afro wigs, can make it difficult to distinguish individuals from the group as they roll by in a flurry of screams and beads. But Powell's wide features and strong smile would be unmistakable, and he was unmistakably missing. In a last-ditch effort to snag my prize, I abandoned all self-made coconut principles and begged the float's final rider for one of his. I watched him feel around inside a white cloth sack as if searching for a missing sock in a laundry bag and then retract his arm slowly, igniting a glimmer of hope. Ultimately, in a move that underlined the prevailing royalty-serf atmosphere during all Carnival parades, he dangled a string of cheap white beads in my face.

I passed, and so did the float. Ambling around its rear end, heart-heavy and wishing I had worn something more revealing than my lucky black cowgirl shirt, I peeked at the other side. There, at the center of the lower level of the second car, was Powell!

The Mississippi River snakes around and through the Crescent City; you can see it from the tops of bridges and levees and from the riverfront that edges the French Quarter, but mostly its brown waters flow invisibly behind warehouses and loading docks, railroads and protective dikes. However hidden, the river is New Orleans' north in that a good citizen always knows where she is in relation to it. It was my sixth Mardi Gras, and I had become cocky about my local's clout until this humbling realization: I had miscalculated the river side of Powell's float, and it had almost cost me a coconut.

Our eyes locked immediately, and before I could register this turn of luck, both my hands stretched upward. It was a moment frozen in anticipation, like standing at the altar on the brink of "I do"—the marching bands silenced, the crowds parted and vanished, and all sensation in my limbs receded even as I jogged to keep up with the float. There was just Powell, me, and the deep purple coconut that passed between us, heavy with milk, sparkling with gold glitter. And then he was gone.

I admired my coconut from every angle and then slipped it into my backpack. It was barely 10 A.M., a long chapter had closed, and the day had just begun.

. . .

Three months after my hallowed moment with Powell, Matt and I bought our first house, on the corner of Constance and Cadiz Streets, just two blocks from where we'd been renting for nearly six years. Because Matt could complete his medical training anywhere, we had toyed with moving away from New Orleans so often that sometimes even our friends seemed surprised to find us still here. But in the year of the coconut we'd agreed to settle, holding one priority while house-hunting: to stay near the parade route. We'd also aimed to keep a Constance Street address, because Constance sounds like just the kind of street you'd always want to come home to.

While our immediate neighborhood becomes staging grounds, dance hall, horse stables, and picnic area during parade season, it's a wasteland on the ultimate day. On Mardi Gras, the action tends away from the river and toward downtown, and I follow it starting at what I consider to be the break of dawn. The Zulus are always scheduled to roll around 8 A.M., and because there are years in which they actually start on time, I must make it to my usual viewing post earlier than the coffee would be kicking in on a normal workday.

Mardi Gras is a pedestrian holiday. No one who can help it traverses the city by car. Major thoroughfares are closed to traffic, and even when driving legally you're bound to be dead-ended by a parade or a walking procession, possibly for hours. People with bicycles wheel around the city instead. I prefer to hoof it, my routine walk on Mardi Gras morning being my favorite exercise of the year.

The initial stretch takes me up Napoleon Avenue, along which the stillness combined with reminders of the previous evening's parades create the impression of a town recently abandoned by Barnum & Bailey. Errant beads sparkle from tree limbs and telephone lines. Trampled stuffed animals pave the street in dirty colors. Silvery MoonPie wrappers and crushed beer cans glint between the tents and chairs that stand empty on the neutral ground. The only signs of life are those revelers stumbling out of Ms. Mae's, and they are not lively.

Turning down all-important St. Charles Avenue, where the Rex parade will roll in a few hours, is like opening C. S. Lewis's wardrobe. For today, this is where the center of an alternate universe begins. Couples sit in low lawn chairs drinking coffee and reading about Rex royalty in the morning paper. Other couples drink Bloody Marys and would no sooner read on this day than live in Pennsylvania. The avenue is splattered with purple, green, and gold, Mardi Gras' garish, gorgeous colors. Representing justice, faith, and power, respectively, the chromatic trinity decorates striped shirts, hats, banners, flags, painted faces, color-sprayed hair, and everything sold by the kinds of cart-pushing traveling salesmen who peddle carnival toys at parades in every town.

On a sidewalk near the bar Fat Harry's, a man fries bacon and scrambles eggs over a propane flame. A few blocks farther down, within the iron-gated front yard of an antebellum home, a catering crew pulls purple, green, and gold linens over tables that in a few hours will heave with fried turkey sandwiches, potato salad, cold Popeye's fried chicken, jambalaya, pickled okra, and red beans and rice. The aromas of sizzling meat and cheese hang over the corner of St. Charles and Louisiana Avenues, the site of what must be the most profitable Philly cheesesteak truck in the land. Down at the Grocery, a corner store shaded by the avenue's live oaks, Cuban sandwiches will soon be handed to customers through a window.

By the time I reach the corner of Jackson Avenue, a block from my Zulu viewing point, I've already encountered two walking clubs—Mondo Kayo, a Caribbean-themed whirlwind of costumes and beats, and the Dixieland clarinetist Pete Fountain's geezerish but spirited Half-Fast Walking Club. The colors and crowds have thickened, and so have the smoke clouds of outdoor cooking. One year I tried to buy a sausage sandwich from a man furiously barbecuing on an industrial-sized grill he had rolled down from the bed of his pickup truck. He rejected me: "This ain't for sale, baby, it's for my family."

When you're as untethered as I am on Mardi Gras, absent a neighborhood and a fixed destination, eating can be problematic. Families and friends gather for picnics, barbecues, and crawfish boils, but restaurants tend to take the day off; for ramblers, meals are catch-as-catch-can. Mardi Gras may be the only day of the year in New Orleans when food isn't automatically the center of attention. To wit, you cannot buy Carnival's only signature food, king cake, on Fat Tuesday in any of the obvious places. Supermarkets that stay open on Christmas batten down for Mardi Gras; smaller bakeries require you to order ahead and pick up on Lundi Gras (the Monday preceding Fat Tuesday) at the latest.

King cake traditions can be traced to the Middle Ages. The local custom of eating them during Carnival and only during Carnival is a souvenir from France, where they are called *galettes des rois*. You can mail-order king cakes throughout the year, but that doesn't make it appropriate. Patient locals wait until Twelfth Night, the fabled occasion on which the Three Kings brought gifts to the Christ Child; New Orleanians express their piety by having Twelfth Night parties and gorging on these visually terrifying pastries.

A ring of baked dough similar to brioche or Danish, a typical New Orleans king cake is frosted with achingly sweet white icing and further sweetened with decorative purple, green, and gold sugars (because if an oversized coffee cake doesn't personify justice, faith, and power, what does?). Some are braided, some bare. Certain bakeries season with cinnamon, and some offer a filled line. I'm partial to those hiding cream cheese or custard, though the Latin American Union Supermarket sells a superior guava-filled king cake, and a small operation in Baton Rouge uses fresh raspberries to killer effect.

A just-made king cake can be attractive, in the way that anything frosted is attractive to a sweet tooth, but rare is the occasion on which you encounter them so fresh. More likely your store-bought king cake will have stewed in a plastic bag for at least a few hours, during which time it will have taken on the countenance of a clown caught in a monsoon. Such was the ticky-tacky appearance of the first king cakes I ever encountered, during a tasting at the catering company where I worked briefly. I expressed my disgust with each one, and my new colleagues nodded even while they ate every crumb. What I didn't understand in the moment was that the tasting was market research: the company was gearing up to develop its own signature king cake for shipping. I met karma when the boss informed me that I would be the baker's assistant. For the duration of my first Carnival season, I made nothing but king cakes. By Mardi Gras you could have buttered your toast with the patina on my forearms.

I attribute my inflated civic pride and weakness for Mardi Gras in part to this early overexposure to yeast dough and unnaturally colored sugars. Before I ever experienced Mardi Gras, I had a hand in preparing for it, and rather than embittering me, the tedious assembly-line baking somehow fostered within me a sweetness for king cakes, all of them, runny sugars included. The same does not apply to catering, which I soon renounced. I looked back only once, the time I attempted to bake a king cake at home and burned out the motor of my household mixer before I could add the eggs.

Plastic, metallic, or ceramic Baby Jesuses (or other symbolic figurines) used to come baked into New Orleans king cakes, until liabilities like choking and broken teeth frightened bakeries into including them on the side instead, to be pushed into the cakes by their owners. According to local custom, whoever bites into the piece that contains the baby is duty-bound to supply the next king cake, whenever the next get-together may be. For most of the season's parades, my friends Sue and Mario Ceravalo, Georgia transplants whose Mardi Gras fervor is unparalleled, set up lawn chairs and ladders (for better bead-catching), coolers and card tables, on the St. Charles Avenue neutral ground. Often there's a king cake on the card table, amid the Zapp's potato chips and the jambalaya wraps, and it's common to see whoever bit into the baby during the previous parade tramping down the avenue with a fresh one.

This ritual makes for juicy office politics. It's one thing to splurge on a king cake for your friends, another to invest in your coworkers, and so while no king cake in the history of Carnival has ever survived a day in the break room, misers employ all manner of tricks to avoid getting caught with the Baby Jesus. There's the stealth move of pushing it into the underside of another piece when no one is looking. A friend who worked for Mississippi Polymer Technologies copped to once hiding Jesus in his cheek until he could make it to the restroom to dispose of it in secret. Surely babies have been swallowed on purpose. It's always a moral dilemma when you cut into a king cake just at the spot that reveals a few of Jesus' protruding fingers or toes—is that piece technically yours? Even if you haven't touched it yet? Word spreads quickly when a known baby-getter shirks her payback responsibilities.

A freelancer with a lonely home office, I participated in the king cake game vicariously one year by conducting an e-mail Q&A with staffers at the offices of *Gambit Weekly*. A cash-strapped writer admitted to throwing one baby in the trash can when no one else was in the break room. "I'm sorry, but it wasn't even a good cake," she wrote. The paper's production director got two babies in one day, a fact she hesitated to admit because it implicated her in having eaten two pieces in one day. A new staffer from the Midwest was horrified to learn about the custom, not at the thought of shelling out for her coworkers but at having to face king cakes throughout Carnival. "I'm more of a salt person," she wrote in explanation. By Mardi Gras, however, her sweet tooth had blossomed and she had begun sending me run-on odes to the pastry, such as "I like the sweet white frosting and the colored ball sprinkles and fresh dough with custard in the middle."

When the low-carb diet debacle infested my sister Stephanie's office, outlawing king cakes one year, she and I took turns buying, sometimes not waiting to find the baby to try the next one. Our mutual favorite was the "queen cake" from Antoine's Bakery, which looked like a wreath of open-face jelly doughnuts, a jewel of different filling embedded into every couple inches of pastry. We also enjoyed the more effete styles, like the eggy rings from McKenzies Bakery, a local chain that went from indispensable to mythical during my first years here. The final McKenzies location went out of business in 2001, but locals refuse to let its memory die. Every year during Carnival the rumor mill buzzes with tips on where to find former McKenzies bakers secretly working from the old recipe, and every year there's public lament. In 2004, a Metairie resident wrote to the *Times-Picayune* pleading for another bakery to recreate McKenzies' "simple delights": "I long for a homely McKenzies king cake with that fine colored sugar and cherries embedded at the ends (where the baby inevitably was stashed). I call on the king cake retailers of the metro New Orleans area to put a stop to the white-icing-cinnamon-laced madness and offer the public a real king cake."

When we first moved to New Orleans, a McKenzies Bakery operated in a sunny corner space a few blocks down St. Charles Avenue from my Zulu viewing post. A barbecue restaurant has taken its place. I make a mental curtsey now when I pass by, as I did while proceeding downtown on Mardi Gras in the year of the coconut.

In order to catch a glimpse of the Mardi Gras Indians before they remove their hot, heavy costumes around midday, you must beat it downtown before the Zulu parade makes it to Canal Street. Arrive a moment too late and the parade will trap you interminably on what long ago was called the "American" side of town (the area downriver from Canal Street was called the "Creole" sector). In the year of the coconut, my girlfriend Cynthia Joyce and I ran late. We did manage to worm our way across Canal between floats, but then hit an absolute dead end farther downtown, where North Claiborne Avenue meets Basin Street and Orleans Avenue beneath the I-10 overpass. In the 1920s, Louis Armstrong sang "Basin Street Blues," and now we could relate.

While there are worse ways to spend Mardi Gras than watching the Zulu parade twice, once uptown and once downtown, missing the Indians is always a blow. Only three dates in a calendar year guarantee the possibility of an Indian sighting—Mardi Gras, St. Joseph's Day (when they mask after dark), and Super Sunday (during an organized second line)—and then only if it doesn't rain or get too windy. Whenever, wherever, a Mardi Gras Indian is a mystical sighting, like spotting a quetzal in the Costa Rican rainforest.

The custom of New Orleans blacks masking as Indians dates back more than a century. The exact moment of origin is fuzzy. Some histories claim that a Buffalo Bill Wild West Show that rolled through town in the 1880s was significant. More important to the Mardi Gras Indians themselves is that their masking traditions honor the Indians who gave shelter to escaped slaves during the colonial period. Many black families in New Orleans have fairly recent Indian ancestry, though it's not required of Mardi Gras Indians.

The Mardi Gras Indian society is insular, with its own hierarchy, symbolism, nonviolent competition, and chanted folk language, which has been incorporated into traditional New Orleans jazz and hip-hop. The inner workings of the Indians' world, like the universe that revolves around debutante balls, I know only through reading. Visible to the public eye is that tribal pride centers on the Indians' spectacular beaded and feathered costumes, which take all year to sew and cost between $3,000 and $10,000 to complete.

In vocalizing the way in which she perceives New Orleanians to be different from people in other places, an older Creole woman once told me, "We love money, but it's a means to an end for us, not an end in itself." I always remember this when I see the Indians, many of whom live in sections of town where the average household income rests at the poverty line. When I manage to be in the right place at the right time to catch them preening down the street like exotic birds, I feel humbled by the generous gift of their chosen "end."

The roadblock we encountered at Basin Street kept us from finding any Mardi Gras Indians that day, but Cynthia and I hit the bull's eye for lunch: competing mobile trailers dispensing barbecue sandwiches, nachos, red beans, and other quick-serve foods. By this point I was wilting inside my long black sleeves, hungover from the adrenaline rush of the coconut exchange, and worn out from the bead peltings during our crowded walk downtown. One of the take-out trucks had just the remedy: a hot, salty soup of protein, noodles, hard-boiled egg, and green onions that you eat with a fork and call ya-ka-mein, if you can pronounce it.

. . .

One of the more interesting, if indelicate, ya-ka-mein anecdotes I've gathered came from a woman in her early thirties who grew up in New Orleans and is now raising three kids here. When I asked about her experience with the dish, she answered, "You mean ghetto pho?" in reference to the Vietnamese beef and noodle soup eaten with chopsticks. What I liked about the comment is that it put expression to a generalization that's consistent with my further observations: at this moment, Vietnamese pho seems to be more accessible to white New Orleans than ya-ka-mein is, even though the latter has been a fixture in the black community here since . . . a long time ago.

Two historical theories dominate casual ya-ka-mein discussions. The first is that black Korean War veterans returned to New Orleans with a taste for noodle soup and ad-libbed their way to a recipe using available ingredients. The other is that Chinese workers imported to build American railroads, including perhaps the Star and Crescent route between Houston and New Orleans, introduced African slaves to a Chinese dish of the same name, also replacing some more authentic ingredients with products available in this country.

More than a century ago, New Orleans even had a Chinatown, around Tulane Avenue downtown, which is said to have been settled by Chinese laborers who came to the region to replace slaves on plantations following emancipation but then found a better life in the city. Chinatown had a legendary and symbiotic relationship with nearby Storyville, opium (and noodle soups?) from the former supplying prostitutes, jazz musicians, and junkies in the latter.

The century that separates the two most common theories of ya-ka-mein's origins indicates how theoretical they are, and in most instances the dish's modern presentation in New Orleans is too obviously not Asian to point directly to either one. While I've found the Korean War hypothesis to be more prevalent anecdotally, the Chinese connection is more consistent with the places where ya-ka-mein thrives: neighborhood groceries and takeaways whose menus also include po-boys, boiled seafood, and Chinese food of the egg roll and fried rice variety.

Additionally convincing are the Chinese cookbooks published in this country before the Korean War that contain recipes for noodle soups similar in name and ingredients to New Orleans' ya-ka-mein. *Madame Chang's Chinese Cookbook*, published in 1941 in Minnesota, instructs garnishing chicken "yet ca mein" with green onions and half a hard-boiled egg. Philipe LaMancusa, the owner of Kitchen Witch Cookbooks in the French Quarter and an amateur ya-ka-mein scholar, remembers seeing an American-published reference to the soup as old as 1936. Philipe doesn't count those recipes that omit the hard-boiled egg as relevant to the discussion, as that ingredient above all seems to define the prevailing version of the soup in New Orleans.

One could argue that ya-ka-mein is no more indigenous to New Orleans, or significant to a discussion of the city's food culture, than burritos are—that it's just another Chinese dish of cheap ingredients and straightforward technique that Americans have adapted to their own tastes by dumbing down the vegetables and turning up the sodium (others in this category would be chop suey, chow mein, and fried rice). But the soup's prevalence in New Orleans is so extreme and its preparations so various as to suggest that passion as much as practicality drives locals to cook and eat it. And isn't it passion plus practicality that creates a food culture anyway?

Sometimes New Orleans ya-ka-mein cooks strive for an overtly Asian aesthetic, as with the ginger-scented version containing shrimp, chicken, carrots, chopped hard-boiled egg, scant noodles, and a year's worth of soy sauce that I ate at Sal's Seafood in the Ninth Ward. Other times its aesthetic goals are more difficult to pinpoint, as with the "yat cha mein" at Mama's Tasty Foods in the Garden District, which hasn't reopened post-Katrina; despite containing an impossible amount of meat scraps, shrimp, noodles, and vegetables, its most outstanding characteristics were the aroma of fried onions and the film of lard its broth slapped over my tongue.

As with gumbo, red beans, and other dishes whose soul arises from the person making them, ya-ka-mein's recipe is flexible and its variations unlimited. Tammi Fleming, a friend who grew up eating the dish at home in the St. Thomas housing projects and now makes it for her own family of eight, laughed when I asked for her recipe. "You know you're not from New Orleans, because you say 'ya-ka-mein.'" Tammi mimicked me by exaggerating the enunciation of every syllable. Then she pronounced it her way, quickly: *ya*kamee. To her ears, her way sounds like *ya*kamea*t*; I asked her to repeat it several times but never could hear the *t*. For a while after that, I tried to imitate Tammi when ordering, but I ultimately found it easier to get my point across by using my own white-girl voice. I still say it incorrectly, but at least it's a familiar mispronunciation.

"If you're economically challenged, you use end-cut pork chops or chicken," which you boil to cook the meat and make a soup stock, Tammi said. For vegetable flavor, she adds finely chopped onions to the broth. Then she looks at what's in the cupboard for seasoning—maybe some chicken bouillon, garlic powder, onion powder, bay leaves, or seasoned salt; Kitchen Bouquet for color.

Tammi serves her ya-ka-mein smorgasbord-style, "like if you were doing tacos." Everyone gets a bowl of broth and noodles ("it should be regular #4 spaghetti") and then adds soy sauce, hot sauce, catsup, hard-boiled eggs, and chopped green onions to taste—"*Lots* of green onions." You can replace the spaghetti with ramen noodles, she said, but that's more for economics than ethnic accuracy. "The kids are doing it nowadays. Ramen's fifteen cents a pack, so you can't go wrong."

Ya-ka-mein in any preparation is one of New Orleans' most cost-effective pot dishes. Prepared quarts of it cost between three and six dollars; made at home, as a mother to six would know, "it stretches," said Tammi. And yet even among the lowest-priced foods there's an economic spectrum.

When Cynthia saw the ya-ka-mein that I bought from the trailer caterer on Mardi Gras, she exclaimed, "That's what Mr. Earl makes!" Mr. Earl is Earl Antwine, a man synonymous with God's Vineyard, a community urban garden started to benefit the St. Thomas Housing Development Community (where Tammi grew up) before the city closed the housing project in 2000. Among the ventures that sprouted from the garden despite the housing project's demise is the kicking St. Thomas Seven Pepper Hot Sauce, which Mr. Earl and boys from the community produce year-round with peppers from the garden. Cynthia met Mr. Earl while volunteer tutoring some of the youth he mentors; during one of the sessions, Mr. Earl whipped up a ya-ka-mein lunch and sent Cynthia home with leftovers. She's never forgotten how it warmed her.

Cynthia's testimony prompted me to call and ask Mr. Earl about his ya-ka-mein method. "I don't make it like y'all make it," he said.

Come again? I was using my white-girl voice, which in the past had made ordering the dish problematic, and now suddenly someone thought I belonged to a group that *made* ya-ka-mein? It was an honor, but an undeserved one. I stuttered a bit, and then Mr. Earl clarified. His food budget is minuscule; what he doesn't grow he gets from Second Harvesters Food Bank, for which God's Vineyard is an agency. When cooking for the boys he mentors, and often for homeless people in the neighborhood, Mr. Earl makes his ya-ka-mein with canned pork.

If there's such thing as high-end ya-ka-mein, I would say that's what I ate at the sit-down Chinese restaurant Imperial Garden in suburban Kenner (where it was spelled *yakkamein* and resembled a pale vegetable soup), because though it cost less than six dollars, it was served in a nondisposable tureen, by a waitress, with spoons.

While ya-ka-mein is a staple in corner store and takeaway culture and on dinner tables in some New Orleans homes, I relate to it best as street food, probably because of the first version I ever tried, on the sidewalk outside Charity Hospital. Amid a flurry of chopped green onion tops, the halves of a hard-boiled egg gazed at me with yellow pupils from beneath a transparent plastic lid; hot, dark broth dripped down the foam sides of its quart container. Crammed with spaghetti noodles and chips of beef, served with a fork, and heavy as a phone book, this was the ya-ka-mein from the mobile trailer of Mitchell's Fruits & Snacks.

Mitchell's setting belied the quality of the food sold there. Fresh shrimp battered and fried to order. Potatoes cut on the spot for French fries. Homemade pralines. A man selling produce beneath the trailer's awning had much redder tomatoes than the produce truck in my neighborhood. Another man, who once entertained me while I waited with stories about the poor eating habits of physicians, saw me inspecting a package of cracklin'. He grimaced and snatched the bag away. "Look at those cracklin's. They look like they were cooked too long, don't they?" I had lived in the South for barely a year; I nodded, for lack of a more educated response. The man shuffled through the selection and came up with another bag "from a better batch" and opened it for me.

Employees from the surrounding hospitals made up Mitchell's steady clientele back then. Only a fraction of them now work in the flood-wracked area, the patient population having scattered and the entire medical system having been restructured; clinics have closed, hospitals have moved. Since Katrina, no one has been born or died within the old gray building known as Charity, a new truth that's as unnatural for some New Orleanians as the loss of lakefront restaurants and the temporarily silent St. Charles Avenue streetcar line is for others. I hadn't visited Mitchell's for two years before the storm, since Matt had graduated from medical school across the street, and now it was gone. As ungrounded as a mobile takeout trailer obviously is, you never expect an institution like Mitchell's to disappear.

The business wasn't listed in my old phone books under any of the obvious names, so I couldn't try calling. Once a month or so I would drive through the ghostly hospital area looking for the trailer, knowing it was a silly mission. Then one afternoon there they were, Frank and Lucinda Mitchell, parked on LaSalle Street alongside an empty hospital, with a line of customers waiting for food. Okra smothered with Creole tomatoes and ham, black-eyed peas with fried chicken, po-boys with Patton's hot sausage, peach cobbler, gumbo, chitterlings, ya-ka-mein—their menu was as strong as ever. When I asked Mr. Mitchell whether business from the neighborhood could sustain them, he said they were making a go of it. This area was home.

Immediately following the storm, it seemed certain that black traditions in New Orleans were in danger of extinction. I thought of those stunning Mardi Gras Indian costumes as much as of their owners as floodwaters submerged the neighborhoods in which they lived, beaded, and met in the streets. Corner stores and takeaways don't exist without neighborhoods to support them, and the 80 percent of the city that flooded had been inhabited largely by blacks (before Katrina, New Orleans' population was 67.5 percent black). Even in the lower-profile flooded areas that never got mentioned on CNN, ya-ka-mein stalwarts showed little hope of revival. Podner's. Broadview. Cajun's. Soul Food Kitchen on South Claiborne Avenue, where the chef, Dennis Dunn, had spelled his lush version *yat-kai-mein*.

That said, the food scene, particularly the indigenous food scene, began to show signs of regeneration as soon as repopulation began, which is to say relatively immediately (relative to the regeneration of schools and traffic lights, for instance). Hundreds of minor food outlets will never open again, for reasons that are too complex and numerous to list here, but others, like Mitchell's, sprouted exactly when and where I least expected to find them.

During the first post-Katrina Mardi Gras, in 2006, I again met the Zulus down at North Claiborne Avenue and Basin Street, this time on purpose. Because New Orleans' police force had been overtaxed since the storm, and because the city had no resources for funding overtime, Mardi Gras parade routes had been limited to make patrolling them more manageable. One consequence was that the Zulus were prohibited from rolling their floats as far as they usually do—past the Lafitte housing projects (which no one had been allowed to move back into since the storm) and Dooky Chase Restaurant (which at the time was undergoing a slow reconstruction) all the way to their clubhouse on Broad Street (which club members had gutted and restored), through a stretch of town that the floodwaters had desecrated. The prohibition was a spiritual blow.

If ever the Sixth Ward needed some color, this year was it. Fortunately, the city and the Zulus reached a compromise: the Zulus would have to descend from their floats downtown at the Convention Center, but they would be allowed to second-line the rest of the way.

I trailed along behind the foot parade with the digital pocket camera I had purchased the previous day. I'd never had an inclination for visual documentation before Katrina, I suppose because before Katrina I'd never experienced the bottomless loss that fills the empty spaces when a flood washes away so much of the backdrop to your life. My best photos from the day are of the Krewe of Saint Anne parade in the Marigny neighborhood, a masked pageant that makes Venice look like a city of fingerpainters; of a few Mardi Gras Indians whose costumes, and spirits, had survived and risen; and of a man standing beside a catering trailer beneath the I-10 overpass, eating ya-ka-mein with a fork.

This dusty area along North Claiborne Avenue may not have appeared so promising since the 1960s, before the construction of the interstate overhead, when it was a tree-lined promenade of black-owned homes and businesses. Among the hundreds of flooded and stripped cars that wouldn't be removed for another few months, young men embraced upon seeing each other for the first time since the storm, multigenerational families staged reunions, and a fleet of trailer caterers I'd never seen before dispensed red beans, burgers, nachos, and quarts of the hot, salty noodle soup.

In addition to the obvious ways in which 2006 was an unusual Mardi Gras, the scene was curious because in my time here, New Orleans' street food culture had been so patchy that the covert Friday suppers trade had seemed conspicuous in comparison. Before the post-Katrina reconstruction era, which has peppered the city with taco trucks and other roadside entrepreneurs, mobile units like Mitchell's had existed in such limited numbers that people tuned in to the subculture of roach coaches could tick off the regulars on one hand. Lucky Dog carts, more cultural than culinary landmarks, had cornered the market on aboveboard street vending in the French Quarter. Steve Himelfarb (known as the Cake Man) peddled his moist cake slices door-to-door; the Roman Candy man, Ron Kottemann, sold his taffy from a mule-drawn cart; the Pie Lady's call echoed through the streets; and I once purchased a warm, square praline from a man who'd wandered into my doctor's waiting room. But as with ice cream trucks and peanut hawkers at baseball games, you used to have to wait for such treats to find you.

Linda Green is a case study of how post-Katrina configurations enabled—and created the need for—low-profile food merchants to make themselves more available. Miss Linda lost her job cooking for the Orleans Parish school system when the school system all but dissolved in the storm. Afterward, while traditional restaurants struggled through the challenges of reopening, she set up shop inside the music club Tipitina's, where she sold a rotation of homemade hot plate lunches from a makeshift buffet line. Tipitina's is a two-minute walk from our house. I stuck her daily menu to the refrigerator: red beans on Monday, smothered turkey wings on Tuesday, spaghetti and meatballs on Wednesday . . . and ya-ka-mein always.

Miss Linda, whose spelling of the dish I've adopted for this book because I had to pick one, already was known as the Ya-Ka-Mein Lady for her consistent presence at second line parades, where she has sold the soup from the back of her van since 1997. In 2005 she reintroduced ya-ka-mein to Jazz Fest; the dish hadn't been part of the food service there since the festival's earliest years. It's a hoot to see the tie-dyed crowds with their folding chairs and sunburns standing around in the heat eating soup with a fork.

Ya-ka-mein first-timers display a range of reactions. On one end are the easy targets, people for whom the soup connects with some deep-seated sensory memory of hot salt and noodles; on the other are the skeptics, people who stop eating after a few bites and ask what kind of snake-oil salesman makes a living selling bouillon and spaghetti anyway. My first impression registered smack between the two. I didn't drag anyone to Mitchell's to show off my new discovery, but I did appreciate how wholesome it tasted, and I looked forward to the next quart. Whenever I eat Miss Linda's ya-ka-mein, made with tender beef roast, I'm reminded of what I liked about it that first time: the peculiar, comforting look of hard-boiled eggs trapped against a see-through lid; the scalding temperature, which seemed reckless given the scalding temperature outside, and yet correct; the broth, which was salty but multidimensional; and the showering of green onions, such thoughtful freshness.

One of my first questions for Miss Linda on the morning when she sat down with me before the lunch rush at Tipitina's was how to pronounce the dish. She says it just like Tammi does. When I told her I couldn't hear the final *t*, she answered, "A lot of people say that."

Miss Linda learned about food from her mother, who used to cook for St. Francis de la Salle Catholic Church on Sundays. "She didn't allow me to go many places, so I, you know, had to stir the pots." In the 1980s and '90s, Miss Linda's mother had another side job, selling ya-ka-mein at a bar that operated on the corner of Sixth and Danneel Streets, flat by where Miss Linda grew up. She was the original Ya-Ka-Mein Lady.

"You got to really work to get that flavor. Because I know my mom, when she made that ya-ka-mein, I used to sit down and think, 'Lord have mercy, that's good. That's real good,'" Miss Linda remembered. "There's something my mom told me—she told me, 'You might be able to do something with this recipe.'"

On one of my first post-Katrina Sundays back in New Orleans, I attended a social aid and pleasure club all-star second line, organized by a hurricane relief fund for musicians. Normally, on Sundays throughout the year, social aid and pleasure clubs with names like Golden Trumpets, Perfect Gentlemen, Money Wasters, Black Men of Labor, and Devastating Ladies take a turn stepping through the streets accompanied by brass bands and followed by whoever feels moved to join in. But New Orleans had a new normal; aside from a modest funeral second line honoring Austin Leslie, the fuzzy-faced king of fried chicken, who had survived a rescue from his flooded home but then died of a heart attack in Atlanta, the streets hadn't been danced in since before the storm.

Witnessing each club's annual outfit debut is part of a second line's excitement. The men wear dapper suits and matching shoes, the women their Sunday best or better, and the kids miniature versions of both; accessories include elaborate handmade satin sashes, hats, parasols, and feather fans. More than half of the city's fifty-plus clubs were represented at the all-star second line, a sober and celebratory event. Members of each one showed their cross-club solidarity by wearing unflashy black T-shirts printed across the chest with "renew orleans." Still homeless in their own city, many of the participants, as well as the spectators, had traveled from their cities of exile to take part in the culturally vital day.

The procession departed from the Treme neighborhood's Backstreet Cultural Museum, a nucleus for New Orleans' second line culture, after a special jazz mass let out from St. Augustine Catholic Church across the street. The second line and the church weren't connected by any sort of doctrine, but in that section of town, Sunday doesn't ever quite get rolling until mass has ended, whether you partake of the service or not.

I did partake and was slow to exit, not wanting to miss the jazz band's final notes inside. As the all-stars had already departed once I got out, I bought a smoked sausage sandwich on white bread from a man grilling in the bed of his pickup truck and walked with other stragglers down North Claiborne Avenue to meet the procession head-on.

Along the way, a young man stopped me. "What's going on here?" he asked, betraying the accent of a Spanish-speaker.

He stood in the doorway of a home that, judging from the brown smudge still visible on its exterior, had taken on water in the flood. His was the only building around that looked to be inhabited. He said that he lived there and that he was Mexican by birth but had lived in this country since he was a teenager. He had come to New Orleans recently to do construction work.

"There's going to be a second line coming down this street," I answered. "Do you know what that is?"

"No. Is it like a parade or something?"

"Sort of. It's like a foot parade with lots of music and dancing."

"Is it Mardi Gras already?"

"Sort of." Technically Mardi Gras wouldn't be for another month and a half, but it *was* Carnival season, and weekend parades would begin rolling soon. This wasn't one of them, though. I explained to him that second lines are a Sunday tradition in New Orleans. This was the first big one since Katrina.

"Is it religious?" he asked.

"Sort of. It started after mass . . ." But then I tried to imagine the pope at a second line. "No," I amended. "Second lines are spiritual but not religious, really."

"I didn't think so," he said. "Because I keep seeing people with beer and stuff."

I thought back to when I'd been that new to New Orleans, back when I'd believed that beer and church were mutually exclusive. I'd also asked people to describe second lines to me. But the explanation doesn't fit entirely into words. Music and dancing in the street sounds like it could happen anyplace a boom box meets a six-pack.

Like Mardi Gras in the neighborhoods and crawfish boils in backyards and a million other place-specific cultural events around the world, a second line is something you begin to understand only once you're in the thick of it—once you've felt a tuba's moan fill out your chest, a trumpet screaming between your ears, and a snare drum tickling the soles of your feet into stepping in directions you never knew existed. And I mean *begin* to understand, because the culture of social aid and pleasure clubs is like the culture of the Mardi Gras Indians: there for the world to see, feel, and even participate in for a few days out of the year but a true lifeblood to a much smaller community the rest of the time.

I ran into the construction worker later that afternoon, as the largest second line I'd ever witnessed carried me back up North Claiborne Avenue, in the shadow of the I-10 overpass, past the spot where five months earlier a photographer for *Time* magazine had captured the image of an anonymous dead man floating facedown in the floodwaters. The Rebirth Brass Band blew so hard I thought our hearts would rupture. All around people waved Crown Royal bottles, jumped and cheered to the horns and the beats, danced on the roofs of flooded cars, and yelled into their cell phones to displaced friends who couldn't make it, "I never seen so many people. New Orleans is *back!*"

"See?" I yelled to the construction worker, who stood beneath the overpass drinking a beer.

"Yeah, I see it," he said.

Alcohol is as much a part of second line culture as you imagine it would be in a subtropical town where the law allows drinking in the street. Empty Heineken bottles and a beer cooler are among the artifacts on display at the Backstreet Cultural Museum. This helps explain why ya-ka-mein is such an appreciated commodity at second lines and, so I learned from Miss Linda, in barrooms. She also calls the dish by an easily pronounced nickname: Old Sober.

"It does something to your body inside, it makes it feel *good*. I've had people come to me and say, 'Miss Linda, thank you so much.' You know, they drank and drank and then they came and got that hot soup, and it sobered them up. It was able to help them get home," she told me.

Ya-ka-mein as a hangover helper may account for the punishing amount of sodium in so many versions, as well as the sealant of lard on the one at Mama's Tasty Foods. I use the same palliatives, only they're called bacon. Adding hot sauce additionally clears the head. Miss Linda's recipe calls for a dab of Tabasco. "There's something about that Tabasco sauce," she said. "That special ingredient they have in there connects with mine, and it's delicious."

Miss Linda had run out of ya-ka-mein by the time my path crossed her van at Yellow Pocahontas Big Chief Tootie Montana's funeral second line in July 2005, one of my final sterling pre-Katrina memories of New Orleans. It felt like we were standing on the surface of the sun, and people were apparently needing soup.

Mr. Montana, known among Mardi Gras Indians as the "chief of chiefs" for his cross-tribal leadership and magnificent costume designs, had suffered a heart attack while addressing the city council in defense of his fellow Indians, whom officers of the New Orleans Police Department had reportedly harassed the previous St. Joseph's Day night. He was pronounced dead soon after at Charity Hospital. The spectacle at his funeral second line, with dozens of Mardi Gras Indians in attendance—from outfitted toddlers to feathered men in wheelchairs—was as historic as his death.

The mood was consistent with that of other funeral second lines I've attended: somber up front, near the horse-drawn hearse that ferried his coffin to St. Louis Cemetery No. 2; trancelike in the middle, with Indians and civilians beating tambourines and chanting together, "Golden crown, golden crown, Tootie Montana got a golden crown"; and euphoric farther back, where brass band musicians blew their respect through their horns.

Of course one of the bands played "When the Saints Go Marching In," the most clichéd and meaningful song in New Orleans' modern history. Traditionally a funeral march, the song now adapts to whatever situation it's played in. Louis Armstrong turned it into a pop tune in the 1930s. They blast it at Saints football games as a rabble-rouser. It's a church song and a tavern song: few jazz bands in either place get away with skipping it—not that they would want to. If a New Orleans compilation CD exists without at least one version, I bet nobody buys it.

Whatever the context, the song always makes me feel fatalistic and weepy about living in this city. People love New Orleans like they love a person. After Katrina, I heard more than one New Orleanian compare watching the city die to losing a parent, a sentiment I gratefully can't confirm from personal experience. When I hear the refrain "I want to be in that number," I always sing along. The lyrics limn the entirety of my attachment: I *want* to be here, in *this* number. "When the sun refuse to shine," as the song goes. "When the moon turns red with blood . . . When the trumpet sounds the call." When the coconuts go to bums. When the king cake sugars run. And definitely at the second line where the ya-ka-mein sells out.

LE BOEUF GRAS

Food Radio, and an Unwitting Mentor

There is no single Mardi Gras. While the spirit of oneness persists throughout the neighborhoods, the particulars of your own experience on that day are as individual as your upbringing. Maybe you take the town by foot, as I've done, or maybe you hole up and watch old salts spin the history of Carnival on public television. You might bicycle to the R Bar after dropping acid with your coffee and then orbit around that corner of the Faubourg Marigny until the Krewe of Saint Anne parade swallows you into its mellow frenzy. Or you might stick uptown for the mother lode of throws launched from the long, boxy floats of the afternoon truck parade. If you partook of the all-night Lundi Gras show at Tipitina's, you'll probably spend the day recovering; if you have small children, you'll probably be run ragged protecting them from head contusions; if you have a French Quarter balcony, you probably won't leave it; if you're a college student on spring break, or repressed, or a pervert, you'll probably see a lot of skin on Bourbon Street; and if you celebrate in the suburbs, you'll probably mention how happy you are not to be inside the feral city.

Most people seem to acquire a Mardi Gras tradition and stick to it. I had to experience the Zulu parade only once to develop a loyalty that dictates how I want my Mardi Gras forever to begin. How it ends has been less certain; later in the day, the rush tends to drop off, as it used to on Christmas once we'd torn open the presents and eaten all the gravy by midafternoon. On my first few Fat Tuesdays in New Orleans, I slumped home before dark, irritable and hungry, and went to bed, because I sure as hell wasn't going to work.

Then one year I discovered a low-profile boeuf gras tradition that met my desire for a more satisfactory, celebratory ending. Deriving from Latin, the word *carnival* means "removal of meat," which is what stricter Catholics do during Lent to mark the forty days that Christ spent in the desert without sustenance. Catholics in New Orleans, a city so close to water it sometimes becomes one with it, torture themselves during Lent by limiting their flesh intake to seafood. But not, in theory at least, before first getting meat out of their systems.

In his book *Lords of Misrule*, the British-born New Orleanian James Gill writes that before the turn of the last century, a live fatted bull—the literal boeuf gras—walked through the streets with the Rex parade. (He also writes that while the bull was meant to provide the last meal before Lent, it actually was eaten, heretically, on Ash Wednesday.) The Carnival club Rex has since replaced the live bull with a gigantic white papier-mâché bull surrounded by float riders masking as chefs. Before I got the hang of interpreting parade float themes, which are sometimes mythical, sometimes wistful, sometimes sarcastic, sometimes political, and still sometimes incomprehensible, I liked the boeuf gras float best because it seemed to present the only coherent idea in all of Carnival. Few things are more forthright than a good steak.

Few steaks are more forthright than the ones at Crescent City Steak House, a Mid-City restaurant circa 1934 that established itself as a harbor for beef back when that was every steak house's chief source of pride (as opposed to, say, million-dollar wine cellars, hidebound appointments, and dancing girls). Crescent City's hexagonal tile floors, white tablecloths, and practical chandeliers suspended from drop ceilings set the classic, endangered tone of a New Orleans neighborhood restaurant. The room's single design flourish is the curtained booths built along one wall. There must be numerous uses for such privacy in a steak house, though laboring over your order is not among them here, as the menu selection fits on a single page and amounts to some steaks, some potatoes, some vegetables, and a blistering sauce of butter, parsley, and al dente garlic that's known in New Orleans as bordelaise.

Opened by the late John Vojkovich, a Croatian immigrant, and maintained essentially as is by his survivors (an extensive post-Katrina renovation changed almost nothing), Crescent City subsists on locals, and especially so on Mardi Gras afternoon, when the room transforms into a festive boeuf gras. In the year of the coconut, 2005, once the parades had wound down, four friends and I tried out the tradition, dipping our spoons into a cereal bowl of bordelaise sauce to dribble over steaks that challenged the strongest of tooth among us. Ribeye, porterhouse, T-bone, sirloin strip—while the beef was prime in grade and flavor, we were grateful for our incisors. Grateful also for onion rings, cottage fries, shoestring potatoes, yolk-orange spinach au gratin, whole cooked button mushrooms, warm bread for sopping up more of the bordelaise, and a sturdy red wine to ease us into the late afternoon fade.

At a certain moment someone on a cell phone cried out to the dining room that a tribe of Mardi Gras Indians was moving up Broad Street. We watched for them through Crescent City's blinds, to no avail; it was but a minor disappointment, as the scene within the restaurant held its own fascinations. A foursome masking as copper-faced Oompa-Loompas (the original, pre–Johnny Depp species) sat in one corner; the president of the Zulu Social Aid and Pleasure Club (so his sash read) ate with his family across the room. In the center, around a succession of pushed-together tables, gathered a civilized bacchanal—a large party of middle-aged men filling out their golf shirts, about half as many women looking tolerant but tired, and at the head their host and the reason we had decided to partake of the boeuf gras that year too: Tom Fitzmorris, restaurant critic, cookbook author, message board moderator, newsletter writer, fiction dabbler, choir member, and my best radio friend.

. . .

For a long time I had more radio friends than actual friends in New Orleans. My golden rule for working at home was no daytime television. No matter how sensational the subject matter, no matter how insidious my sloth, no exceptions—and especially not the Food Network, the most pornographic channel of them all. I neglected to freelancer-proof the radio, though, and 1350 WSMB soon became my social unit. Clark Howard, Laura Schlessinger, Art Bell, Phil Hendrie, Dean Edell, Bill O'Reilly, whoever was on—they followed me into the bathroom when I showered, they strolled with me around the Audubon Park loop, and they kept me company during long, lost hours in the car hunting down catfish in Marrero, pupusas in Kenner, and pizza in Westwego, always stubbornly without a map.

When Matt returned from class or work, he could tell whom I had been spending time with by my mood—frugal, self-righteous, hypochondriachal, anxious about shadow people. One day he accused WSMB of stealing my soul. I listened more defensively after that, switching over to National Public Radio on FM when I heard his key in the door, or before exiting from my car, in case he drove it next. Unless it was Tom Fitzmorris's *Food Show;* I didn't need to hide that. Call it enabling or love, Matt always encouraged my radio friendship with Tom. He even abetted my celebrity stalking of him on a few occasions when I wanted a visual. Once, when Tom announced that he was broadcasting from an Indian restaurant in our neighborhood, Matt wandered over and engaged him in an on-air conversation about the acrimonious flavor of acorns so that I could take a long look.

Over time, I made real friends who didn't get it—my AM radio habit or my Tom fixation. They performed the same eye-roll when I began a sentence "Tom says" as when I related a valid point made in the No Spin Zone. "When do you find the time to listen to that trash?" they would ask me. "When you're working," I would answer.

If I may self-analyze, my indiscriminate predilection for talk radio stems from my hypersensitivity to music with lyrics, which taps too easily into my shallow emotional font. Thirty minutes of the classic rock station and the rest of my day is swallowed in reminiscence. Don't get me started on WWOZ, the peerless, always-struggling FM station in New Orleans that plays mostly local music. Even before Katrina turned us all into blubbering boosters, it wrecked me to listen. In contrast, the incessant banter of talk radio curbs deep introspection; the ranting, pontificating, and preaching of others mercifully silences the voices in my own head. Radio advice shows are the best, the sadistic voyeurism into other people's problems falsely, yet deliciously, minimizing my own.

The depth of my talk-radio dependence hit home once when, after a week of worrisome symptoms, I found myself at Diagnostic Imaging Services, shivering in a papery gown, on the verge of rolling inside the penne tube of a pulsing MRI machine. A technician clamped a pair of globular headphones over my ears, conveniently muffling the news that he would have to roll me back out midway through the procedure to inject cold radioactive dye into my arm. Then he asked for my station preference. It was after 4 P.M. Tom's show was on. "WSMB, please," I said. "What's that?" he asked. The MRI showed my brain to be normal, but the consensus was that my radio habits weren't all that healthy.

At the beginning of my listenership, Tom's show served a specific and educational use. Having landed a job as a restaurant critic within months of moving to perhaps the most provincial and food-driven city in the country, I was desperate to tap into the minds and palates of people who had been eating here forever. What luck, then, that New Orleans also was the sort of town that supported three hours of food banter on the radio every day.

Like every public personality, Tom has sycophants and critics, the latter being the louder and more persistent voices, as is usually the case with negativity. Tom's opponents doubt his professional ethics and pick apart the minutiae of his opinions: his taste in restaurants, his halfhearted attempts at maintaining anonymity when dining out, his pronunciation of *poor boy*, his reluctance to try brand-new restaurants, his choice and treatment of advertisers on his radio show.

But it wasn't the niggling details of Tom's public existence that met my needs early on; it was his existence itself. The theme of Tom's radio program is food, but he is its main character, and he is above any other title a New Orleanian. Included in Tom's favorite conversation topics are gumbo, his high school, and great New Orleans people and places that don't exist anymore. He talks about what he had for dinner last night, every day. He refers to his mom's red beans, as a standard. And he loves his city, to a fault. If a native exists who doesn't hold these same interests, I haven't met him. Obsessively listening to Tom, and to the community of everyday eaters who called in to his radio program, became my crash course in New Orleanianism.

The *Food Show*'s food content isn't as broad as it could be, considering the fifteen-plus hours per week that it airs (at least). While any food-related topic technically is fair game, and while listeners do sometimes call for vacation-dining recommendations in Napa Valley or for instructions on where to purchase kaffir lime leaves, mostly the conversation narrows in on local flavors, restaurants, and history (with a big exception for wine, one of Tom's obsessions).

Looking back, Tom's show has such focus that it introduced me to just a parcel of New Orleans, *his* New Orleans. Your New Orleans is as individual as your Mardi Gras. Tom couldn't tell me where to find the best Big Mama–style gumbo any more than he would be in the acid-dropping group on Mardi Gras morning. Rather, he recommended the red beans at Dunbar's, the chicken and andouille gumbo at Bozo's, and the boeuf gras at Crescent City Steak House. Because he was the unwitting mentor to my early New Orleans education, I followed almost every tip.

When Tom falls short in his coverage of the local food scene, his radio listeners, and those who post on a Web message board he used to moderate, let him—and, by extension, me—know about it. It was a *Food Show* caller's tip that first steered me to Hillbilly Bar-B-Q, an instantaneously mythical cinderblock palace of smoked meats out in the suburb of River Ridge where the pulled pork doubled my quality of life. Another caller gave me Taqueria Mexicana, in Terrytown, and my gratitude grew with every weekend bowl of posole. Six message board posters responded to my query for an Italian baked oyster recipe during my post-Katrina exile in New York City, and I was significantly less homesick after making it.

Tom looks like that uncle who you can't imagine ever was a teenager but who simultaneously never ages: perpetually graying but not yet gray hair and beard; dark-frame eyeglasses that ride to the midline of his nose when he talks; an ample waist; a Tabasco tie. He's shaped like a bon vivant, but one with height on his side. By New Orleans gourmand standards, he's a big man but not a fat one. He'd like to be thinner, if only he could keep away from the doughnuts. When you sing in the church choir, it's impossible to avoid doughnuts.

Tom (he's been my radio friend for too long for me to refer to him more formally) doesn't always choose the Tabasco tie, but he usually does wear one. It makes him crotchety to see underdressed diners at fine restaurants, and he admits to looking like a salesman next to the younger, pierced-and-tattooed deejays at the station (WSMB is owned by a conglomerate that also runs a variety of other local stations, AM and FM). If he could get away with it, he'd wear a jacket to Jazz Fest, where he abhors the vista. "If I can go the rest of my life without seeing a fat middle-age guy in a U-shirt or his equally out-of-shape girlfriend in a halter top, my happiness will have been incremented distinctly," he wrote in "The New Orleans Menu Daily," an on-line newsletter and one of numerous means besides his radio show through which I've entered Tom's world.

The campus newspaper of what is now the University of New Orleans published Tom's first restaurant review when he was twenty-one years old, and from that foundational piece grew a long career in food journalism. He's in his fifties now. The review column has traveled through numerous New Orleans publications over the decades, most recently landing in *New Orleans City Business* and on his own Web site. Tom believes, and frequently reiterates, that his is the longest-running single-author weekly restaurant review column in the world, though he admits there's no way to prove it.

In 1997, the year I learned to surf the Internet and two years before I figured out how to e-mail, he compiled some of his writings into the "Menu Daily," which he circulated via e-mail for free until Katrina, after which he asked subscribers to begin paying a self-set fee. I offered twenty-five dollars and received two years of unlimited access.

These days the "Menu Daily" includes passages from a food almanac; a Q&A sidebar; a rated restaurant report; an original recipe; a diary entry in which Tom divulges more about his personal life than I tell my mother about myself (sorry, Mom); restaurant and event advertisements; a profile of an extinct restaurant; the next segment of Tom's fictional work, "Back to the Wall"; several links to his other food-related projects (Eat Club dinners, a Mediterranean cruise, a cookbook); and his signature sign-off, "I hope you have a great New Orleans meal today!" Lately the newsletter has topped five thousand words, not including sidebars. It's not all original prose, and it's not always spell-checked, but that doesn't keep it from intimidating some of us who call five thousand words a chapter. It's always startling to meet someone in New Orleans who doesn't know where Tom likes to eat red beans, as the accessibility of his experiences and opinions—and his confidence in publicizing them—is comparable to the political platform of an active campaign.

For years before I met Tom, I knew details about his life that some people would file under "too much information." I found every tidbit fascinating. I knew that he was born on Mardi Gras. He weighed 232 pounds on January 1, 2005. He didn't vote in the last presidential election, though he did posit that Kerry made Nixon look like a liberal. He bought a PT Cruiser. He loves traveling by train. He and his wife, Mary Ann, spent their wedding night at the English-manor-elegant Windsor Court Hotel; they returned on a recent anniversary and watched an episode of *Jackass* on television before falling asleep. Until recently, Tom occasionally still wore a retro Scout uniform, while attending something called a camporee with his son. He had a dog named Popcorn. Eating popcorn gives him blood-pressure headaches. Eating escolar gives him intestinal distress. His left big toe is arthritic.

At the height of my anonymous, media-enabled relationship with Tom, I sometimes spent more than four hours a day in his world—three listening to his radio program and an hour or more reading his newsletter and scanning his message board. My immoderation went uncensored, but not unnoticed, by those closest to me. Stephanie busted me once for listening to the *Food Show* while practicing my warrior pose. "Tom Fitzmorris is *not* yogic," she said.

Indiscriminate talk-radio dependence and desperation for information were the main reasons for my *Food Show* routine, but I wouldn't have wasted my time if Tom hadn't been a skilled radio entertainer. Goofy, sure, but capable of carrying it off. He's a radio geek himself, listening to recordings of antique programs, frequently mentioning radio trivia, and lowering the bass on his voice for dramatic effect. He has filled in as a pinch-hitter host during nonfood-related times of crisis, such as during the mass evacuation in anticipation of Hurricane Ivan in 2004. While the rest of us hunkered down or fled the city by automobile, Tom kept us company by discussing the weather (another passion) and fielding phone calls from anxious drivers along the Gulf Coast. He kept me awake all the way to Memphis.

Tom's radio talents were never so apparent as when WSMB's management instituted a format change and replaced all my other radio friends with "progressive talk" shows (Tom kept his 4 P.M to 7 P.M time slot). Despite the fact that my sociopolitical beliefs tend in a direction that supports progressive talk, I could not listen long. Solid, well-adjusted, responsible conversation does not make the best radio. Controversy and egomaniacs make the best radio. Cases in point: the supreme successes of Rush Limbaugh, Laura Schlessinger, and Howard Stern; also, to a lesser extreme, Tom.

At this moment in time, the *Food Show* is the greatest literal example of the ongoing conversation about food, cooking, and dining in New Orleans that makes this such an exhilarating place to eat, and

Tom is the most consistent, accessible, and inexpensive medium for that conversation. If I were to write his obituary, I would have to credit him for being, after big eater and radio nerd, a cultural philanthropist. And then I would have to run like the wind from his many detractors, who would pummel me.

In writing so fondly about Tom, I risk losing credibility among my peers, both literary and culinary. Anecdotal evidence suggests that even the few who don't have contempt for Tom prefer NPR. "I didn't know anyone could milk so much out of a lousy career, resting on his laurels," one friend in the restaurant business railed. But New Orleans itself rests on its laurels; the city's fusty, crumbling, blinkered tendencies have always been among its greatest weaknesses and defining beauties. That Tom reflects these characteristics with his old-line rituals, his formal dress, his nostalgic bent, is, I think, precisely why he has been able to build a career here.

His knowledge of New Orleans food and restaurants is encyclopedic, of a size and depth you might expect from an academic wheezing through his final volume rather than a professional windbag raising teenagers. With or without eloquence (he accomplishes both), he will report which hamburger joint, on which back-street corner, offers the city's best-tasting hot dogs; then he will report on how the hot dogs are cooked, where the owner went to high school, and what the burger joint looked like thirty years ago. And he can do so, I'm guessing, without consulting his notes first, before his second café au lait of the day kicks in.

Tom's capacity for yesteryear is so strong that he must edit his reviews by lopping off their first paragraphs. "The first thing that comes to mind is all the history: what restaurant used to be there, what the building was once, who the chef was twenty years ago. But nobody gives a shit. It's all buzzing around in my mind and I have to get rid of it," Tom told me once.

Not everyone appreciates this particular talent. A recent post on a competing local food message board launched a familiar assault: "Fitzmorris is losing it! We need a young, more energetic person to replace that tired old hack!" The poster had fallen into a common misunderstanding, and in so doing failed to grasp the most basic and interesting fact about Tom's position: he's essentially self-employed. No one ever hired him to be the most prolific—and in some circles the most powerful—food commentator in the city, and anyone can try to dethrone him. Before Katrina, he told me that his show brought in 50 percent of the radio station's ad revenues, a figure that speaks to his economic impact on the city's restaurants as well as on the station's coffers. Outside the radio gig, he's an independent operator. No time clock, no expense account.

Despite the length of Tom's experience with the food and restaurants of New Orleans and the at-your-fingertips nature of his work, local media rarely consult him as an expert, with the exception of the publications for which he writes. While researching for this book, I couldn't find a single full-length article published locally about his first cookbook in more than twenty years, *Tom Fitzmorris's New Orleans Food,* which he completed during his Katrina-enforced exile in Washington, D.C.

Tom is tepid, sometimes even vicious, regarding other local food media. Once, during the *Food Show*, he began a thought with "That lady at *Gambit* . . . ," meaning me. My reflexes were quick: I switched off the radio, frightened of what would come next.

I considered holding back from writing about him too. I thought about the people who don't respect him, and who might not respect me by association. I thought about how I talked Matt and Stephanie into attending one of Tom's Eat Club dinners once, and about how the food wasn't very good, and about how Tom skipped our table while making the rounds even though we'd made sure to save him a seat. I thought about how much air time he gives to unworthy restaurants, which I won't name here, because many of them pay him for it. I thought about how he sometimes snaps at his callers, and how he used to censor the message board, and about how he gives iced-tea drinkers a hard time, not bothering to ask whether they aren't allowed to drink or have admirably quit drinking alcohol with dinner. I thought about how people who have lived in New Orleans longer than I have say that Tom makes stuff up, that he inflates, and that he demands free meals when he dines out.

But then I remembered a radio moment during which Tom

admitted that his sensitivity level is comparable to a cold toilet seat. I found this confession, and others like it, endearing. Most of the time he manages to balance his egocentricity with just enough self-scrutiny to keep this fan.

And anyway, if I didn't credit Tom for his huge contribution to my New Orleans culinary and cultural education, my conscience would probably force me to dedicate this book to him instead, which would be weird. Or I would have to add something like this to the bibliography: "Tom Fitzmorris, *Food Show*, 'Menu Daily,' message board, two Eat Club dinners, plus all callers and posters. New Orleans, LA, almost every day 1999–2006." And that wouldn't explain the half of it.

It took me about three years to hear it all. New Orleans is different from other great American food cities, like San Francisco and New York, where new restaurants open and prosper like dandelions. There's always movement here—native son Adolfo Garcia opens an Argentinean steak house, Todd English lends his name to a Harrah's Casino restaurant, the Windsor Court Hotel chef serves risotto with white truffle ice cream and Parmesan foam—but it's a bigger news day when Galatoire's fires a beloved waiter, or Casamento's reopens for high oyster season, or a former nurse sets up a bake sale in an annex at Café Reconcile. While keeping up on selected openings and changes in the dining scene, Tom plays to the New Orleanian tendency toward reminiscence and stagnation, and so after a while a fanatical listener begins to hear the same stories twice . . . okay, a half-dozen times.

As my knowledge of New Orleans and its food culture deepened, my dependence on him waned, and I began to think of Tom less as a celebrity than as another important person in my life. Which was odd, because he wasn't a person in my life; he was a *voice* in my life. I hadn't even introduced myself during the boeuf gras. No longer so intimidated, and wanting to confirm some facts before writing about him, I e-mailed and requested a tête-à-tête. That Thursday we shared a table at Philip Chan's Asian Cajun Bistro.

Nothing happened, really. It wasn't like meeting Beck, which I imagine would be life-changing because we'd run away together. And it wasn't like meeting Ernest Hemingway, which I imagine would have sucked because he would have been too wasted to talk. It went as I imagine meeting any everyday idol would go—some chitchat, some sizing up, some uncomfortable silences. Tom wore a yellow tie with colorful daisylike flowers on it. He didn't drink any of his water, only beer and wine. He used his fingers a lot when he ate. So did I.

He seemed perplexed at first by why I'd wanted to meet him, but he politely answered my questions, repeating some stories I'd already heard or read (my shame, not his; when a man publishes his journal and you read every detail, it's your own fault for being overinformed). The chef sent out course after course—stir-fried andouille and snap peas, frog legs with peanuts and asparagus, black rice with crawfish tails, lobster bisque. When we finished, the waiter refused to bring a bill. Tom handed over his credit card and told him to charge a big tip to it; he refused to take any money from me. And then it was over. I went home without an autograph.

Our uneventful get-to-know-you dinner paved a smooth road to my real coming out two weeks later, when I attended another one of Tom's Eat Club dinners, this time alone. None of my friends would commit to dropping sixty-five dollars on the promise of an audience with Tom and several courses at Tujague's restaurant. It didn't matter; I finally felt comfortable enough with my maturing inner New Orleanian to mingle with Tom's other listeners and readers without any hand-holding. At our first Eat Club dinner, Matt, Stephanie, and I had felt like the albino alligator at the aquarium downtown: isolated, cagy, of slightly embarrassing DNA. We hadn't spoken to anyone. But now I was eager to know whether Eat Clubbers and I had anything in common besides Tom. After all, these were people I had been trying to emulate for nearly six years.

Upon entering Tujague's wood-paneled, tile-floored dining room, I took the first solo seat available that wasn't beside a man wearing a tuxedo shirt and a bow tie (some in Tom's Eat Club crowd follow his fashion lead). This put me at the head of a long table, beside a middle-aged man in a golf shirt who coincidentally was also my neighbor in Uptown. Across the table from us sat three suburbanites. All of us turned out to be AM radioheads, and we wasted no time before commiserating about WSMB's new format and the loss of all our old radio friends. Tom visited with us during his rounds, swinging a wine bottle in each hand, but it wasn't a highlight. I'd found my community.

Dinner itself was classic Tujague's, beginning with two styles of shrimp rémoulade, one white and tangy, the other deep orange and peppery; a cup of seafood and sausage gumbo reinforced with a weighty shellfish stock; hot, downy, New Orleans–style French bread; and the homely but remarkable house specialty of salty boiled beef brisket with orange horseradish sauce. Next came a round of poorly executed main courses served family-style, followed by grasshopper cocktails and glasses of coffee and chicory with hot milk.

The air inside Tujague's is chewably thick with history, and if it's sometimes more palatable than the crawfish étouffée, oh well. Established before the Civil War, Tujague's is a New Orleans institution like the Crescent City Steak House and Tom are New Orleans institutions: no matter whether you like them, New Orleans would be a little less New Orleans if they weren't here.

Tom sent out an e-mail blast soon after Katrina to say that his family had evacuated to Atlanta and would be moving temporarily to Washington, D.C., where his son and daughter would begin the school year. I had been checking his message board constantly since the storm, the error screen a reminder that New Orleans had become an unknown place. Picturing Tom working in D.C. was like picturing Tujague's in Las Vegas—possible but all wrong.

I added Tom's hurricane diary to my daily Web route, the Web being the new New Orleans for evacuees with access to computers. On day nine after the storm, Tom drove back to the Northshore briefly for a look at his house, which hadn't flooded. On day twenty-two, after having spoken with a wholesale seafood distributor, he announced that Louisiana seafood was safe to eat. On day twenty-four, the message board went back up and regular posters gave one another virtual hugs. At four weeks, Tom urged everyone to calm down about Ruth's Chris Steak House (the New Orleans–founded company moved its corporate headquarters to Orlando after the storm, angering New Orleanians, who felt abandoned on so many levels). On day thirty-two, he reported that Chef Austin Leslie had passed away in Atlanta. And on day forty-three, Tom moved home, alone, leaving his kids to attend school in D.C. and his wife to look after them. He wrote that his evacuation had been "the longest time I've been absent from New Orleans in my fifty-four years."

Fifty-three days after the storm, with 209 New Orleans–area restaurants back open, Tom decided to retire his hurricane diary and get back to eating, cooking, and dining and talking about all three through a lens of pure optimism. It was clear by this date that whatever else would prove to have survived the ordeal, the restaurant industry and the food culture it draws on would lead the city's recovery by example. It was comforting to have him back in form.

AM radio in New Orleans had experienced a renaissance. The sister station to Tom's WSMB, 870 WWL, had broadcast throughout the hurricane chaos, providing the only source of anything resembling information for people within the city who had stocked up on batteries. It continues to be as valuable a news source as—and a better medium for discussion than—the newspaper. When I returned from my own exile, even my AM-wary friends knew the names of the local hosts (Garland! Spud! Tommy! Bob! Deke! Vinnie! Oh, Vinnie . . .). The storm and the all-consuming recovery, which will last decades, has further isolated a city that already sometimes felt as though it existed in its own hemisphere. The extreme localism that Tom personified before the storm now infects everyone.

It's a common refrain in post-Katrina New Orleans that the food and restaurant culture is keeping the city alive, spiritually as well as literally. Even lukewarm restaurant news carries hope, and Tom has kept track of what he knows via an on-line reopened restaurant index and a separate page with information—some anecdotal, some factual—about restaurants that remain closed.

In December 2005, the *Times-Picayune* published a piece by Brett Anderson titled "Can the Restaurants Save Us?" Woven into its lovely, difficult vignettes was a hesitant "yes?" Posters on Tom's message board took up a discussion about the article. Some of them were optimistic, others despondent even through their antidepressants. One poster with the pen name Pilaf expressed a sentiment that mirrored my own: "It is hard to resist, at this point, a rant on what is lacking in terms of saving our city as a whole. But I will resist, and instead make plans to go out to dinner tonight." Amid the systematic and constant breakdown of critical resources—FEMA, the criminal justice system, underground water and gas lines—damn it, dinner still worked.

In a characteristic display of self-promotion, Tom added to the discussion by writing that the newspaper article wasn't news, that *he* had been saying as much about New Orleans restaurants for months. The last part was true. Tom had predicted the invincibility of his city's food culture, and by extension his own livelihood, in the second entry of his hurricane diary. In those dark days of early September 2005, with most of New Orleans still submerged, Tom had written from Washington, D.C.: "Say it, and it becomes true. I say the serious eaters of the world cannot live without New Orleans food. And that when we give it to them again, it will be the best we've ever had."

COFFEE AND CHICORY

In Reverence of Things Past

Among the reams of his "Menu Daily" newsletters that I've printed and saved over the years, Tom Fitzmorris laments the dwindling of the New Orleans café au lait. "I hate to see great bits of the past left behind. Or, perhaps, I hate the idea that I could be left behind, myself," he writes. And then he proceeds to defend the threatened beverage tradition that incorporates a mud-dark brew of coffee and chicory mixed with an equal amount of boiled whole milk and, if you follow his recipe, some sugar.

A casual visitor to the city might not immediately perceive that the café au lait is endangered, because casual visitors inevitably wind up at Café Du Monde, where a New Orleans café au lait is the entire point (second to the beignets, I mean). Likewise, old-timer New Orleanians who have awoken every day since kindergarten with mugs of home-brewed coffee and chicory are unlikely to notice the beverage's fragile status; local supermarkets still stock their caffeine sections with more choices for coffee and chicory blends than seem necessary. I nevertheless side with Tom. False confidence is a real and present danger. Because for every Café Du Monde in New Orleans, there's a militia of coffeehouses like Rue de la Course.

Two baristas slouch against the scratched-up wooden counter at the Rue de la Course on upper Magazine Street, otherwise known as "the Big Rue" or, among its regulars, just "the Rue." (A "Little

Rue" used to operate farther down Magazine Street, at the corner of Race Street in the Garden District, where Mojo Coffee House is now.) One wears a five o'clock shadow, plush for his tender age. The other, a young woman, shows off more growth: two hummocks of cleavage that seem to have their own respiratory system, heaving and panting and otherwise distracting her colleague.

It is my pleasure to interrupt. "Do you have coffee and chicory?"

I already know that they don't, but it's almost noon and I've yet to caffeinate. I'm desperate to release some of the aggression brought on by withdrawal, and I'm not up for the other option, pounding my forehead against the cement floor.

The baristas exchange a smirk. Her breasts gasp. He fights back. "Do you even know what chicory *is*?"

"As a matter of fact, chicory is a root—"

"Yeah, it's a root, all right." The unshaven one cuts me off. "It grows underground, and when they pull it out, they scrape off all the dirt"—he pantomimes the action of peeling a carrot—"and that's what they put in your coffee."

The four of them (two baristas, two breasts) commence panting and snickering like a better-looking coed version of Beavis and Butthead. I order a double latte as usual.

Forget that the Rue is the only New Orleans coffeehouse in which my rear end ever meets a chair's seat. Ignore also that if it weren't for the Rue's wide tables, green banker's lamps, and productive atmosphere mingling quiet jazz and (until 2007) cigarette smoke, I might never have met a single writing deadline. Never mind that deep down I enjoy entering the orbit of the Rue's young, brooding, intimidating staff more than I apparently value my lungs. More critical for this argument is that, as evidenced by my squabble with the baristas, the Rue and other coffeehouses of its chicory-free genre threaten to stomp dead not merely the city's venerable café au lait custom but the very spirit of nostalgia that enables such customs to thrive here.

Nostalgia is a sixth sense in New Orleans. It works just like the other five. When functioning optimally, nostalgia deepens your experience of the city. In a gym recently, I overheard a beefcake quoting Count Arnaud Cazenave, the founder of Arnaud's Restaurant, who died more than a half-century ago. When he finished with the count, he talked quietly to his trainer about family secrets from the early days at Brennan's Restaurant, and he told her how absinthe used to be as legal as water in the French Quarter—all in a tone of voice that I believe was meant to be seductive. Historical gossip is everyday conversation in New Orleans, at gyms, in line at the snoball stand, with your bank teller, and whenever I overhear it, I can't help believing that by caring about antiquated hearsay, the participants are creating a more dramatic setting for their lives.

On the flip side, the city's contentment in replaying its past and dwelling there has been one of its most stunting weaknesses. Before Katrina delivered material too compelling to ignore to the national press, its coverage of New Orleans one year was the same as it had been the previous year, and the year before that, and two decades before that: ghost stories, jazz funerals, political corruption, flashing breasts. At first I wondered why locals never revolted against the monotony, but pre-Katrina New Orleans just wasn't a place that put progress before a solid, well-rehearsed story. (The jury is still out on how much the storm has changed this.) Perhaps they knew what it took me some humiliation to learn: that what was considered news in pre-Katrina New Orleans was about as interesting to the rest of civilization as what Count Arnaud said to his housekeeper eighty years ago.

Over the years, I've worked with a few national food magazines, most of which are fashion magazines in disguise, primarily driven by what's hot the moment the presses begin to roll. The focus of these publications rarely intersects with the interests of the average New Orleanian, who I suspect will always prefer a Sazerac to a sake martini, a fried seafood platter to a crème brulée of sea urchin, and hollandaise sauce to foie gras foam. Eventually I stopped caring about my rejected pitches, the courteous, weary replies from New York editors, such as "That pasta Milanese you eat on St. Joseph's Day sounds divine, but we covered red sauce in the 1970s" and "Thanks for the history lesson on Creole cream cheese, but we don't do culture pieces. Try any exciting new Asian ingredients lately?"

Does ginger count?

I've been a poor national freelance writer in part because I tend to find more intrigue in the city's culinary parochialism than I find in its attempts at advancement. I long to see better schools, smooth streets, revolutionary leaders, and levees that hold, but I also gloat a little every time the city's cultural pride is used against it. Misunderstood places are as alluring as misunderstood people when you're one of the privileged who gets them. I humbly count myself in that number regarding New Orleans.

The custom of drinking coffee and chicory is perhaps the most conspicuous illustration of this city's rampant nostalgia. Why else would the inhabitants of a major American coffee port choose an impure brew when they can grab the uncut stuff off the docks? In most coffee-drinking cultures, chicory is considered inferior, and with reason: it contains no caffeine. But as with Barq's root beer (the local king of sodas, even though by all accounts it's a lesser product now than when it was manufactured in New Orleans) and McKenzies king cakes (which were tasty but hardly the holy grail that sentimental New Orleanians make them out to be), nostalgia breeds taste preferences down here.

Biologically speaking, chicory is a plant, different from but related to Belgian endive, which is also sometimes called chicory. The chicory that eventually finds its way into coffee cups begins as a bitter root that resembles a white carrot until it is cut up, kiln-dried, roasted, and ground, at which point it looks like Folgers and smells full and sweet. It tastes somewhat sweet at this point too, as the process of roasting caramelizes the root and reduces its inherent bitterness.

Brewed with hot water, a blend of ground coffee and chicory produces a liquid that's more syrupy than straight coffee tends to be, and darker. It laps at the sides of a white ceramic coffee cup like motor oil, glowing around its circumference with a sinister golden halo. While chicory is responsible for this arguably unappetizing veneer, it's not to blame for the acrid flavor that gives coffee and chicory a bad rap among uneducated tasters of the drink. That would be low-grade coffee, which is too often part of the equation. As the chicory (typically imported from Europe) is preground, the coffee must be too, and apparently the temptation to throw in whatever freeze-dried flavor crystals happen to be lying around the warehouse is great. Fortunately, some of the old-line Louisiana coffee distributors have developed standards, and so have a couple of boutique coffee roasters in the area. A café au lait made with quality coffee and chicory and sweetened is as smooth and nonabrasive as hot cocoa.

With coffeeshops on every other street corner and "cappuccino" machines in highway minimarts, it's difficult to imagine a time when coffee was in short supply. But it happened in the early 1800s in France, when Napoleon instituted the Continental Blockade, and it happened during the American Civil War and World War II, when labor, transportation, and money, and thus coffee, were scarce in this country. History books tell us that during such desperate periods, addicts lengthened their coffee rations, and sometimes replaced coffee altogether, with second-rate noncaffeinated substitutes, including chicory.

It's difficult to say whether New Orleans' taste for coffee and chicory evolved from immigrants' desire to maintain their European heritage or from economic necessity during wartimes. Evidence exists for both possibilities.

In his funny little book *Coffee, Tea, and Chocolate: their influence upon the health, the intellect, and the moral health of man*, translated from the French in 1846, Dr. A. Saint-Arroman writes that "coffee of chick-peas and of sucory [chicory] have been in fashion [in France] for some years." Certainly it's possible that coffee fashions rode the same transatlantic waves as French perfumes and hats did at that time. And then stayed in New Orleans, just as French street names, French language on menus, and French celebrations like Reveillon and Twelfth Night remained.

Ersatz in the Confederacy, published in the 1950s, lists chicory (as well as rye, acorns, and okra seeds) as one of the American Civil War era's coffee substitutes. The author does not mention whether New Orleanians had already established a taste for chicory before that war commenced.

Café Du Monde 's Web site offers one more possibility for the origins of Louisiana's chicory habit: the Cajuns. The site asserts that the Acadians, having developed a taste for chicory in their original homeland of France, carried it with them when they were ousted from Canada. If this theory is true, chicory would have arrived in the New Orleans area much earlier than either the American Civil War or the writing of Dr. Saint-Arroman's book.

By whatever means chicory took hold here, it remains true that France ditched its chicory dependence eons ago, that the American Civil War ended in 1865, that chicory today is pricier than some coffees, and that many Cajuns now prefer their coffee pure—dark as night, but without chicory. Only nostalgia can explain why the additive remains revered here. And perhaps flavor too, but most coffee drinkers need more incentive than flavor to sacrifice caffeine content. And in "most coffee drinkers," I include myself.

Full disclosure: my affection for Old New Orleans does not preclude my nostalgia for my faithful stainless steel French press pot, and my own home coffee-drinking ritual therefore doesn't include chicory at all. I level my scoops, measure my water to the ounce, set the timer to four minutes, wait, and plunge. Coffee and chicory blends are ground too fine to brew using the French press method, and so for years Matt and I have ordered whole coffee beans from a company in San Francisco. Every now and again I resolve to turn over a new leaf. To walk the walk, as they say. Drink the drink. I buy another drip machine (inevitably having thrown out the last one in disgust), consult Tom's method (his favorite coffee-chicory blend is Union), and press the little red button. But the resolution, like most resolutions, never lasts long. My coffee and chicory always comes out too weak, and I find electric coffeemakers depressing and noisy in the morning. I hate that little hot plate and the way it burns the glass carafe, which never comes clean. A few days and I'm back on the 800 line, ordering another pound of Major Dickason's Blend from Peet's.

When I began writing this chapter, I made yet another resolution to become a regular coffee and chicory drinker, one that held more weight than my previous resolutions for two reasons. First, I *really* wanted to be able to write that I drink coffee and chicory every morning, without lying. Second, I had become ever more afraid that the total dissolution of chicory-drinking in New Orleans was a real threat. Restaurants that I could swear had served coffee and chicory when I moved to town suddenly had developed vicious, chicoryless coffee programs. I can't seem to pinpoint when it happened, but suddenly restaurateurs of otherwise respectable establishments seemed to have formed a behind-the-scenes malevolent society of coffee loathing, all agreeing to serve the same locally roasted chicory-free blend that my coffee-loving, native New Orleanian friend Kevin Molony correctly likens to the flavor of burned twigs. Which, no matter how you feel about chicory, is not an improvement. This wretched-coffee plague was infesting even those restaurants where the bartenders made proper Sazeracs, where the airy bread was of brittle crust, and where the French language was sprinkled among menu descriptions. And so I resolved, again, to take a stand. But this time, no hot plates.

The Writers' Project of the Works Progress Administration, established during the Great Depression, documented this coffee-brewing method in the book *Louisiana: A Guide to the State*: "Many natives will not travel without a supply of coffee and their own coffee pot. There is an old Creole saying that 'good coffee and the Protestant religion can seldom if ever be found together.' Creole coffee differs from 'Northern' coffee in that it is a darker roast, is ground for finer dripping, and contains 10 to 20 per cent chicory, from which it derives body."

The sort of portable coffeepot to which this passage refers is an old, French-style, white ceramic drip pot that locals call a "biggin." As I'm a northerner by birth (though, in my defense, *not* a Protestant), my dowry contained no such pot; I would have to buy one. The task did not prove simple. Several New Orleans natives directed me to a mom-and-pop hardware store on Jefferson Highway, close to the Huey P. Long Bridge. Anything close to the Huey P. feels like thoroughbred Louisiana to me, and sure enough, this store stocked turkey frying pots large enough to fit two whole birds, not just cast-iron skillets but entire pot-and-pan sets in cast iron, and even some crawfish boil seasoning mixes, right beside the camp stoves. No enamel coffee pots, though. A worker at the store told me that his supplier's supplier had stopped producing them. He thought I might still be able to find one or two defective ones floating around shops in the French Quarter.

Over the succeeding months, I signed my name to waiting lists on retail Web sites and at antique stores, including Lucullus, a French culinary antiques store that poses more danger to the credit report of someone like me than Prada. Lucullus had one enamel drip pot in stock, and I would have paid the $125 for it, in the name of research, even though it was red, except that it was missing its innards. The mesh part that's meant to hold the coffee grounds as the hot water drips through them wasn't there. "But it would make a beautiful flower vase," the sales clerk pointed out.

Onward I went. And then Katrina.

I know it seems petty to mention the derailing of my biggin search in the context of the awful ways the storm affected New Orleans and its people, but that cursed hurricane also upset loads of relatively inconsequential plans—birthday parties, naps, camping trips, movie dates, first days of school, last pickings off the tomato plants, trips to Target—and I'd like to publicly hold her accountable for those too.

In an ironic twist of events, sometime in the immediate poststorm haze during which I lived technically in Manhattan but virtually on the Internet, a long-awaited e-mail popped into my in box: someone at the Cajun Connection, a Web-based store, had written to inform me that they finally had more biggins in stock. Not heavy-duty ones; the two-cup, not the four-cup, kind. My heart fluttered with hope, but not knowing at the time whether I'd ever be able to function on partially caffeinated coffee again, I filed the e-mail in my "think about later" folder.

A few months afterward, back in New Orleans and spending way too much time at the Rue, I finally ordered myself a minibiggin in white. I haven't fired my stainless steel French press pot, but I swear that on the day the biggin arrived, my kitchen echoed with the viscous drip-drip of chicory liquor against enamel. I followed the instructions of my Creole friend Annou Olivier, who kindly transcribed the instructions that her family's cook used to follow: "As she fixed a meal she would pour a couple of tablespoons of boiling water onto the grounds. When the water had time to drip down, she would pour in another couple of tablespoons. It was very thick—not at all transparent the way pure coffee is. It took some time, but that's the way all the Creoles I knew did it." Annou emphasized that Creole coffee and chicory must be drunk hot but never boiled. In the evenings, after dinner, her family would enjoy it sweetened but without milk, poured into demitasse cups.

Even in New Orleans, not everyone has the talent—or the patience, or the biggin—for making coffee and chicory properly. Thank goodness, then, for Café Du Monde.

Café Du Monde is a riddle. The enchanted outdoor café has a Disneylike magnetism for tourists and cameras, and yet it also hits the nostalgic g-spot of locals. Before every visit, I'm convinced that the tourists will have used all the napkins, the pigeons will have roosted beneath the chairs, the sidewalk musicians will be playing classic rock, the servers will all be high school cuties, the café au lait will be weak, and the beignets will be flat and cold. But after nearly a century and a half, no number of busloads from Topeka or station wagons from Bethesda seem to break the café's stride; the French Market, where Café Du Monde originated (along with the American notion of the coffee break, some say), may have morphed into the less desirable aspects of a flea market (though it's now in the throes of a multimillion-dollar revitalization), but the spirit of the café appears immovable. Even while the neighborhood is sold off to wealthy (and largely absent) out-of-towners, Café Du Monde's service staff upholds the French Quarter's reputation for the eccentric. On a recent visit, my waiter/tress showed off a generous bustline, a pencil-line mustache, and a head ornamented with rollers. The cement underfoot was sticky, as it should be, from an eternal slurry produced when the condensation from glasses of ice water drips to the ground and mingles with the powdered sugar that snows from each bite of beignet.

Café Du Monde's menu describes its beignets as "orders of three French doughnuts," which is a simpler way of saying three dense, rectangular, yeast-risen pockets of fried dough on which powdered sugar has been dumped in amounts that call to mind an avalanche. Each one hits my system like a 50-yard dash: my heart revs, my stomach heaves, and some deeply animal impulse persuades me to do it again—to eat another one. I'd never finished an entire order of beignets on my own until I met a friend visiting from Kentucky for a midmorning snack. She wasn't old, but she was retired and much smaller than me, and yet she finished her three beignets as if they had been a bunch of grapes. White sugar dusted her yellow shirt, and not a glint of shame shone in her eyes as she told me that this was her second order of beignets in twelve hours—she'd visited the café the previous evening before checking into her hotel. I felt a pang of envy, as I often do, at the reminder of how honest and easy a southerner's relationship to fried things can be.

In another guilty pleasure, the novel *Dinner at Antoine's* by Frances Parkinson Keyes, the character Ruth Avery says to her date for the evening, "Do you know, I like this better than any place we've been yet . . . This Café du Monde couldn't be anywhere except in New Orleans, like Antoine's and Mardi Gras, it isn't only unique. It's—it's *real.*" I've saved this quote since I first read it, forever ago, because it's so nostalgic, so cheesy, and so true: there is no place like Café Du Monde.

Unless you're at Morning Call.

Morning Call Coffee Stand opened two blocks from Café Du Monde in the French Quarter in 1870. It remains the second most famous place in which to eat beignets and drink café au lait in the New Orleans area, second because in the 1970s it moved to a strip mall in the suburb of Metairie. The current location contains the café's original sign, illuminated by vanity bulbs arching over a central dining counter. For the rest, the café is suburban anonymous. But what Morning Call lacks in architectural and geographic atmosphere, it recovers with its offerings—hand-rolled beignets and café au lait poured from dented silver pots—and with its client base, which is strictly local.

The scene from a recent visit: a snowy-haired woman in a houndstooth skirt and jacket enters on her husband's arm. Without waiting for a server to notice her, she walks to a gap in the wall between the dining room and the kitchen and calls in an order of beignets. "Shake them up in a bag with the sugar, will you?" she hollers. "Make sure they're nice and hot, now!" Without acknowledging the request, a man in the kitchen lifts the lid on a bin of beignets that appear to have been fried last week. His shoulders rise and fall in a sigh. The woman catches this, stands up beside the table where she and her husband have taken a seat, and strains to see into the beignet bin. Just as she opens her mouth to protest, the waiter closes the lid and shuffles over to a cook who is working a length of soft dough rolled out on a table before him, flour snowed over his feet. The waiter shakes his head as the two commune. The cook shakes his head back; then he turns and tosses three fresh dough pillows into hot oil.

Morning Call's café au lait is a regular part of my Metairie routine—in this chicory-phobic age, you've got to take it where you can get it, and you can get it good and thick out there—but I was dismayed on another recent visit to receive my beignets naked. The only powdered sugar in the vicinity was on the table in a shaker canister with holes that apparently had been poked through with a safety pin. I shook it over my beignets, but only an insulting wisp of sugar dust fluttered out.

It was about six months after the storm at the time, and I wondered whether management was trying to conserve sugar. Louisiana sugar farmers had taken two hits, from Katrina and then Rita. Perhaps we were living in a time of rations. I queried my waitress, who said she had been working at Morning Call for nineteen years and that never in her time had the beignets come sugared by the kitchen. "You must be thinking of Café Du Monde," she said. This woman couldn't have been older than thirty, which would have put her at about eleven when she started working at Morning Call, which I was sure was a fib, along with that "fact" about the sugar. I'd had beignets here before; I would remember if they had been naked. Like a defiant juvenile, I twisted the lid off the shaker canister and dumped a sandbox of powdered sugar onto my plate. A mushroom cloud billowed and then settled onto my gray sweater.

Done flawlessly, as these were, New Orleans beignets are deceivingly light. When I bit down, steam escaped from the fried dough pockets and fogged up my eyeglasses. I finished all three and then, of course, regretted it.

Afterward, I contacted a few New Orleans natives and food professionals to ask for their oldest Morning Call beignet memories: naked or sugared? Everyone had an answer, and they were split. For every memory of a Morning Call Coffee Stand that had left the beignet-sugaring up to customers was another that insisted that the kitchen had always bulldozed drifts of white over them before serving. I continue to pose the question to old-timer audiences when I think of it. I know I could just phone up Morning Call's management and ask for the truth, but facts aren't the goal of this examination. I'm a born-again New Orleanian—this is an exercise in nostalgia.

RED BEANS AND RICE

Rising to the Occasion

Like savvy politicians, food is equally powerful as a divider and a uniter. North Carolina, for instance, would be a more peaceful place if the state could just officially sever down the middle, with whole-hog barbecue eaters on one side and those who prefer pork shoulder on the other. Fingernails are sharpened for family reunions in Louisiana, where the shade of one's roux gumbo is noted and discussed and sometimes battled over. Matt and I stood divided on the po-boy, unable to share one until I finally agreed that mayonnaise is not the devil's condiment.

Unlike politicians, however, food unites with complete sincerity. It harbors no ulterior motives; its power is irreversible. Red beans and rice is my best example.

Compared with its cooking time, which according to lore ought to take an entire Monday, red beans and rice, the consummate New Orleans dish, requires virtually no prep work. You rinse the beans following an overnight soak (an optional though recommended step); you chop some vegetables and any combination of sausage, tasso, ham, pickle meat, and pig tails; you add water, fire, and possibly a cracked ham bone; and then you walk away to fold laundry, work the crossword, crawl under the covers, or begin whatever other activity consumes your usual Monday. Any New Orleanian who cooks by tradition could produce a pot of red beans while also tending to a gumbo and smothering a chicken, which made it all the more embarrassing one Monday when, along with the brown smudge on a stalk of celery that had aged in my refrigerator since the last pot of beans, I cut off the tip of my thumb.

"How much? Does it look like a fish scale or a pencil eraser?" Matt asked over the phone.

During the nearly six years I had worked as a professional cook, I had cut and burned myself so often that I no longer recall which incident caused which scar, divot, and speck of permanent numbness that now plot the landscape of my arms and hands. But I had never before foraged through a pile of diced vegetables to find a former piece of myself of a size that could be compared to a No. 2 pencil eraser.

"I'll be there in ten minutes," Matt said.

It was six o'clock in the evening, too late to be starting a pot of red beans anyway, but it was Monday and my friend Pableaux hadn't called. After swaddling my estranged flesh in plastic wrap and setting it on ice inside a Mason jar for portability (a move that later won me laughs, if not a single painkiller, from the emergency room staff), I kept my mind off the throbbing by calling and berating him: "From now on, I'm *always* invited to red beans!"

If there was a first pot of red beans in New Orleans, documentation of it hasn't been found. Everyone here knows, though, that whether true or myth, red beans and rice became a Monday staple for two reasons: it made good use of the ham bone from Sunday dinner, and cooks could stir the low-maintenance dish infrequently while tending to housework back when Monday was laundry day and people still set their washtubs over charcoal furnaces in the backyard.

Some sources point to African slaves, who survived on beans and rice, a protein-rich combination, during their nightmarish trips to this country and who later, when they began cooking in plantation kitchens, used the same ingredients as a canvas for expressing the heritage of their homeland. (The African American cultural transference helps explain other regional food preparations, like okra gumbos, rice fritters called calas, and smoking techniques.) Other sources credit the French Canadians ousted from Canada for introducing the red bean when they relocated to southwestern Louisiana, though the Monday red beans ritual is weaker in other parts of the state today, which suggests that it's always been more of a city dish.

The origin of red beans and rice means little to most modern New Orleanians, who care only that no Monday passes without at least one helping. I count myself in that number, and I blame and thank my friend and neighbor Pableaux Johnson for what became a Monday habit on good weeks and a desperation on others.

A native of New Iberia, a pretty town that idles along Bayou Teche in Cajun country, Pableaux (né Paul) moved to New Orleans roughly a year after Matt and I did. I met him through a mutual friend, though if she hadn't introduced us we would have met through another friend, or in a café, or at the dentist's. It's virtually impossible *not* to meet Pableaux, a magnetic extrovert, and once you're in, you're in. "Wanna come over for red beans on Monday?" he asks, and you agree at once, so convinced by his enthusiasm that you neglect to run his name through Google first.

Five years after my first taste of his red beans, I thought to ask why he began cooking for strangers when he moved to town. "Because I knew they would come. And this table needs to be fed once a week," he said, resting his palm on the long, homely oval slab of laminated wood around which he and his grandmother's other twenty-three grandchildren grew up eating. They were the second generation to do so. It's not happenstance that Pableaux is the one member of his sprawling clan who wanted the table, given the fitting way he describes himself: "a Cajun grandmother with a beard." On red beans Mondays, during deadline crises, and for the duration of hurricane evacuations, during which he corrals friends inside a one-room church he domesticated in St. Martinville, Pableaux displays the herding instincts of a border collie and the cooking abilities of a woman who knits between shots of hot sauce. I've met no finer onion smotherer, no more ardent devotee of the andouille link, no better tamer of the red bean.

To begin a batch, Pableaux eyeballs a measure of red beans, dumps them into a pot, and covers them with water for a quickie couple-hour soak. By observing the contents of other shoppers' grocery carts, I learned early that the only beans suitable for making New Orleans red beans and rice are the ones packaged in chunky, cellophane-wrapped rolls and marked with the classic Camellia-brand red rose. While Camellia's packaging calls the legumes within "red kidney beans," Camellia red beans are unlike any other kidney beans I've ever cooked. For one thing, they exhibit a dusky dark pink color, a lighter shade of pink than regular kidney beans, which have a more maroonish hue; also, they're squatter, more compact, not so kidney-shaped. Camellia's red beans have thinner skins than other kidneys, which is not to call them weak; on the contrary, they bloat with hot pepper and pork fat like a blistered ballerina on opening night, with stoicism and delicacy.

When I once mentioned my Camellia preference to Pableaux, never imagining that there was another side to the argument, he balked. "What? Red beans, kidney beans—they're all the same. I use whatever I got, whatever kind is cheapest that week." And then he accused me of being a red bean brandist.

To settle the score, I phoned up Camellia's packaging plant in Harahan. The receptionist, unwilling to weigh in herself, transferred me to a woman who apparently thought I was issuing a quiz when I posed the question "What's the difference between a Camellia red bean and an ordinary kidney bean?"

"Is it that we only use Grade A beans?" she asked.

I tried to clarify, explaining that I wasn't looking for secret formulas, just for confirmation that Camellia beans were somehow special—their genes grafted from some long-lost beanstalk, their waterings dictated by some obscure lunar chart, their growing soil fertilized with fairy dust, anything. The woman assured me that no, Camellia beans are just ordinary kidneys. When I pressed further, she excused herself. "We're really busy. Maybe if you can call back in a few days . . ."

It was so odd. An informal survey of other New Orleanians

assured me that I wasn't the only red bean brand partisan. Willie Mae Seaton, the nonagenarian who served red beans every weekday at her Scotch House restaurant before it flooded (the restaurant reopened, but Willie Mae has retired) sided with me over a cup of coffee and chicory one morning. "No red beans taste like the Camellia beans," she confirmed. When I told Willie Mae about Pableaux and the woman at the packaging plant, she commiserated. "That's all right, because you know the difference, don't you?"

Other ingredients are not so arbitrary at Pableaux's house, which until recently he shared with his wife, Ariana French, a subtler though equally generous personality. There, red beans are always made with Louisiana andouille, a hard, heavily smoked and seasoned pork sausage—except when there's a small side pot of vegetarian beans, which the rare guest requires. (The vegetarians must know that Pableaux's pots are too well seasoned with lard ever to cook meatless honestly.) It's always a banner Monday when pork lust has driven Pableaux thirty miles northwest to Laplace, known locally as the Andouille Capital of the World, where the *charcutiers* at Jacob's World Famous Andouille smoke their mighty, garlic-powered links so hardily over pecan wood they turn almost black.

Even on regular Mondays, when the andouille comes from Langenstein's or Zara's, neighborhood markets partial to local products, Pableaux's beans might get an extra concentrated kick of red pepper and warm spices from tasso, a seasoned and smoked pork shoulder product that's difficult to find outside Louisiana. Tasso is leaner and more like jerky than sausage, tangy and primarily used as a flavoring agent, like salt pork or pancetta; sometimes it's made with turkey instead. Pableaux might also throw in some hot sausage or bacon fat. He's not of the ham bone school, whose marrow fetish produces the creamiest beans in town, but some weeks his red beans are so meaty you do wonder whether there's still a pig living in the state.

I could pick Pableaux's red beans from a lineup according to other signatures: dried sweet basil, bay leaves, and acid (lemon juice, vinegar, Tabasco) zinging across the surface of the pork-swollen richness. You smell all these things before you cross the threshold of his second-floor apartment; I've caught whiffs of the aromatic simmering from the driveway. Rendered pork fat, weeping garlic, collapsing beans. This is the smell of a Monday in New Orleans, the all-day reminder of what you want to be eating. The aromas thicken as you wind up Pableaux's staircase, cringing past a Nordik Trak, stomach groaning. By the time you descend those same stairs a few hours later, the smells are braided into your hair, woven among the fibers of your clothing, clinging to your skin.

Most red bean recipes call for all or some combination of the local holy trinity of vegetables: onion, celery, and green bell pepper. Also garlic, which may not have a place in the trinity but is no less hallowed. New Orleanians call these starter vegetables their seasoning, as in "I save some of my seasoning to add at the end of cooking for more flavor." So many regional staple dishes build upon an identical seasoning base that you can cheat and buy the vegetables prechopped by the pint in the produce section of any supermarket here. Before moving to New Orleans, I defined *seasoning* as the dried herbs and spices sold in small overpriced bottles in the baking goods aisle. It took me years to embrace the local usage of the word, and it wasn't until I whacked off the tip of my thumb that I worked this advanced New Orleans–speak into conversation. The injury turned out to be superficial, but I kept the outsized white dressing on my hand for five days anyway, as bait for sympathetic questions, to which I couldn't wait to reply, "Oh, the knife slipped while I was chopping my seasoning."

Whereas some cooks don't even bother sautéing their vegetables, opting simply to boil them with the beans, Pableaux sweats his to a sweet golden jam. Then he adds them to his chopped pork products, which have been similarly cooked on the stovetop, rendered of their fat, and singed with a dark caramely varnish on all sides. At this point he calls anyone in the vicinity to the stove. "Look at this!" he yells, by which he means, Stick your nose inside this pot and take a whiff. "Is there anything better?" Not much.

The final essential components of a proper pot of red beans, and of an infinite number of other traditional Louisiana dishes, are chopped green onion tops and parsley—"the green stuff," as Matt calls them. At Pableaux's, these are added at the end of cooking and also passed around the table for garnishing, and they are the only fresh vegetables you will eat during Monday dinner if he's in charge. Crystal hot sauce counts as a side dish. In deference to the ways of his Cajun people (the Creoles do it too), there's always butter and hot French bread on the table.

And then there's rice, without which the dish wouldn't be complete and Mondays wouldn't smell quite right. Rice is one of Louisiana's most important agricultural products, after sugarcane and cotton. At first I found Louisiana table rice to be comparable to the parboiled rice I grew up eating with pepper steak and in tuna fish casseroles in Wisconsin. I snubbed it, driving to an imports store in Metairie for basmati by the bushel, but eventually I came to agree with diehard locals who argue that the discrete grains and muted flavor of Louisiana rice make it a perfect foil for the state's heavy and heavily seasoned beans, étouffées, jambalayas, and gumbos. (In some parts of the state, the preference is for stickier rice.) A rice cooker in the corner of Pableaux's kitchen chugs steam clouds aromatic with a twiggy, popcornlike perfume. When the sensor clicks, indicating that the rice is ready, you grab a porcelain bowl, marry rice from the cooker with beans from the stove in a proportion that has become your own Monday signature, then head for a seat at the long oval table. That is, providing you've been invited.

In his book *The Great Good Place: Cafés, Coffee Shops, Bookstores, Bars, Hair Salons, and Other Hangouts at the Heart of a Community*, the author Ray Oldenburg discusses the importance and disappearance of the "third place" in modern America. A third place, he writes, is an informal gathering spot that helps create a sense of community, a place where neighbors can unwind, meet, perhaps eat or drink, and momentarily break from their first and second places, which are home and work, respectively. While the author correctly laments that third places have steadily faded from the American landscape since World War II, the abundance of timeworn neighborhood restaurants in New Orleans, all of which serve roughly the same food, including red beans and rice every Monday, ensures that third places aren't obsolete here.

Then again, since a favorite neighborhood restaurant is something passed down through New Orleans families like cemetery crypts, many of them seem to cultivate a sort of members-only air. This social phenomenon is fascinating to observe, but it's not so welcoming for a newcomer. Simply frequenting a third place doesn't make it your own, as Matt and I learned after doing time in every bar, café, and restaurant within walking distance of our home when we moved here. Though my restaurant reviewing job sent us to restaurants all over town, we didn't establish a third place in New Orleans until we met Pableaux.

We never knew whom we would meet around the rice cooker. Pableaux's red bean guest list on any given Monday could include his sister and two nephews visiting from Baton Rouge, a screenwriter he met at the coffee shop, a couple who I always suspected invited him to their wedding to secure future red bean invitations, married sociology professors, a female Protestant minister, his college roommate, Ariana, and whoever he had met that afternoon. His grandmother's table thus became Oldenburg's "social condenser," a place where we developed friendships, discussed social and political issues, and debated the superiority of local hot sauce brands. Like Matt and me, in the beginning the majority of Pableaux's red bean invitees were transplants to the city, often fresh from the U-Haul. Because his ritual was identical to what New Orleans natives also do on Mondays, including those who open cans of Blue Runner red beans, for many of us the first red bean Monday at Pableaux's marked the first time we felt like active, meaningful participants in the local culture of domestic eating. I don't think it's exaggerating to say that through the humble red bean, Pableaux single-handedly helped countless people begin to love living in this city.

Matt and I were not unique in finding our third place in his dining room, and therein lies a sticking point, a flaw in the third-place ideal. As Pableaux's grandmotherly qualities aren't limited by biology, over time his red bean black book exceeded his own grandmother's brood and continued to grow. As the table seats only ten comfortably, no matter how tight you are with Pableaux, he can't feed you every week.

Whereas mythology would have New Orleans red beans simmering from dawn to dusk, a sputtering pressure cooker allows Pableaux to make last-minute plans. An invitation might come as late as four o'clock on Monday afternoon—or not—just late enough to mess you up if you haven't formulated a backup dinner plan. I've run into other red bean semiregulars on Mondays at the supermarket, wondering what to cook. "You didn't get a call either, huh? Who do you think is there?" we ask each other, admitting that it makes us feel better about ourselves to see others who haven't made the cut. One friend who was never invited as often as she would have liked asked me once, "What did I ever do to Pableaux? I even ate seconds last time. Should I buy him sausage or something?" I suggested that she try calling him on Monday afternoons, to trigger his memory of her. Not that I ever stooped so low, letting red bean paranoia get the better of me.

One Monday, Pableaux called early with an invitation, and I paged Matt at work to deliver the good news. Then, late in the afternoon, he called back to cancel: "The stove broke." I'm sure it says more about my character than his that I didn't believe him. I heard kitchen noises in the background, and he sounded excited and happy, which is not the same as disappointed and apologetic. I irrationally concluded that he must have made alternate plans without including us. A small part of me worried that he'd found someone better to take our seats. Forever.

Pableaux and Ariana lived five blocks from us, which was too close to resist for someone who once spent an entire summer successfully stalking her wayward boyfriend. As the sun set that Monday, I commissioned Stephanie, another red bean semiregular and an obedient younger sibling, to creep past their house with me. We looked for lights in the kitchen and sniffed the air outside for that telltale aroma. We detected neither, which was only mildly comforting, because we thought we could hear voices coming from the second-story patio. I never found out what really happened that night, and I've never told Pableaux about the lapse of composure his red beans triggered. I trust that he'll take it as a compliment. His little joke turned out to be a prophecy: he has become like a grandmother. No one else's red beans taste quite right.

The ordinariness of red beans and the unfussy process of preparing them to local tastes do not prohibit chefs from building entire careers on the dish. Buster Holmes, whose Buster Holmes Restaurant on Burgundy Street in the French Quarter closed before my time, cooked red beans for the first-ever Jazz Fest and became known internationally for his reportedly top-notch version. According to his cookbook, he used only seven ingredients, one of them being half a stick of margarine, which his recipe instructs should be melted into the beans five minutes before serving.

"I know better not to put a pot on the stove unless I have red beans," Willie Mae Seaton, whose favorite red bean seasoning meat is pickle tips with the gristle bone, told me once. While Miss Willie Mae is perhaps more lauded for the chicken that she butchered herself and then fried so thoroughly that even the bones crackled in your teeth, red beans are closer to her heart. "I just love me some red beans," she said. "This is a red bean city here. If you don't have no red beans, you just *out*."

On August 29, 2005, none of the reliable, necessary red beans and rice preparations that New Orleanians had known for entire lifetimes were available. Not the ones I liked at Crabby Jack's, thick and creamy as softened butter. Not the ones crowned with a behemoth ham shank at Smilie's. Not the free ones at Donna's Bar and Grill, where the New Orleans jazzman Bob French had a standing Monday night gig. Not the gravylike ones in Mandich's red bean soup, shot through with rice and sausage. Not Tom Fitzmorris's favorite at

Dunbar's. Not the ones at Mandina's, or Franky & Johnny's, or Praline Connection, or Joey K's . . .

It was Katrina Monday. New Orleans was just *out*.

Pableaux and I cover the same beat, New Orleans food, only he's better at it. A superior byline for the job does not exist, and he applies the same quality that has so many of us dying to crowd around his table on Monday nights to connecting with editors, which makes him a darling—or a disturbance, depending on your position—of the freelance food writing world.

While I'd like to think it's my solid sense of self-worth that quells my envy, it's more likely Pableaux's bigheartedness, and his red beans, that have kept us friends. It's true, that cliché that cookbook writers, old-timer head-shakers, and pushers of family values preach: dinner matters. Cooking for one another and gathering around a table together to eat brings people eye to eye, literally and figuratively. It forges alliances, it eases conversation, and it can be the only palliative during desperate times.

It's not unusual in New Orleans to eat three meals a day composed of native foods and combinations that are unknown, or at least unattainable, in the rest of the world. Katrina drove that home even while she drove us away. During the days immediately following the storm—first when no one remaining could get out of the city, and then when everyone was forced to leave—it was spirit-crushing to think of losing the city's rich food culture, but it was infinitely worse to imagine everyone there who just needed to eat. Morally correct or not, I did think about red beans on Katrina Monday; by the following Monday, I was longing for them. In monitoring the Internet for news of the city and its displaced, I found I wasn't alone.

In September 2005, the *Times-Picayune* ran a story by Michael Perlstein about hurricane refugees who had been flown, not by choice, to shelters in Milwaukee, Wisconsin. For some of them it had been a first-ever plane flight, and probably for many a first-ever week without red beans. "It's a nice town and all, but I don't think I could live here. I'm hungry for some red beans and rice real bad," one woman said. In closing the article with her quote, the New Orleans reporter, also displaced in Milwaukee, betrayed how much he also missed home.

In Hawaii, another reporter interviewed a manager from Popeye's, the fried chicken chain founded in New Orleans, which serves startlingly tasty red beans (moles say the secret is lard). The manager had been transferred in the wake of the storm, and he remained flabbergasted, not by Hawaii's beauty or its beaches but by its sticky rice. "I can't eat this rice with nothing on it," he told the reporter, Jarvis DeBerry. "I just can't seem to eat rice without beans, green beans, or gumbo on it. I just can't." He said he had broken in the kitchen of his new Hawaiian apartment by making a pot of red beans, but he hadn't been able to locate Camellia beans or Louisiana smoked sausage on the island. "They were good, but they're just not the same."

In the meantime, Pableaux and Ariana had holed up in their church-turned-country-house in St. Martinville, forming their own hurricane shelter and acting as a triage station for friends—some homeless, some just hungry. Red beans became everyday food, for the same reason that the dish has remained a New Orleans staple for so long: one pound of beans plus sausage and some rice can stretch to feed and console an extended family, a neighborhood, a congregation. I received reports from their hurricane commune while cozied into my in-laws' New York apartment, where I had developed a raging case of homesickness and a throbbing, impossible hunger for red beans and rice, even though I was eating shamefully well.

Unlike the hundreds of thousands of other New Orleanians who had lost their homes, their jobs, and their lives, I soon moved back to New Orleans, where Pableaux had resumed his Monday ritual. For a couple of months he cooked them in our house, as my roommate. He and Ariana had split—amicably, as they say in Hollywood, only this time for real. She remained a regular at his red beans table.

Inevitably, the one-year anniversary of Katrina rolled around, and with it, for many of us, the impossible task of deciding how to spend the day. Gospel concerts had been scheduled, second lines, memorials, prayer services, vigils, relief dinners, television specials. But the difficult post-Katrina era was not over, wouldn't be over for years—ever?—and so commemoration felt premature—not inappropriate, but not settling either. Too much had changed and too much hadn't. What, we wondered, could possibly feel meaningful? Even the prospect of eating, the most common means of both celebrating and mourning in this city, sounded indulgent. And yet wouldn't it be missing the point to spend the day alone? Being here and being together were two of the few things New Orleanians who had been able to return still had in their favor.

And then someone remembered that most of us had missed eating red beans and rice on Katrina Monday the previous year. We had been in hotel rooms or cars or shelters or foreign states or hospitals or attics or pain. Many New Orleanians had been hungry that day; others had lost their appetite. Realizing this, Pableaux decided to observe the sad turning of a year by making Tuesday, August 29, 2006, an honorary Monday. He cooked a triple batch of red beans with andouille from Laplace and invited everyone he saw, table space be damned.

OYSTERS

Size Matters

A favorite game around the Monday red beans table, once city politics and hot sauce debates have run their course, is this: cake or pie? You must answer with your gut, immediately, the idea being that your gut reaction says something profound about your character. We've never discussed what. So, quick, cake or pie? (Cake? Me too.) On really slow nights, or on fast ones when the Abita has flowed a bit too freely, the game turns silly. Pudding or custard? Whiskey or gin? Crab or shrimp? One night someone asked the table whether we'd sooner give up oysters forever or have our lives cut short by ten years. This wasn't a split-second kind of question; the group fell silent. Then someone piped up, "I wouldn't do ten, but five sounds right." Yes, five sounds right, we agreed all around. We'd give five for oysters.

Do people talk like this in other cities?

If it's not too late, I need to amend my answer. Probably it was clear at the table at the time, given our coordinates, but for the record, I'd give five for *Gulf* oysters. The kind you get at Casamento's.

If there's a downside to reviewing restaurants in a city like New Orleans, it's the impracticability of becoming a true regular anywhere. The duty to maintain anonymity and to keep abreast of the dining scene by eating in as many different restaurants as possible all but prohibits it. The position's perks are obvious, but it can get lonely. As I contemplated relinquishing my review column after four and a half years, I realized how I still yearned to belong, to have an Oldenburgian third-place restaurant, to become a regular somewhere.

Restaurants are public spaces of terrific intimacy. Life decisions are deliberated, proposals are accepted, food and its artistry transfer from one person's hand to another's mouth, desires are fulfilled for the unspoken promise of a tip. If you partake in this exchange anonymously, you dine; become a member of a restaurant's extended family and you eat. Similar to human-to-human relationships, the difference is one of comfort level and acknowledged mutual commitment. When I quit reviewing restaurants, I chose one place for myself, Casamento's. I chose it for its solid character and for its proximity to our house, but mostly for its oysters.

In her essay "Consider the Oyster," M.F.K. Fisher catalogs the mollusk's numerous adversaries: the duck, the slipper, the mussel, the black drum, the leech, the sponge, the borer, and the starfish. "She has eight enemies," Fisher writes, "not counting man who is the greatest, since he protects her from the others only to eat her himself."

It's a hard-knock life for sure. And to think of the lengths to which the Gulf oyster in particular goes in order to make herself undesirable (or himself—an oyster changes sexual orientation as if it's eye shadow). She seals herself inside a bedrock-solid shell, she makes herself the color of cement, she's wet and slimy, she occasionally harbors worms, and once in a while she kills a vulnerable diner. No wonder Ms. Fisher wrote with such awe and respect.

Oh, but wait, there's a caveat in "Consider the Oyster" that I missed the first time I read it, probably because at the time I was living in California, where Gulf oysters are outlawed. In her exposition, Ms. Fisher likens southern oysters to southern ladies: "delicate and listless." What's more, she declares that "on the Mexican Gulf they are definitely better cooked" than raw.

Clearly Ms. Fisher never visited Casamento's in December.

Casamento's is a perfect New Orleans restaurant. It's a family-run enterprise, from the obsolete cash register up front to the gleaming white kitchen in back; it's content to do just a few dishes well; and there are always more customers than there are tables, thereby ensuring that you're never alone. The restaurant is so wholly steeped in the old-fashioned (the Italian immigrant Joe Casamento opened it in 1919, when it looked much like it does now) that its neon signage, art deco light fixtures, and wall-to-wall tiles suggesting an era when hygiene was a novelty are almost too good to trust. It's a cash-only holdout, and like any New Orleans institution worth pondering, it's the object of mythology and longing; the restaurant closes during the hottest months every year, and the break has a libidinous effect on its devotees.

And then there are the oysters, as choice and consistent as the shuckers who open them. Casamento's shuckers work behind a short, standing-room-only bar, raking the rough mollusks from a top-loaded metal bin that resembles a furnace but keeps them cold. The oysters tumble into the shuckers' trough like dirt-covered rocks or potatoes freshly unearthed; opened, their glimmering lobes can be as small as quarters or mighty enough to clog a drainpipe. They're sometimes salty, sometimes not, depending on how the wind is blowing, and they always taste of the sea: cool, raw, damp, and alive.

For some people, the Louisiana oyster is an acquired taste. Others, like Ms. Fisher, never acquire it. The Gulf oyster has opponents all up and down the more vertical coasts, who call it names like "warm-water," "dangerous," and "listless." I was one of them once. Following my first visit to Casamento's, shortly after moving to New Orleans, I wrote in my notes that the oysters "look like just the sorts of things people in other parts of the country would—and should—fear." I got over myself after learning three facts. First, oysters from the Gulf are the last wild oysters in America. Second, the potentially harmful bacteria, *Vibrio vulnificus*, are not present in dangerous amounts in oysters harvested from water cooler than sixty-five degrees; check the temperature of the Gulf, and as long as you're healthy otherwise, you're safe. Finally, Gulf oysters are *delicious*. Now the debate is not whether to brave the raw ones but instead, six or a dozen? Abita or Dixie? Naked or dunked?

Whatever else I might order at Casamento's—the delicate oyster milk stew with its buttery film; the fried trout, for which lard is a savory ingredient, not just a medium for heat; the seasonal soft-shell crabs, their availability posted on a sign in the front window—I always have at least half a dozen raw. I've worked out a technique for managing the big ones, cupping one hand over my mouth to restrain the tidal wave of seawater cut loose with the first bite. And I've developed a methodology for assessing the profile of a given day's catch: taste the first one bare, the second with a squeeze of lemon, and the third with the locally preferred orgy of condiments: ketchup, hot sauce, horseradish, and lemon stirred together in a little plastic cup. After that, the winner takes all. New Orleanians up the challenge of eating oysters gracefully by transporting them to their mouths on saltine cracker rafts, sometimes dunking the whole shebang into their self-styled cocktail sauces and eating them like canapés.

One Casamento's meal in particular marked a milestone in my evolution into a spiritual New Orleanian. A friend who thought he was being chivalrous offered me the smallest oyster on the platter. "I don't like the small ones," I said with a defiance, and a love of the big ones, I hadn't known I possessed. It was one of those happy, enlightened, fully present "moments of being" that Virginia Woolf writes about. I knew then and there that I was meant to be here.

There's so much more to be said about oysters in this town. Hardly a restaurant exists without serving them in one glorious form or another: Rockefeller at Antoine's, Gabie at Gabrielle (closed since Katrina), panéed at Tommy's Cuisine, cold-smoked at GW Fins, Bienville at Pascal's Manale, fried and raw at Bozo's, chargrilled at Drago's, in chowder at Dick & Jenny's. And then there are the people who devote their lives to fishing them, hardscrabble people, many of them of Croatian heritage, who took such a hit financially, physically, and spiritually during Katrina that the future of oyster fishing in this area is a story yet to be written.

But that moment of being pretty much does it for me here. This, I think, is a time for leaving things be special, to borrow the wise words of Leah Chase. Because besides the people of New Orleans, who are so good, the oysters are what I will miss most about living in this city.

For a few days after Matt got accepted into a residency program at the University of Pennsylvania, in Philadelphia, after Katrina blew his career path right out of New Orleans, I wondered how many women had ever left their husbands for a city. He let me wonder, I think without ever doubting what I would choose, which is why I could only choose him. Matt started his new job in January 2006, the same week I moved back to New Orleans to wrap up this book and our lives here. It's September already, and in a couple of weeks I will pack up my Saturn, have a final dozen raw and a final dozen fried at Casamento's, and drive east on I-10, way beyond Vietnam.

I've scheduled my departure for exactly seven years from when I arrived, on an October day so scorching that I stopped at a mall outside Biloxi to buy a skirt. When I arrived around dinnertime, Matt took me out for California-style burritos, because that was what we knew then. How far we've come.

We're not selling our house here, which makes moving to a street called Croskey slightly more palatable. No offense, Philly, but it really doesn't have the same ring as Constance, which is just the sort of street you always want to come home to. It was on Constance Street that I took my first roux beyond the creamy shade of résumé paper; that I stitched my first turducken, not entirely by myself; that I blacked out from my first fried-potato po-boy; that we displayed our first Zulu coconut on a mantelpiece above a nonworking fireplace; that I boiled my first crawfish; that I turned thirty; that Matt proposed; that I met a neighbor who stuffed artichokes; that Stephanie took a pregnancy test and then announced my pending aunthood; that we bought our first house, found our first cat, had our first porch swing, heard our first Carnival parades, learned to make

Sazeracs. It's difficult to come up with a meaningful moment together that doesn't somehow trace back to this street.

It hasn't been the same, these past eight months, without Matt here. The line at Hansen's has been lonely without him. There's been no one to monitor my radio addiction. I haven't been cooking enough. This was our New Orleans. Then again, the city was a faithful companion and cook during my double widowhoods, first medical school and then one residency. I don't doubt that Matt and I were better off as a couple for it. Certainly we ate better, lived lighter, than most doctors-in-training do.

I cannot stress enough that these are my New Orleans food stories. New Orleans is a city of friends and neighbors, restaurants and cooking, and it swells with stories about how they all interact. Put yourself in the middle of them and you become part of the story yourself. Eat an Italian salad, take a long lunch at Galatoire's, cook a pot of red beans, and you're in. There's no admission price, no required reading. Food and the people who cook it, and the rituals that honor it, and the places that serve it, and the reasons for preserving it—that's what happens here, who we are, what matters.

The other day I drove past a canary-yellow mobile sno-ball stand in a corner of the Warehouse District that's newly buzzing with construction and commerce. I'd never seen the stand before, and it warmed me to imagine that it was about to become the Hansen's Sno-Bliz for some contractor from Alabama or some electrician from Connecticut or some cabinetmaker from Mexico. All the while I've been hunched over this computer, trying to finish writing so that I could move (has there ever been a less motivating prospect?), new New Orleanians have been discovering restaurants where I may never eat, taco trucks I've never seen. They're choosing Tony Angelo's over Venezia, and they're eating the rabbit salad that ought to be mine. The food culture of New Orleans has proven that as long as the city survives, it will thrive. And by New Orleans' food culture, of course I mean its very heart.

I do not want to move away from New Orleans. It's a real hurt. But it's important to remember—and I've reminded myself every day—how many people have not been able to return to their city since Katrina, to eat a po-boy or to see a friend, for reasons too many to list. I have had the luxury of a long, peaceful farewell, and I am grateful for it.

I'm heartened a little too by knowing that I've become a better eater here, a better cook, a better person. That was inevitable. And this city has taught me what I believe to be the strongest and most liberating lesson in my life so far: that the power of place is not limited to where; it can also be a why and a how. New Orleans, you're coming with me.

AFTERWORD

TURKEY BONE GUMBO

You Can *Take It with You*

JANUARY 2007

On the morning that I surrendered my New Orleans citizenship by leaving my house keys with a property manager and then driving toward my husband, I stopped for coffee. And a lagniappe. Almost as soon as Katrina hit, I began stockpiling New Orleans mementos, starting with any old cookbook I could find in Manhattan's used-book stores. Once I returned to New Orleans, I expanded my range: rarer cookbooks, bumper stickers, photographs, oyster shells, a bottle of Mississippi River water. The frantic collecting was as much an endeavor to hold on to my own identity as it was to preserve what I loved about the city. As I waited for my coffee on that ultimate morning, I scanned the café for a last-minute souvenir, something symbolic that would help make sense of the day, and I found it rolled up in a basket on the floor: an earthy clay-colored T-shirt with "Be a New Orleanian Wherever You Are" printed across the chest in orange lettering.

The phrase had become a mantra for many New Orleanians who had reluctantly started their lives anew elsewhere after Katrina, first because their homes hadn't survived and then later because of lost jobs, poor schools, uninhabited neighborhoods, unhappy spouses, mental and physical health concerns, better career opportunities, common sense. I had already collected a pile of stickers with the same slogan, and I intended to vandalize Philadelphia with them.

When I tried to imagine what it would mean to be a New Orleanian wherever I was, creating my own Monday red beans and rice ritual by inviting our new neighbors to dinner came to mind. Shrimp boils in the courtyard of our rented townhouse came to mind. Also baking fig cakes and building my own altar to Saint Joseph on March 19; gumbo z'herbes on Holy Thursday; another resolution to make coffee and chicory my morning wake-up beverage. In other words, I would eat and drink like a New Orleanian wherever I was, which seemed thematically appropriate, considering how I had bonded with the city.

So on the day before my departure, I went grocery shopping, heading first to Angelo Brocato's in Mid-City for cookies, then out to Jacob's in Laplace for andouille, tasso, smoked turkey legs, and beef jerky for the drive. On the way back into New Orleans, I stopped at Dorignac's supermarket in Metairie, where the shelves always heave with local staples: Cajun Crawtator potato chips from Zapp's, hot pickled okra, smoked and fresh hot sausage, Louisiana pecans, Bulgarian-style yogurt from Bittersweet Plantation Dairy, honey from a beehive in Uptown, Union coffee and chicory, pickle meat, crab boil, Creole mustard, Tony Chachere's seasoning, and Camellia brand red beans. At the checkout, the cashier glanced at my loot and said, "Oh baby, you must be leaving town."

A final dozen raw and a final dozen fried at Casamento's, that coffee stop, a farewell wave to the Superdome, and that was it. If I hadn't been bolstered by wearing my "Be a New Orleanian" T-shirt while crossing the Potomac—that damn Yankee river—I'm certain I would have turned around.

I continued to wear the T-shirt in Philadelphia, but the message began to lose its hold on my resolve immediately. Such as once I learned that you can't buy beer on Sundays here or legally drink anything alcoholic while walking down the street. And once I learned that navigating the city according to the position of the Schuylkill River doesn't get you where you want to go—Philadelphia streets fall into a tidy grid pattern, with right angles and signs at every corner, an efficient system so unfamiliar after seven years in the Crescent (shaped) City that my inner compass refused to adjust. When a rusted seal broke on a water pipe in our basement in the middle of the night, causing a flood to soak all the belongings that had remained dry during Katrina, it felt somehow poetic. When I had to relinquish my Louisiana ID in order to get a Pennsylvania driver's license, in order to get a Pennsylvania license plate, in order to get a parking permit, in order not to get towed—that was the final nail. My identity had officially been jacked.

The worst of it was that somewhere during the move I had misplaced my will to cook like a New Orleanian. I had shoved those groceries from Jacob's and Dorignac's into the freezer upon my arrival, and there they had stayed. I wasn't in New Orleans anymore, wasn't a New Orleanian anymore, no matter how often I wore that T-shirt, so what would a pot of red beans prove? Why bother the stomach with cayenne? What was the point of pickle meat? What *was* pickle meat? Instead I tried my hand at curry cauliflower pasta, lamb stew, pork tenderloin, broccoli soup, and roast chicken. And it was awful, all of it. Food without a narrative just tasted like food. Matt lost weight; I was lost.

I did experience some moments of emotional clarity during this period, moments when I understood that I was not making New Orleans proud. What kind of born-again loses her faith the first time her prayers aren't answered? Where was all that wisdom I reportedly had gained while learning to like mayonnaise, kill crawfish, manage silver-dollar-sized oysters in one mouthful, eat soup with a fork? I despised my stupid T-shirt, because it reminded me of where I wasn't; at the same time, I knew that there must be some way to repossess my inner New Orleanian—to remember why partaking in tradition, delighting in community, and finding meaning in family had seemed so obviously the best way to live.

During one of those clear moments, in mid-November, a solution startled me out of the dark side: turkey bone gumbo. An e-mail exchange with my dad's brother Danny, still the turkey chief in our family, gave me hope. Danny agreed to save me two turkey carcasses from the Thanksgiving dinner we would eat together in three weeks, and I resolved to save myself by making turkey bone gumbo out of them. Settled.

...

In preparation for another cross-country drive, this time from Pennsylvania to Wisconsin, Matt and I repacked the car with the andouille from Jacob's, a baggie of Louisiana bay leaves (which are milder than the California variety), and a canister of seasoning mix called Slap Ya Mama, which, despite the fact that I had never used it before, I hadn't been able to leave Dorignac's without buying.

A few days later, in the afterglow of our traditional Thanksgiving mish-mash-mush, Danny placed the two turkey carcasses in a white garbage bag, and I hauled them across town to my parents' house.

Turkey bone gumbo is not a specialty of Louisiana as much as it is a given there. Like turkey and cranberry sauce sandwiches, cold pumpkin pie, and Stove Top re-mish-mash-mushed with creamed onions and sweet potatoes, turkey bone gumbo is what you make from Thanksgiving leftovers, because they are there and because Thanksgiving dinner is always better the second time around no matter where you live.

The next day I woke early to fire up a stock using the turkey bones plus some onions, celery, and bay leaves. It simmered while the rest of the family and I joined my dad's other brother, Jay, in his favorite event of Thanksgiving weekend: a typical Wisconsin tavern lunch of beer and brats. My uncle Jay is the only one of the three Roahen brothers who moved away from Wisconsin as a young adult, and it's never seemed accidental that he's the one who drives the most Wisconsin-centric ritual of our family's annual reunion. Place-specific traditions allow you to hold on to home—to taste it, even—long after you don't have a bed there anymore.

As usual, I didn't allow enough cushion time to make the gumbo myself without risking the loss of another thumb tip. You can't do anything else while you're preparing your roux—no phone calls, no bathroom breaks, no pleasantries—and so it was a happy coincidence that the family's newest babies went down for naps just as I was beginning the process. This freed up Stephanie and our cousin Jenny to cull the good turkey meat from the two boiled carcasses, separating out the bones, a fussy job. Matt worked at the counter alongside them, peeling potatoes and hard-boiled eggs for the potato salad that he insists accompany any gumbo we make at home. I manned the stove, a slave to my roux, while the three of them chattered behind me.

"Is this an onion or a tendon?" I heard Jenny ask as she picked through the strained stock remains.

We're in that important middle generation now—Stephanie, Jenny, Matt, me. The generation that gets fewer presents and less sleep; the generation charged with carrying on those little traditions that have been passed down from our parents and grandparents, so that our own children, and their children, can begin to understand where we all came from. So that *we* can understand where we all came from. Listening to them prattle on like kids in art class as they pitched in to help me make this dinner, I experienced one of those full, soul-moving, Virginia Woolfian moments of being. Here we were, establishing a new tradition for our family: Thanksgiving weekend turkey bone gumbo. How important and gratifying. As long as I didn't burn the roux.

Shoot, the roux!

Some Louisianians believe that making a proper roux requires hours of continuous stirring over a low flame. I learned to make roux using a more aggressive, borderline violent method by following the instructions in a Paul Prudhomme cookbook to cook the fat and flour together quickly over high heat. I always wear long sleeves for safety, and I acquire the gastronomic equivalent of a runner's high in the process. This time was no exception. My mom's steel whisk clanged against her heaviest-bottomed aluminum pan at a frantic tempo as I conjured up the photographs of differently colored rouxs printed in Chef Paul's cookbook, so as to recall the difference between brown and burned.

You must rely on your nose as well as your eyes, though judging a roux by its aroma is trickier, as the smell of *burning* nuts is a good sign when making a roux while the smell of *burned* nuts is the kiss of death, and only a millisecond separates the two. I called Matt over to take a whiff as the nutty aroma peaked. "You better stop now! You better stop now!" he yelled. "Not yet, not yet!" I yelled back, as is our roux-making routine. Then, just a moment before absolute terror, I dumped my chopped seasoning vegetables into the pot, stopping the roux from cooking any further and inducing a puff of moist, earthy, caramel-scented steam. My roux never approaches black like I want it to, but this one was nevertheless a pride. A respectable brown.

Next I added the stock; an hour later, in went the turkey and the andouille. An hour after that, the company began to arrive, twenty-nine people in all. Every one of them tried the gumbo. Even children who had been too finicky for plain roast turkey on Thanksgiving tried the gumbo. Some people slapped some Slap Ya Mama on theirs. Others garnished with Tabasco. I set out a bowl of "the green stuff"—chopped green onion tops and parsley. Matt persuaded nearly everyone to marry their gumbo and their potato salad in the same bowl, and no one seemed to find it offensive. I watched the room from a stool at the kitchen counter, content for the first time in a long time. Here were all my people, eating like all my other people. My dad served brandy old-fashioneds.

When I lived in New Orleans, I believed that a meal like this—Louisiana turkey bone gumbo made and eaten in Wisconsin—was less relevant because it was out of context. Though I haven't changed my mind entirely, I know that I experienced an emotional breakthrough the night that twenty-nine members of my extended family partook of my Louisiana turkey bone gumbo in Wisconsin, and I know it was possible only because of what living in New Orleans had taught me about connecting with people by cooking and eating together.

I've never loved books with happy endings, and this isn't one of them. But new beginnings are important. And what is a roux if not a new beginning? What is a New Orleanian, wherever she is, without a reason for gumbo?

Gratitude

I am most grateful to Gail Roub, whose guidance I still rely on, in writing and in living. And to Mathieu de Schutter, my best editor and best friend: thank you for bringing me to New Orleans.

Thank you also to Nathan Harrison, for bringing my sister down to New Orleans too, and for sharing in so much of this book. And to Stephanie, of course, for always sharing everything.

Thanks to my parents, Marcie and David (Fud) Roahen, for their acceptance and their humor, and most of all their patience. And to my extended family members on both sides, none of whom has ever asked me to shut up about our drinking habits.

I could not have completed this project without the warm writing spaces lent to me by Maëlle de Schutter and Barry Burchell, Laure-Anne Bosselaar and Kurt Brown, and the Writers Room in Manhattan. And certainly not without my thorough readers and consultants, both cultural and literary: Gene Bourg, Annou Olivier, Jonathan Gold, Michelle Wildgen, and Sarah Rothbard.

Thanks to my SFA friends and colleagues, for the inspiration and the pork—and especially to John T Edge for leading by example.

Thank you to all the people of New Orleans. If ever our paths crossed, you contributed to my experience of the city. And especially to the following New Orleanians: David Buehler, for Constance Street; Donna Sacknoff, for defining the perfect New Orleans neighbor; Carol Allen Feinsilber, for all the hookups; our postmen, Huey Moss and Kenneth Powell; the Fagots, the Hansens, and

Pableaux Johnson, for opening up their lives to me; Susan Tucker, for the research help; and Michael Tisserand, David Lee Simmons, and Shala Carlson—first for the job, then the friendship. May we meet again at Mosca's.

I need to thank all the dear friends and acquaintances who lived through these stories with me and made them real. Most of you are in here, and I'd name you again a hundred times if I didn't think it would be overkill. A few of you are heretofore unnamed but shall not remain unthanked: Billy Sothern and Nikki Page (Perino's!); Dianna Cottier (the world's best king cake baker); Katy Wallenter, Dora Sison, and Shannon LeBoeuf (king cake gossips); Todd and Andrea Price (roommates extraordinaire); Robb Walsh (Gulf oyster expert and eater); Lorin Gaudin, for the beignet consult; and Becky Lloyd, for managing to keep my back from ruining my life.

I am grateful to Liz Duvall for the expert copy editing.

And finally, thank you to my agent, Esmond Harmsworth, and to my editor at W. W. Norton, Maria Guarnaschelli, for the obvious.

I acquired much of the backstory for this book while working on an oral history project for the Southern Foodways Alliance. To learn more about some of the pillars of New Orleans' food culture, visit the oral history section at www.southernfoodways.com.

Bibliography

Allen, Carol. *Leah Chase: Listen I Say Like This*. Gretna, La.: Pelican, 2002.

Arthur, Stanley Clisby. *Famous New Orleans Drinks and How to Mix 'Em*. New Orleans: Goldman Label, 1937.

Bienvenu, Marcelle. *Who's Your Mama, Are You Catholic, and Can You Make a Roux? The Sequel*. Lafayette, La.: Thomson Acadiana, 1998.

Bienvenu, Marcelle, Carl. A. Brasseaux, and Ryan A. Brasseaux. *Stir the Pot: The History of Cajun Cuisine*. New York: Hippocrene, 2005.

Bourg, Gene. "Our Daily Bread." *Culinary Concierge*, June-July 2002.

Bremer, Mary Moore. *New Orleans Recipes*. New Orleans: Dorothea Thompson, 1944.

Brite, Poppy Z. *The Devil You Know*. Colorado Springs, Colo.: Gauntlet, 2005.

Burton, Marda, and Kenneth Holditch. *Galatoire's: Biography of a Bistro*. Athens, Ga.: Hill Street Press, 2004.

Burton, Nathaniel, and Rudy Lombard. *Creole Feast: 15 Master Chefs of New Orleans Reveal Their Secrets*. New York: Random House, 1978.

Chase, Leah. *The Dooky Chase Cookbook*. Gretna, La.: Pelican, 2000.

Collin, Richard H. *The New Orleans Underground Gourmet: Where to Find Great Meals in New Orleans for Less than $3.75 and as Little as 50¢*. New York: Simon & Schuster, 1970.

Collin, Rima, and Richard Collin. *The New Orleans Cookbook: The Most Authentic and Reliable Gathering of Great Cajun and Creole Recipes from the City's Grand Restaurants and Modest Cafés, from Mansions and from Country Kitchens*. New York: Knopf, 1987.

Denker, Joel. *The World on a Plate: A Tour Through the History of America's Ethnic Cuisine*. Boulder, Colo.: Westview, 2003.

Feibleman, Peter S., and the editors of Time-Life Books. *American Cooking: Creole and Acadian*. New York: Time-Life Books, 1971.

Fitzmorris, Tom. *Tom Fitzmorris's New Orleans Food: More than 225 of the City's Best Recipes to Cook at Home*. New York: Stewart, Tabori & Chang, 2006.

Folse, John D. *The Encyclopedia of Cajun & Creole Cuisine*. Gonzales, La.: Chef John Folse, 2004.

Gill, James. *Lords of Misrule: Mardi Gras and the Politics of Race in New Orleans*. Jackson: University Press of Mississippi, 1997.

Green, Phil. "Antoine Amédée Peychaud." *Mixologist: The Journal of the American Cocktail* (2005).

Grimes, William. *Straight Up or On the Rocks: The Story of the American Cocktail*. New York: North Point, 2001.

Hansen, Harry. *Louisiana: A Guide to the State*. New York: Hastings House, 1971 [reprint].

Harris, Jessica B. *The Welcome Table: African-American Heritage Cooking*. New York: Fireside, 1995.

Hazan, Marcella. *Essentials of Classic Italian Cooking*. New York: Knopf, 2000.

Hearn, Lafcadio. *Lafcadio Hearn's Creole Cook Book*. Gretna, La.: Pelican, 1990 [reprint].

Hellman, Lillian, and Peter S. Feibleman. *Eating Together: Recipes and Recollections*. Boston: Little, Brown, 1984.

Holmes, Buster. *The Buster Holmes Restaurant Cookbook: New Orleans Handmade Cookin'*. Gretna, La.: Pelican, 1983.

Kennedy, Diana. *From My Mexican Kitchen: Techniques and Ingredients*. New York: Clarkson Potter, 2003.

Kirk, Michael, and Bywater Neighborhood Association. *Mirliton and Other Neighborhood Favorites*. Leawood, Kan.: Circulation Service, 1995.

Lagasse, Emeril, and Jessie Tirsch. *Emeril's New New Orleans Cooking*. New York: William Morrow, 1993.

Lemotte, Justin G. T. *New Orleans Talkin': A Guide to Yat, Creole and Some Cajun*. New Orleans: Channel, 1998.

Margavio, Anthony V., and Jerome J. Salomone. *Bread and Respect: The Italians of Louisiana*. Gretna, La.: Pelican, 2002.

Martin, Ti Adelaide, and Jamie Shannon. *Commander's Kitchen: Take Home the True Tastes of New Orleans with More than 150 Recipes from Commander's Palace Restaurant*. New York: Broadway, 2000.

Maselli, Joseph, and Dominic Candeloro. *Images of America: Italians in New Orleans*. Mount Pleasant, S.C.: Arcadia, 2004.

Massey, Mary Elizabeth. *Ersatz in the Confederacy*. Columbia: University of South Carolina Press, 1952.

McCaffety, Kerri. *Etouffée, Mon Amour: The Great Restaurants of New Orleans*. Gretna, La.: Pelican, 2002.

———. *Obituary Cocktail: The Great Saloons of New Orleans*. New Orleans: Vissi d'Arte, 2001.

———. *St. Joseph Altars*. Gretna, La.: Pelican, 2003.

Oldenburg, Ray. *The Great Good Place: Cafes, Coffeee Shops, Bookstores, Bars, Hair Salons, and Other Hangouts at the Heart of a Community*. New York: Marlowe, 1989.

The Picayune Original Creole Cook Book. New Orleans: Times-Picayune Publishing, 1971.

Prudhomme, Paul. *Chef Paul Prudhomme's Louisiana Kitchen*. New York: William Morrow, 1984.

———. *The Prudhomme Family Cookbook: Old-Time Louisiana Recipes by the Eleven Prudhomme Brothers and Sisters and Chef Paul Prudhomme*. New York: William Morrow, 1987.

Reckdahl, Katy. "Chief of Chiefs." *Gambit Weekly*, July 7, 2005.

———. "St. Joseph's Night Gone Blue." *Gambit Weekly*, March 29, 2005.

Rodrigue, Melvin, and Jyl Benson. *Galatoire's Cookbook: Recipes and Family History from the Time-Honored New Orleans Restaurant*. New York: Clarkson Potter, 2005.

Rombauer, Irma S., Marion Rombauer Becker, and Ethan Becker. *The All New All Purpose Joy of Cooking*. New York: Scribner's, 1997.

Saint-Arroman, A. *Coffee, Tea and Chocolate: Their Influence upon the Health, the Intellect, and the Moral Health of Man*. Philadelphia: Townsend Ward, 1846.

St. Joseph Guild. *Viva San Giuseppe: A Guide for St. Joseph Altars*. New Orleans: St. Joseph Guild, 1985.

Saxon, Lyle, Edward Dreyer, and Robert Tallant. *Gumbo Ya-Ya: A Collection of Louisiana Folk Tales*. Gretna, La.: Pelican, 1987.

Scott, Natalie, and Caroline Merrick Jones. *Famous Drinks and Foods from the Carnival City (New Orleans)*. Pamphlet, publisher and date unknown.

Tusa, Marie Lupo. *Marie's Melting Pot*. New Orleans: Spielman, 1980.

Uglesich, John. *Uglesich's Restaurant Cookbook*. Gretna, La.: Pelican, 2004.

Vollen, Lola, and Chris Ying. *Voices from the Storm: The People of New Orleans on Hurricane Katrina and Its Aftermath (Voices of Witness)*. San Francisco: McSweeney's, 2006.

Wilson, Justin. *Justin Wilson Looking Back: A Cajun Cookbook*. Gretna, La.: Pelican, 1997.

———. *Justin Wilson's Homegrown Louisiana Cookin'*. New York: Macmillan, 1990.

Women of All Saints Episcopal Church. *La Bonne Cuisine: Cooking New Orleans Style*. Memphis: Mercury, 1997.

Zulu 2005 Social Aid & Pleasure Club Inc., Official Souvenir Book. 2005.

INDEX

A NOTE ABOUT THE AUTHOR

Sara Roahen's work has appeared in *Tin House*, *Oxford American*, and *Food & Wine*. Roahen and her husband moved back to New Orleans in the spring of 2008.

WWW.SARAROAHEN.COM